Intimacy

Julian Rathbone is the author of twenty-three novels, two
of which (*King Fisher Lives* and *Joseph*) were shortlisted for
the Booker Prize; his other work includes a TVM screen
play (*Dangerous Games*). He has been awarded short-story,
crime fiction and poetry prizes and has been translated into
fourteen languages. He lives in Hampshire.

JULIAN RATHBONE

Intimacy

INDIGO

First published in Great Britain 1995
by Victor Gollancz

This Indigo edition published 1996
Indigo is an imprint of the Cassell Group
Wellington House, 125 Strand, London WC2R 0BB

© Julian Rathbone 1995

The right of Julian Rathbone to be identified as author
of this work has been asserted by him in accordance with
the Copyright, Designs and Patents Act, 1988.

A catalogue record for this book is
available from the British Library.

ISBN 0 575 40019 6

Printed and bound in Great Britain by
Guernsey Press Co. Ltd,
Guernsey, Channel Isles

96 97 98 99   10 9 8 7 6 5 4 3 2 1

The main character of this novel is called Querubín. This is the Spanish for Cherub. The 'Qu' is pronounced like an English 'K'. Please, dear English reader, say to yourself Kerrroobeeen, all through. Not Kwerubin.

In attempting to present aspects of life in Madrid between 1932 and 1936 I used several standard texts. The one to which I owe a very particular debt is Ian Gibson's splendid biography of the poet Lorca – *Federico García Lorca*, published by Faber & Faber. I am grateful too to Ian for allowing me to quote the three sentences which appear in the text of *Intimacy*.

Acknowledgements

My heartfelt and affectionately offered thanks are due to my cousin, Day McAusland. Drawing on her distinguished career as a singer, especially of baroque music, she provided invaluable help with all of the musical background to this book and especially with the lessons Querubín gives Petra. Any errors that are left are mine. She was, moreover, an inspiration and a source of great encouragement at a very difficult time, a time when only she, together with my partner Alayne Pullen and my friend Thomas Wörtche, remained confident that this was a book worth writing. My thanks again, to all.

J.R.

PART ONE

Villa Melchor

I

David Querubín died late at night on the thirty-first of May 1994, just two days after Dr Caridad Rocío Lorca had come with the hospital laboratory report which confirmed the lump in his throat was a malignant carcinoma. The doctor (mid-thirties, new Spain, designer jeans with a soft leather jacket, drove a black Toyota Celica) spent an hour with the old man discussing the situation. She returned the next day with a packet of white pills and a small bottle filled with dark blue capsules. She told Petra the old man might like to die quite soon and that when the moment came he would tell Petra. She was then to grind ten of the pills using the kitchen pestle and mortar, mix the powder with the contents of five of the capsules and dissolve the result in ten centilitres of undiluted sweet anis. Before giving him his final drink, Petra was to get him to swallow a lump of sugar impregnated with five millilitres of an anti-vomiting agent. She was to flush what was left of the anti-vomiting agent down the toilet, wash out the container and leave it in a public litter bin at least as far away as Campanillas, the nearest village.

At ten o'clock, Carmen, Querubín's housekeeper, brought him his supper: a thin gruel made from *migas*, the Andalusian wheat polenta, and chicken stock. He refused to eat any, and asked to see Petra. She came and leant over his tired white head. Speech was now a painful business, but he had only three words to say.

'*¿Esta noche, sí?*'

Tonight.

Petra mixed up the brew in the big kitchen. Carmen and her husband, Paco, who looked after the gardens and the fabric of the villa, watched, knew what Petra was doing, and stoically approved. They were Catholics but too they were peasants: they knew about babies smothered when there was not enough food to go round, and old people when their ailments became insupportable both to themselves and their carers. Carmen dabbed her eyes with her apron, but not a lot. Petra asked them if they would like to be present, but they said no. They preferred to remember their master and friend of twelve years alive, rather than dying, and, anyway, it was not their place . . .

Petra helped Querubín to get upright against the pillows, and held him there with her arm round his shoulders. Taking them from the bedside table with her other hand she gave him the lump of prepared sugar on a spoon, and then, when he was ready, the drink. He drank it off in one, grimaced and signalled that he would like more anis: to take away the taste. This time he sipped it slowly.

When it was gone Petra let his back and head sink into the pillows, and handed him his newest and best toy, a Sony Discman, the latest model. Petra helped him put on the cans, larger and better than the ones that were sold with it. He settled himself, lifted his right hand. Petra took it, squeezed, then kissed him on both cheeks. She sat down in a wooden armchair by the side of the big bed. He pressed the play button, smiled, and closed his eyes. The *Kyrie* that opens Mozart's C minor Mass filled his ears and mind.

They remained like that for half an hour. Occasionally Petra could hear the tinny tinkle of the louder passages, nothing more. Querubín's breathing became heavier, noisier, then shallow, with a sort of whisper in it. Then it rattled in his murderous throat and died, and so did David Querubín. Petra stopped the CD and took the cans from his head.

Later she played the disc for a second or two on from where it had stopped: it was the beginning of the *Credo*, and that pleased her because it meant he had almost certainly heard the *Domine* in the middle of the *Gloria*: a wonderfully sensual intertwining of soprano voices in which they seem to soar and swing in and out of each other in lilting lines of song that echo and answer each other, pleading with such seductive perfection that the Lamb of God should be merciful that no one can doubt He will be.

The next morning, after Dr Rocío Lorca had called and certified that Querubín had died from an overdose which she was prepared to say was accidentally self-administered, Petra helped Carmen wash him, though there was very little need. He had eaten hardly anything for days, only fluids. She marvelled at how thin and frail his body had become, quite unlike the sturdy figure who had welcomed her two years before.

Both women were curious to see the cut that had created or preserved the most magnificent voice this century has heard: beneath a shrivelled uncircumcised penis, no bigger than a boy's, but surrounded by thin tufts of hair, mostly white (there are few sights sadder than grizzled pubic hair), the skin was puckered along a brown scar about three inches long. That was all it had taken to do it, fifty-eight years earlier, not long after his fourteenth birthday.

They put him in a dazzlingly white and immaculately pressed night-shirt, folded his hands on his breast, and then filled the room with his favourite roses, white tinged with pink, a floribunda called English Mist. All day people came to see him. First of all friends and acquaintances from nearby, then the big cars from Malaga, Marbella and Granada crunched through the gravel outside; one or two made it from Madrid and even from abroad. Most stayed for the funeral on the third of June and Carmen and Petra put up those they had room for, chosen from among the familiars he had welcomed most readily; the rest filled the village's small hotel, its *fondas* and *pensiones*.

It was quite a grand affair, the whole village turned up as well, though out of respect for the deceased's professed atheism the parochial priest kept the religious side to the barest minimum.

Petra left a week later. She was booked to sing Nerone in Monteverdi's *L'incoronazione di Poppea* in the Lufthansa Festival of Baroque Music in London, and all through the rest of the summer that role and others at various festivals across the world. She would be hailed as a worthy successor to the man whose pupil she had been for more than two years: indeed that had already been the case over the previous six months. But this time it would be different. Not his successor, they would say, but the new David Querubín. Then year by year the memory of him would fade, he would be a name, a sound on CD or tape, a reputation which a few would recall when they heard her sing. But less and less so as she ceased to recreate his interpretations and developed her own. Then they would come to hear not the reincarnation of Querubín, but Petra Von Stürm – in her own right.

II

Her real name was Petronella Stumff. Stumff is a perfectly ordinary name to Germanic ears but rouses mirth amongst English speakers, and Petronella is a mouthful in any language. So, professionally and indeed to her intimates, she became Petra, Petra Von Stürm.

Her father, Heinrich Stumff, lived in a small castle surrounded by vineyards above a river with mountains nearby. He had holdings in AEG, Siemens, and Hoechst. He was a tall, loose-limbed, fair man with a melancholy disposition, a melancholy which deepened when Petronella's mother died in a car accident for which he was partly responsible. Petronella was still only twelve. Her mother had been English, from a West Country family of Old Catholics, and she had met Stumff at the Salzburg festival when she was eighteen and at a Swiss boarding school. She had been short, dark, jolly and plump. Petronella took after her father. They were both desolated when his wife, her mother, died, and over the next two years both of them found refuge in madness.

After her mother, and then Petronella herself, music was Stumff's passion, though he stopped at Beethoven. The rot, he used to say, set in with Beethoven. For a time, including the first few years of Petronella's life, he played a valveless French horn with the Münchener Band, a chamber orchestra who attempted authentic performances of baroque music for their own delight if no one else's. They were also pleased to have a horn player they did not have to pay. But to maintain an *embouchure* that will achieve chromatics without valves requires six hours' practice a day and can lead to a particularly nasty repetitive strain injury. He gave it up before Petronella's ninth birthday. However, he was also a competent keyboard player, owned a small collection of seventeenth- and eighteenth-century instruments, and by the time she was ten was accompanying her in eighteenth-century songs and later simplified arias from *opera seria*, baroque cantatas, and so on.

The relationship between musicians who play and sing together on a one-to-one basis can become very close in a way which is not exactly spiritual, for the ecstasies that can occur are physical. There is a throbbing excitement, a sense that one is communicating at a depth beyond normal human experience. This excitement, this pleasure, is even more intense if there are other ties too. After Petronella's mother died she and her father were never apart except when, for maybe only half the time the law required, she attended school. He changed the schools twice or three times a year. For the rest of the time they sang and played together, went to concerts and theatres together, all over the world. And during the last year or so David Querubín became an obsession. The last year that is before Stumff shot himself.

Querubín was coming to the end of thirty years as the world's foremost interpreter of the major castrato roles created by all the great composers from Monteverdi to Mozart. Though he refused to confirm or deny it he was presumed by almost everyone to be a castrato, the last castrato singer on the international stage. In 1981 he announced his retirement. His final role would be Ulisse, Ulysses or Odysseus, in Monteverdi's *Il ritorno d'Ulisse in patria*: a daring choice, since it has always in modern times been sung by a tenor and the evidence it was written for a male soprano is slight or non-existent. And he would sing it at the end of the 1982 season at the Metropolitan, New York, with set and costumes by David Hockney. Stumff paid a fortune for second-circle seats at the last performance.

Petronella was almost fifteen, tall, thin, blonde, with hair long and straight. She had reached puberty and when she made love with herself she imagined that she was with her father.

Querubín's performance was unbearably exciting and intensely moving, and during the final duet with Penelope, with those two soprano voices alternating and occasionally melding, Petronella formed the resolve that one day she would sing like Querubín. Back at the Waldorf Astoria she told her morose father that this was what she wanted to do.

Stumff, however, felt that Querubín's final performance

marked the end of an era. He did not believe that it was possible for any woman to develop the power a genuine castrato can draw on, nor develop a timbre that will distinguish her voice from that of the female sopranos and mezzos she will sing with. His refusal to believe that he would one day hear the castrato roles sung again as well as Querubín had sung them, and by his daughter at that, exasperated and inflamed her.

She used the shower that separated their adjoining rooms, and then went through the connecting door. He was already in his bed, but awake, staring at the ceiling. She turned off the lights, dropped her towel, pulled back his duvet, flung herself astride him, and, yes, she sang. Stumff was still only just forty years old. It seemed to him that the fleshly wraith whose surging loins embraced his was a succubus in the guise of his daughter, summoned perhaps by the power of his own repressed fantasies.

Later she became pregnant. Stumff, devout Catholic though he was, procured an abortion for her. He sincerely believed that for what he had done he deserved an eternity in the innermost circle of Hell along with Judas and the other betrayers. To make sure he got there he committed the final, unforgivable sin and committed suicide.

Petronella remained determined to sing Querubín's roles and sing them as well as he had, make them hers. There would be no point otherwise, no point at all, in anything.

III

Nine years later she drove her small red BMW cabriolet down the N323 from Granada to the coast. It was a foul road through decayed extended villages made up of dwellings and shabby shops stuccoed in greyish brown, cracked and crumbling. In the spaces between there were tobacco fields, a military airfield, and new urbanizations of white terraced cottages dumped into the foothills of the Sierra Nevada. As she drove, her mind hovered between the past and the future. The future was a year, at least, as Querubín's live-in student, the past was . . .

The past had begun with three years of horror in the same Swiss boarding school her mother had attended. It taught her to hate institutionalized authority, the first time she had experienced it in any inescapable way. However, building on a foundation laid by her father, she also became fluent in French and Italian, which, with the German and English she already had, gave her the languages she wanted to sing in. The music teaching was awful, and the private tuition her guardians, cousins of her mother, arranged for her scarcely better. They knew she could sing. They wanted her to sing Brünnhilde and Isolde, Strauss and Mahler. They even hired a psychiatrist who tried to persuade her that her fixation on baroque castrati roles was the result of psychosis caused by the events leading up to her father's suicide.

At the Swiss school she also learnt to enjoy love with other girls but failed to form a lasting attachment.

On her eighteenth birthday she shed her guardians and embarked on a campaign to persuade Querubín that she should be his pupil. It was not easy. The process was long and expensive and almost exhausted what was left of her inheritance: her father had already used up much of it in that mad year or so when they had been Querubín groupies, pursuing him round the globe and always sitting in the best seats and returning to the best hotels. And after that the Swiss school had been paid for out of her money, not her guardians'. But she did it. The last preparation was a summer course at a language school in Madrid, trying to convert her Italian into Spitalian. One of the first things Querubín told her was that on that at least she had wasted her money. But before that she went to Rio de Janeiro where an elderly but fashionable surgeon reduced the size of her breasts, perhaps the only physical feature she had inherited from her mother, to a size compatible with the roles she wanted to sing.

How had she persuaded Querubín to accept her? She went to America and then back to Britain and took the best tuition money could buy. She bombarded him with tapes, commentaries, references, photographs.

∽

Thirty kilometres or so from Granada the N323 winds round the western massif of the Sierra Nevada through gorges dynamited out of the rock. To the right, the west, the ground is broken up in tumbled hills: orchards surround smallholdings; there are groves of olive, citrus and almond; stands of poplar and eucalyptus cluster round small white villages. Beyond them the next sierra climbs into the sky. It does not match the Nevada but nevertheless it is imposing. Through it meanders a serpentine lake, created by one of the hundreds of dams Franco caused to be built all over Spain. Following Querubín's instructions, written in florid handwriting, legible in spite of excuses that his sight was poor, Petra took a right down a minor road which crossed the dam. Then she drove back up the other side of the lake for a kilometre or so, before climbing a wide river valley with occasional fig trees, low but spreading and laden with purple or yellow fruit.

It was September and still very hot and in many ways the worst time of year with the oranges not yet ripe, the summer wild flowers gone. But the villages were splendid with banks of nicotiana, bougainvillaea, pale blue plumbago, geraniums and roses; and across the mountainsides above the orchards oleander, pink and white, still bloomed above wild rosemary in its second, autumnal flowering.

Presently she drove through a small white village called Campanillas: a church, two supermarkets, a post office and two banks, later she got to know it well, and then two kilometres on, with the valley closing in now, she came to Villa Melchor.

Approaching from the village she saw a complex of ochre rectangles perched across a bluff of brown rock which was almost sheer to the north where the river wound round it, but to the south tumbled more gently through ancient Moorish terraces into untended orchards behind low dry-stone walls. Around it and showing above tiled roofs were tall dark cypresses and palm trees with their pale gold swags of fruit amongst the high fronds. Access was on the far side: coming from Campanillas she had to circle the cliff which was hung with morning glory and emerald ferns, pass through an ungated gateway and climb a steep track beneath sweet-chestnut trees to a patch of gravel shaded by a high wall supporting deep eaves. In front of her, though she did not really take it in that first time, there was a low, modern garage, big enough to take four vehicles, one of which was a small tractor. There were other outhouses as well.

The high stuccoed wall was pierced by four shuttered windows. One, above big arched double doors made from silvered cedar wood, was larger than the others. The doors were wide enough and high enough to take a hay-cart. Her approach had been marked: six white doves circled the air above the roofs before swinging on clacking wings back to their places on the tiles.

A wrought-iron bell-pull was fixed to the honey-coloured stone. The tug she gave it set off a distant but just audible jangle.

IV

Querubín listened to the rumble of her car as it climbed the stony, rutted track below; he heard the jangle of the bell. He swung legs, the varicose veins discreet beneath silk pyjamas, to the floor, and wrapped himself in a dark red silk dressing gown embroidered in gold with prancing oriental cats, padded across marble slabs and stationed himself in the corner of the window embrasure, pushing the slatted blind a little more widely open so he could watch her first entrance into his domain.

Elegant pillars supported four arches forming a Moorish cloister which ran along the wall she would come through. It was not original. The previous owner, Gabriel Melchor, had torn out the barns that the high doors led into and replaced them with an imitation based on the Patio of Myrtles in the Alhambra, but leaving the big hayloft above more or less untouched apart from opening up the north-facing lights. Melchor had been a painter, and the hayloft his studio. In front of the cloister, but angled quite noticeably off the right-angle, an almost rectangular pool half-filled the space below Querubín, a pool perhaps twenty-five metres by ten. Deep enough to swim in at the far end, it sloped up to the cloister so you could walk rather than step into it. It was surrounded by beds filled with an apparently haphazard arrangement of lilies, roses, bougainvil laea, plumbago, and topiaried citrus amongst whose dark oily green leaves small lime-green fruits had just taken on a first blush of gold.

Carmen, short and tubby, dressed in black, with iron hair scraped back in a bun, trotted out of a side door, along the cloister, through yellow light and violet shadow, and so to the big double door which was fastened with a thick square beam of Spanish oak. This she slid into the cavity of the double wall. It was the only barrier to intruders – but as effective as any number of chains, Yales, mortices.

Already Querubín approved Petra Von Stürm. As she came

through the doorway and into the cloister, he was impressed. His eyes, failing badly at distances under two metres, were still tolerably functional at the thirty or so which separated them. He saw a tall young woman. Her feet were small and neat in simple black slip-ons; on her long legs she wore cropped leggings in some dark material and above them a simple blouse in terracotta silk, loose and tied above her waist. Her hair was fair, not far off white, and very short. He took all this in, and as he did so she pulled off unassertive shades, and gasped.

As well she might, he thought, knowing what she saw.

She took off her shades and gasped. On either side the buildings of Villa Melchor soared into square towers or tumbled in a confusion of sloping roofs set at the oddest angles. The roofs were russet red, the walls warm ochre stucco or rosy stone. There were galleries above ground level with doors and windows, and walls pierced only with tiny ventilation holes or arrow slits. Through shrubberies of rose and citrus she could see more cloisters like the one she stood in. There was a short section on the second floor to her right with modern windows and modern glazing, but done with the sensitivity of a good architect: it did not blend, it was not meant to, it took its place without assertion.

The levels dropped beyond the pool; to her left a final square tower framed the cypresses and palms and the blue and violet spaces between her and the sierra, four, five kilometres away across the valley she had driven up. And in the wide spaces between the buildings there were first the pool and a riot of flowers and shrubs, then a small simple fountain, off-centre, its single jet luminously white against the distant cliffs.

Swifts scoured the deep blue above, in lower layers of air house martins flashed rumps enamelled white. Swallows skimmed the surface of the water, sipped from its liquid skin. Behind her the doves she had disturbed cr-crr-croooed, and crickets laid in a ground. The air was heavy with the scent of lilies, jasmine, and the full-blown roses.

She turned at last to the thickset woman who had opened the magic door for her.

'*Gracias,*' she said. A mistake for . . .

'*De nada . . .*' Carmen took her elbow in a tightly clamped grasp and, with a long flow of Andalusian Spanish, steered her off to the right.

'Flow' is quite the wrong word. Andalusian does not flow: it chatters crisply like liquid castanets, especially from between the lips of the older women, and while every syllable is pure and enunciated carefully, like the quiet but percussive clap *al presto* of the subtler flamenco artists, it is impossible to follow if your Spanish is anything less than very competent indeed. But Petra caught the gist. El señor required that Carmen should show her over most of the domain before he welcomed her in person.

At the end of the cloister there was a lobby with three wooden doors and the bottom steps of a spiral stair. One Carmen threw open for only a moment: Petra caught a glimpse of a room white and gleaming, filled with unpolished silvery timber furniture, stoves and cookers, a deep-freeze, washing machine and so on. There were tinned copper pans and gleaming utensils on the walls or hanging from the ceiling, but also air-cured mountain hams, salamis and sausages in strings, ropes of garlic and onions, bunches of herbs, whose fragrances swam out on the life-enhancing odour of oil from olives just crushed and pressed, no more than that.

Amongst it all a small stout man with a haze of white stubble on his cheeks, in a short-sleeved white shirt and tan slacks, was sitting at the big scrubbed table. He looked up from his newspaper, touched the rim of his shattered straw panama . . . but before he could rise to be introduced, Carmen had shut the door and flung open another. Petra gathered that he was Carmen's husband Paco, an old fool, a touch *loco*, and Carmen tapped her forehead.

Petra was now looking down a long, dark, shuttered hall. The ceiling was high and coved, with three transverse wooden beams. The wall to her left was pierced with four large, high, shuttered embrasures which yet leaked a little light. Carmen went to the nearest and hauled partially open the glazed door that filled it and then pushed the floor to ceiling shutter which squealed across the stone flags. A big brown cricket whirred about them in evasive flight. Carmen chased after it, batted at it until it guessed what she wanted and zoomed out over the pool where a red-rumped swallow claimed it for a late lunch. Above the pool, behind a blind slatted but luminous in sunlight, Petra caught a glimpse of a crimson robe. Querubín? Surely. But Carmen's tongue clattered on, and politeness demanded she should try to understand.

They were in a *biblioteca*, a library, an archive. Set on grey shiny flags of a stone which had a soapy look to it, a long black table filled the middle. High black bookstacks leant against the wall facing the casements, with a big black fireplace in the middle. There were hundreds, perhaps thousands of books some haphazardly pushed on to the shelves but few with their spines facing outward in the conventional way. Many had been left on the table in uneven piles, some still bound with string. Near these, chests, the old-fashioned ones lined with tin-foil in which tea was once transported across oceans, still stood, half-filled with yet more books.

There were also box files, nearly all a faded crimson, with cryptic labels, the coded indices of their contents, hand-written in Spanish italic on their backs. Some of these were on the table or floor, others were stacked on the shelves.

It was not as dusty, nor as cobwebby as the chaos suggested it should be. Petra used her inadequate Spitalian to stumble out a comment to that effect, and Carmen's sibilant clatter came back at her, accompanied by swift, short, expressive gestures of the spread hands, made as if to move on a passing fly rather than do it any harm.

Petra thought Carmen was simply telling her that she swept and dusted the big room once a month though no one ever came in and the gesture described the motions of her cleaning. But later she learnt that in this part of Andalusia these gestures are very typical, have infinite variations though there is a basic meaning: what can we do about it? Police, landlords, officials, bank-clerks, shopkeepers, doctors, dentists, midwives and nurses, the mad old lady next door, God, the priest and the

Pope, the man who runs the post office are/is an idiot, but what can we do? The same applies to frost, heatwave, earthquake, flood, arthritis, and God again. Nothing to be done, forget them.

Carmen turned to leave and Petra, turning with her, found herself facing a painting on the wall beside the door. It was big, a full-length portrait, just about life-size, framed in fluted wood glossily lacquered in black. At the corners carved mouldings figured simple stylized but swirling leaf patterns: *modernismo* – the moment in Spain when art nouveau became art deco.

The painting was of a girl: fifteen, sixteen? She had her back to the painter, one knee on the seat of a high-backed chair, her forearms spread aross the top, and she was looking into a tall mirror that reflected her face but darkly. She was slim, wore a white blouse over a full crimson skirt gathered at the waist. Her long dark hair had auburn highlights and was worn up, but coils and loops hung over her white and vulnerable neck. The mirror reflected a beautiful but secret smile, the twist of her waist between buttocks and torso was provocative. Not only was the technique exemplary, the stated and suggested messages were clear too. 'I am rich, for my father would not have been able to afford a painter as good as this if I were not. The painter is deeply attracted to me and I to him, and to please him I put on this subtly provocative pose, and as he paints me he sighs and sighs again . . .' But the painter, though indeed he had fallen in love – the painting would not have been so good had he not – had a commission to fulfil and he kept in mind what he had been employed to do.

This instant analysis was good, but, Petra discovered later, flawed.

'*Su madre,*' Carmen muttered, and moved to close the shutter. Before she did Petra was able to read the flamboyant signature in the bottom-right-hand corner and the date: Gabriel Melchor, 1914. She wondered. Villa Melchor? *Su madre* – his mother. Querubín's mother? She supposed so.

Hearing the creak of the shutter Querubín returned to his vantage point to see the two women emerge into the little corner lobby opposite, blinking at the sunlight after the darkness of the library. In his mind's eye he followed their progress up narrow spiral steps made of flagstones set in the central pillar. At the top no doubt they paused: would Carmen explain that the door they now faced led into Melchor's old studio, and was never, ever opened? Would Petra's Spanish be good enough to understand? Would she ask why the room was forbidden? Carmen would shrug broad shoulders and reply, 'No sé' – I don't know.

And here they were coming along the gallery above the library: built from ilex timbers it was supported by thick stone pillars with capitals coarsely carved with leaf patterns. Carmen was chattering away, the German/English girl followed, head craned forward over the older woman's shoulder, strenuously, it seemed, trying to make sense of what she said. Then they paused and Petra turned, hands on the wooden balcony. She straightened, head up, breathed in the warmth, the fragrances, the loveliness of it all.

Yes, Querubín thought with a sigh, she is beautiful, more beautiful than the photographs suggested. A sexless beauty: straight, slender, strong. If I can get her to sing, if she can act, she'll do.

The gallery ended in a modern door which Carmen opened into the small suite of rooms which would be Petra's for as long as she stayed. Everything here was light, airy, modern: a small study with a bookcase, a desk, a Yamaha upright piano, the furniture black, elegantly functional, the walls white, but on the desk a bright beaten copper jug, Moroccan, filled with the blushing roses that were his favourite. He had tried to cut them himself but had had to ask Paco to help.

And now Carmen would be showing her the bedroom, the large bed covered with a heavy white cotton spread, with a raised woven pattern, also from Morocco, the simple white bathroom, the cupboards and so on. Impossible that she should not be pleased, delighted.

Time now he prepared himself to meet his visitor, whose tour would soon end in his sitting room, where he had told Carmen he would be waiting to receive her. He felt a tremor of nervousness, anxiety, but also a subtle thrill of expectation. Turning from the shuttered window, he shed his dressing gown and pyjamas, took a brief post-siesta shower, and then, towelling himself, paused in front of a tall mirror. What would she make of him? He peered closely, stood back – his damned eyes, they seemed worse each day.

But he knew, knew what she would see and too what she would not see. Short white hair, an open lightly tanned face, more lined than his sixty-nine years would lead you to expect, just a touch oriental around baggy eyelids, a body succumbing prematurely to old age, arms thin and a little saggy, the torso heavy, the barrel chest that had given his voice such power falling away from the prominent breast-bone, and a loose-skinned stomach. At the height of his career diet had been a terrible problem; often he had had to waste himself like a jockey, refusing to appear in heroic, even romantic roles looking like a fat old queen. Then, above legs now spindly and with veins like ivy branches, the mutilated genitalia: well, it was not likely she would ever see him as he really was. He put aside the towel, reached for a cotton polo shirt, dark blue, silk boxers, pale slacks and loafers.

He welcomed her briefly, with courteous formality, asking how her journey had been, and suggested that Paco should take her cases to her room. She should spend the rest of the day settling in, unpacking, resting, exploring, whatever. Carmen would bring her supper or anything else she required. They would meet again in the morning, at ten, in the music room.

V

She woke at seven, showered, breakfasted off the *churros* and chocolate Carmen brought – far too rich – and then did two hours of voice exercises before going down to the music room.

This was a hollow cube of stone with a fine acoustic. Probably, Querubín explained as he welcomed her over the threshold, it had been the guard room of the small Moorish fort that was the nucleus of the whole complex and which now formed the wing which also held his study and, above, his bedroom and bathroom with a couple of smaller guest rooms. The fort had been built on a spur overlooking the road at the point where the valley widened and spread itself into fertile fields. No doubt the soldiers took tribute from travellers who entered the domain of the Sultan of Granada, and protected the peasants from marauders who came down from the mountains.

Shelves filled with scores lined the walls to the two metres to which Querubín could comfortably reach. He was shorter than Petra had expected, and later admitted that he had almost always worn lifts on stage. A couple of fine Turkey rugs covered most of the stone floor, there were four or five functional chairs and stools, a couple of music-stands and the instruments he kept to accompany singers who came to him for masterclasses. The chief of these was a portative organ, with two manuals, flues and reeds, early eighteenth century. It was very pretty, with intricate lattice work covering the pipes, and mother-of-pearl inlay on the panels.

'She's nice, don't you think? And she doesn't need retuning.' Then the tone shifted, became jocularly guilty. 'But I've had her converted: the bellows operate electrically.'

There was also a modern clavichord he did not much like, though it did stay in tune for weeks at a time, and another upright Yamaha piano.

'Of course I'd like a harpsichord, but . . .' he shrugged. 'I have a car and a chauffeur. But the chauffeur is also my gardener, whereas a tuner . . .'

Finally a seventeenth-century guitar, small, the hole in its sound-board filled with gilded fretwork, first cousin to the one in Vermeer's *The Guitar Player*, sat in the single upholstered armchair done out in green velvet.

Over the fireplace there was an oil painting framed in faded gilt, again a portrait. It depicted the head and torso of a handsome but severe man in late middle age wearing mid-seventeenth-century costume – a padded striped jerkin with a simple lace-edged collar falling over the shoulders. He had a high forehead with receding hair, white at the temples, severe eyebrows, searching intelligent eyes, a good nose spreading slightly at the tip, and the moustache, beard and lean cheeks one associates with Don Quixote. The countenance, however, though unsmiling, was decidedly not doleful. Sharp, enquiring, purposeful, it was the face of a man who knew he was going into places where no one had been before, an explorer not of the physical world but of the mind.

'Claudio Monteverdi.' Petra, having recognized the face, took in the rich dark colours, the mastery of the brushwork. 'It looks contemporary.'

'It is.'

'Goodness.'

On that first occasion there was awkwardness between them, between master and pupil, hierophant and acolyte, not unlike the moment between lovers when both know they will answer yes, but which of them will ask? To defuse it she moved to pick up the guitar. 'May I?'

He shrugged assent but she guessed he would rather she did not.

'It's very beautiful.'

'It was,' he said, 'my mother's. She took it up after my father's death . . . I believe.'

In conversation his voice was richer, deeper than she had expected, but just then she was struck by a break in it and a sort of faltering uncertainty. She shook off the awkwardness, left the guitar where it was.

'All right. My voice is warmed up. I'm ready if you are.'

She did not want to sound pushy, but nor did she want to have to repeat exercises she had already done.

He sat at the clavichord, played a rippling chord and then an intro she recognized: Handel, Solomon. She did her best, but blew it after the first few bars. He pushed back his chair, folded his arms.

'I heard you warm up,' he said, peering at her through the thick half-lenses he had put on, 'and of course I have heard your tapes. You have a pretty voice. It can be a good voice. You have power, or at any rate the possibility of power. And I think a very wide range which really is encouraging. But my dear you sing as if you had yellow plaits, a horned helmet, and a shield.' He shook his head, dolefully, making a meal of it. 'You don't, you do not yet, sing baroque.'

She said to herself, I must not be fazed, he's just letting me know who's in charge.

'But you can teach me? You will teach me to sing baroque?'

'We'll see. We'll see. Now we shall take it a phrase at a time, all right?'

From all the languages they spoke they settled on English. His German was awful, her Italian fair, her Spanish awful, but his English was very good, with an old-fashioned, pre-war, upper-class accent.

When the lesson ended two hours later she had to conceal from him unshed tears, born of frustration and anger rather than his remorseless nagging and attention to minute detail. She made her way back to her room, threw herself on the bed and then, when she had recovered, ran through relaxing exercises before doing some simple yoga. At two, precisely, she made her way to the dining room.

This was an imperfectly rectangular room with ochreish stone walls set between the big entrance Carmen had first opened for her and the kitchen. It was under the locked studio. The furniture was simple: a round black wooden table, large enough for eight, with eight carved high-backed chairs, only one of which had arms and a cushion – the one Querubín used. There was also a big black Castilian dresser with Moroccan bowls and plates patterned with free designs in greens and blues. These were often used – for fruit, and occasionally for wonderful stews served with *migas*.

The vast open stone fireplace was filled with oleander blossom placed in a big beaten copper cauldron polished to shine like burnished red gold. Later, through January and February, it was replaced with boles of olive wood which smouldered slowly, occasionally brightened with yellow fig boughs and pink pomegranate, both of which gave off spicy fumes.

Once more there was a painting. Bolder and with a far more vibrant palette than the portrait of Querubín's mother, it again bore Melchor's flamboyant signature. It was dated 1936. It was clearly a picture of the pool outside, with a bed of lily-like flowers in the background. Their trumpeting vermilion petals clashed with crimson shade and spears of emerald green leaves. In the foreground a naked youth sliced a sheet of water from the surface, blue, green and white, with a vigorous, open-palmed push. A woman swung away from him with arms flung up in an arc above her turning head. Although she seemed to scream, it was a scream of laughter, even joy. Petra judged the male to be adolescent, because the movement of his body was precisely the movement one sees at the seaside or in swimming pools when a young lad seeks to splash a friend, usually a girl-friend, and because his body and not yet fully formed genitals were also those of a thirteen or fourteen year old. The woman was older, with ripe, well-formed breasts and black luxuriant hair, but how much older was hard to tell since much of her face was masked by her arm and by the sheeting water. It was a picture full of movement, light and excitement and yet it filled Petra with a deep nostalgia for something she had never known.

If, she thought, she had known a boy like that when she was nearly fifteen, in an ambience as filled with hedonistic freedom as these two painted figures shared, she would not have seduced her father and he would not have killed himself.

*

31

He asked, 'Do you like the soup?'

'It's delicious.'

And so it was. Nothing to it but almonds, garlic, saffron, olive oil, but . . . delicious.

'And the wine?' He lifted his glass, the gesture a toast to her arrival.

She sipped. It was a brownish rosé, dry, tangy, different, strong.

'After the first glass I always add Casera.'

Lemonade, but not too sweet, just carbonated mineral water with a hint of lemon and lime.

When he went to put the glass down its round base just clipped the handle of his unused knife. It toppled, but Petra caught it before it spilled, righted it. She was not sure if he noticed what had happened.

'This is a very simple establishment,' he continued. 'Don Paco and his wife Carmen look after me, the house and the gardens, though they get a little help in from the village too, since they are almost as old as I am. I never tell them what I want to eat, though I have told them what I will not eat. Tripe and pigs' trotters, to both of which they are partial. You will find the cuisine to be Andalusian peasant. Is that all right?'

'Not too much fried, I hope. A year ago I battled to lose five kilos, and I am very anxious indeed not to put them back on.'

'Quite right. I shall warn them. Always I too had to fight off the spare tyre so I know what you had to put up with. In 1964 I was asked to sing the title role in Cesti's *Endimion*. Imagine my consternation when I discovered that the costumes were to be minimal. I had a spare tyre three inches thick, and bosoms to match . . . far bigger than yours. And I was meant to be an adolescent shepherd boy whose beauty had seduced the Moon herself!'

She felt a slight flush rise. Was it coarse of him to mention her breasts? Did a eunuch of nearly seventy still dwell on such things? Did he know, could he know what she had had done? She came back to earth with a plate of small pieces of chicken deep fried with slivers of garlic, and . . . chips.

'I can ask them to do something else for you . . .?'

'No. I am quite good at avoiding the occasion of sin. But once temptation is placed in front of me . . . '

And that made him laugh, which was good, and from then on they were more relaxed. And though she ate up her chips, and marvellous they were too, since they were cut thin and had been slow fried in olive oil from the local press, she was spared four or five of the chicken bits. A silver tabby, lean and elegant with a thin face and huge eyes, had materialized round her ankles, rubbing against them.

'I am afraid we feed her at table. Do you mind?'

'Certainly not. She's quite lovely. What is she called?'

'Molí.' Molleee. 'Look at her forehead and you'll see why.'

A clear large black 'M'. Petra slipped her a portion of chicken wing and was rewarded by the sound of small bones cracked.

VI

'After lunch, I take a siesta. I advise you to do the same. You may swim in the pool if you wish. Although it has no filters or pumps Paco fishes out the leaves and any other detritus almost daily. It was originally built as an irrigation tank, of course, filled by a spring which now provides the little fountain at the far end. Through the summer we empty it once a week, siphoning it into the channels, making sure that each plot gets what it needs. Then it's refilled and for a day or so the water is quite cold, but it soon warms up.'

She took his advice, though on that first afternoon found the shady gloom of her room unattractive, the hot sunlight outside irresistible. She was moreover still in a state of agitation, excitement over all that had happened in the preceding twenty-four hours. To have achieved an ambition conceived nearly ten years before, to have found that in many ways it exceeded all her expectations, but in others had already turned out unpleasantly problematical, and all in this glorious setting, had left her exhausted but febrile, drained but still high; a doze on her bed was out of the question.

She pulled on a simple one-piece bathing costume, scooped up a big bath towel, a novel by Christa Wolf and pushed her feet into espadrilles. Then remembering dear dead Mama warning her against swimming after meals, she wandered down the sun-filled arcades, crossed the end of the pool and stood for a moment between it and the little fountain. The basin itself was grey stone, about half a metre high, two metres square, the lip smoothly rounded. In the middle was a shallow circular bowl with a diameter of about a metre filled from a central jet whose unwavering force reached the height of her shoulder before splashing back. The water, clear, cold and pure, overflowed its rim into the square which, on the far side, had a narrow outlet with a wrought-iron mesh fine enough to retain plump goldfish. There were water-lily pads, but, in September, no flowers.

She walked round to the other side of the fountain and looked out over the view spread in front of her. She was on a low terrace which she guessed had been built up to the spring when it was enclosed to make the fountain. It was paved with cracked mossy flags, kept moist by blown spray. There were two high terracotta urns filled with pelargoniums round which danced nymphs and graces in low relief, the folds of their diaphanous gowns moulding breasts, buttocks and even navels. Their hair was wild in what she guessed was a wind as hot as the one that now swept up the valley from the Granada Vega. She felt a tug at her heart and let her hand caress the porous smoothness of the warm, baked clay, but still could not fight off the angst of all this newness, nor a sense of doubt, self-doubt.

Nearby, but closer to the boundary wall, stood some of the palms and cypresses she had seen from her car the day before. Below her terraces tumbled down the hill: citrus of all sorts, pomegranate, quince, two fig trees, and on the lower levels big ancient olives. The breeze drifted through the silvery leaves and the sun-bleached grasses beneath them and she could hear distant goat-bells, outside the domain, and an occasional hoarse but high treble shout '¡Cabra, cabr-eee-to!', and then, nearer, the chuckle of running water. The overflow from the fountain. That was where she would go: where the water went.

She walked down the transverse steps from the terrace, and soon found it, a small thread, brown over stones, liquid silver where the light caught it. She followed it into the orchards and where the trickle of water finally shrank and disappeared found she was facing one of the big, spreading fig trees. Its silvery boughs curved like the branches of a giant candelabra, the lower ones weighed down by purple fruit and huge leaves to touch the tops of the grasses. Stooping, she pushed through them and found she could stand by the big trunk, wrinkled and grey, like an elephant's leg.

Thick roots wound out from its base and two of them cupped a round hollow space. She cleared out three figs that had dropped there, spread the towel and lay back on it, her head on the bole of the tree, her arms on the roots. Looking up, she found she was beneath a dome of brilliant sun-filled green, a vault ribbed with silver branches, whose twigs ended in the soft purple fruits. The air was heavy with the smell of sweet fig. There were no flies and so far no ants: a pair of bronze, lithe lizards were probably the reason for their absence. They basked in a sunny patch on a nearby boulder, staring at her with unblinking eyes that glistened like black pearls.

She felt sweat between her shoulder-blades and tasted the salt on her top lip. She knew she could not be seen. Only the distant goatherd, banned from this paradise, would be up and about at this time of day. Without rising, she peeled off the costume, then closing her eyes to make a vermilion screen between her and the leaves she began by playing with her stunted breasts. Presently her right hand moved down to her groin. Desire rose and throbbed, spread in warm pulsing tides down her thighs and tingled in the skin of her buttocks. At last she flung a thigh over one of the roots, thrust a fold of the towel between the bark and her sex, mounted the root, threw herself along it, clung to it. At first the nightmare returned, the lean quixotic middle-aged man beneath her who twisted, screamed even, but refused to push her off, reject her; then her mind's eye sought out the image of the boy in Melchor's painting, fixed on his partially tumescent penis, made it rise and with that vision roughly forced herself to climax.

Heart still racing, she rolled back on to the towel, sat up, shook perspiration from her eyes, rubbed her forehead on her forearm, spread her knees, waited for the faint dizziness to recede, then wondered at the lacerations on her inner thighs, the storm of passion which had brought them but which had left her glowing with gentle delight. Plop on cue, a large purple fig landed perfectly in the space between her knees. She laughed a little, then chortled as she slowly peeled down the purple skin, and let her tongue catch a tear of juice and tickle the sweet seeds beneath. She glanced across at the sunlit boulder: the lizards had gone, hardly surprising really, she thought, and she giggled again.

*

Shoes off, stretched out on a woven cotton bedspread, Querubín lay in twilight behind slatted shutters closed but which allowed bars of light to lie across the floor. Presently Molí leapt on to the bed beside him, licked herself about a bit, and settled with a purr like a distant Harley Davidson. He tickled her chin, by way of a hello. The ceiling shimmered with a gentler light which bounced from the surface of the pool. In the fullness of an Andalusian afternoon in hot early September the silence was almost perfect: both birds and cicadas observed the siesta, only the bees in the plumbago outside his window kept up their steady drone. Unbidden, the soprano line of a madrigal flickered in his mind, the lilting cadences, dolorous for a love long gone.

'*Due belli occhi fur l'armu onde traffita* . . .'

'Two lovely eyes were the weapons that
wounded this afflicted soul
so, for a long season,
it has shed blood in place of bitter tears . . .'

The lilting melody came round again, hovered on a trill, died, and, almost as if he had switched it on, a dream-like memory played itself out behind his lids, perfect in every detail, total recall . . .

ᔓ

A hollow time in a hollow house. They move, the four of them, like planets in space, each in its orbit, observing, watching, circling each other beneath high moulded ceilings, bright chandeliers, round big lumps of furniture that sit like islands in a frozen sea, across marble floors, but never connecting. Doña Pili, the cook-housekeeper-maid, crosses their orbits but, like Halley's comet, is predictable enough to be ignored.

María Dolores is always in black, black heavy silks that rustle, swing only inches above the floor. Condemned by Saturno to wear black, she refuses the new fashions. She says, when asked: the girls in El Corte Inglés wear short black dresses and black stockings. I would not wish to be taken for a shop girl.

37

Miguel is usually in grey, jacketed, breeched and booted, the uniform of a cadet at the Escuela Militar. When he puts his cap on, with its red piping and tassel, Dolí comes close, stands very close, in front of the big mirror by the door to the outer world, and reaches up a little, for Miguel's hard grey eyes are already, at sixteen, level with the top of her head. She straightens the cap, and gives the tassel a little flick to make it swing. Then she smooths the palms of her long white hands down the front of his jacket, checking a pocket button beneath its flap, lingering, a little, before tiptoeing to kiss his lips.

This time (and David is watching through the open door of the dining room, from the high-backed mahogany chair he sits in) she suddenly gathers Miguel's face in her hands, presses her body against his, and lets him feel her tongue. Miguel's hands, big and red – like weapons they are, and David knows them as such for Miguel cuffs and punches him when no one else is there to see – lift, and for a moment David thinks they might close on his mother's waist, return the embrace, but no, they seize her shoulders and shove, push her so the antlers of the big hat- and coat-stand rock above her as she crashes into it.

David turns back to his homework: Felipe II succeeds his abdicated father, goes to England to marry his cousin, María Tudor. Both are grandchildren of Fernando and Isabel . . . the marriage makes him King Consort of England, and is designed to help the reluctant Protestants of that country back into the Catholic fold.

The door to the outside world slams and his mother, distracted, flushed, storms down the hall. David can hear her moving through the big apartment, opening and shutting doors and windows with heavy purple velvet drapes embossed with carnation patterns. In another room Jorge, fifteen, in white shirt and black trousers, grips his cello between his knees, and with his bow drags lugubrious cries from its heart. Oh yes, David remembers, remembers it all, too well, too well.

∾

38

He dozed, slept. But a discreet splash in the pool opened his eyes again and, straining to focus, he made out how the reflected light on the ceiling swung and shifted. Petra. She must now be taking a swim. The lack of noise and the flickering of the light suggested neat athleticism, a smooth crawl, making as little disturbance as possible but fast too, like a dolphin. She would be beautiful, even more beautiful in the water; he would like to see her but balked at being a peeping Tom whose eyes would probably betray him anyway. He turned back to a past forgotten, like a locked room to which dream has the only key.

∽

Miguel masturbates. He kneels on his bed, with his knees a little apart and from between them falsely coy women with big bottoms, big breasts and shadowy crotches look up at him from monochrome sepia postcards. David sees him doing it, because Miguel probably wants him to see, has left his door ajar on purpose. David does not know what is happening, but he knows it is wrong because every time he goes to confession, which he hates, Father Jaime always asks him if he has played with his penis. An hour earlier, before lunch, Miguel pulled David's ears until his eyes ran with tears. So he silently slips away down the corridor and knocks quietly on his mother's door. Ariel, Miguel's huge Irish wolfhound, lean, shaggy and grey, pads behind him, but is not a threat.

María Dolores is sitting in her window seat with a book on her lap, Lorca's *Poeta en Nueva York*, but is looking out and down into the avenue of acacia trees, at the shops and the cafés, aching to be part of the bustle and hustle of the city which is denied her. She spends much of the day thus. David, with a finger to his lips, tiptoes across the Turkey carpets that cover her floor until he is close enough to smell the wonderful perfumes she uses. He whispers.

'Miguel is doing something very naughty indeed.'

'What?'

'Go and see.'

39

Frowning slightly, she puts aside her book, gathers up the silks of her long dress so they cannot betray her, and glides silently out and down the corridor. Ariel pads behind her. She pushes open Miguel's door. David slips back into his own room, lies on his bed, waits . . .

∽

The old man lay on his bed with his cat. In the quietness and balmy warmth of the Andalusian afternoon, he recalled every detail.

∽

'Make yourself decent. Come to my room.'

David waits until Miguel's boots click down the polished marble, then he swings his legs off his bed and pushes open the door. It all works out better even than he hoped.

'You are disgusting,' she says. And her voice is like steel slicing ice. 'I hate you. Every day you grow more like your father . . . You should be whipped.'

But since a whipping is not on the cards, Miguel decides not to let her have it all her own way.

'You killed my father.'

'He died in the arms of a whore.'

'Where he would not have been if you had let him into your bed. I need money.'

'I never denied him my bed. The whore he was with was scarcely in her teens. He liked young girls. You have all the money you need.'

'No. My friends who have fathers have money to go to the whores in Barco. Their fathers give them the money.'

There is a long silence. David then and David now wonders what filled it, what movements, what expressions cross the face of his mother and her eldest son.

At last he hears her say: 'If I had my way I would never see you again.'

David then hugs himself with delight but is back on his bed with his door pushed to before Miguel's boots click back, not to his room, but out through the door, down the stairs and into the streets. Ariel, the tall lean bitch, follows him. Perhaps Mama has given him money. Perhaps he is on his way to Calle del Barco in spite of the shots that ring out a couple of streets away. At all events their mother will never kiss her oldest son again.

VII

After the first awkwardnesses they quickly found a routine. Petra woke early. First she went for a short run following the boundaries of the villa's grounds, down into the orchards where the dried grasses shed white seeds as she passed and some stuck to her socks or, when the mornings became a touch chill, her track-suit trousers. Often a hoopoe swung from fig to orange tree ahead of her and then rowed its magpie-like wings across the valley to the fields that bordered the river, still misty from the dawn. Down one side she ran then climbed the other, panting now but still leaping across old irrigation ditches and the tumbled boulders of dry-stone walls.

Back in her rooms she'd shower, then breakfast off the *tostadas*, coffee and a freshly picked orange she had persuaded Carmen to provide instead of fried *churros* and hot thick chocolate. Then she spent at least an hour on the warm-up exercises Querubín had redesigned for her. At eleven she made her way to the music room for the one extended practical lesson of the day.

They would work for two hours, sometimes two and a half, for much of it with great intensity, but if he felt it was too much he would find an excuse to break off into a discourse on theory, even, after some weeks, discussion.

'Authentic performance? Well, in the first place it remains very uncertain, conjectural. You know how it is: an expert makes a statement about, oh, melisma, for instance, and produces text and argument to prove it. Then three years later along comes someone else who shows the first scholar's texts were corrupt, or his argument lacked logic . . . Secondly, even supposing we got it perfectly right, it would not work. Why not? Because the audience does not, cannot have an authentic *ear*. You understand? No longer do we have an authentic ear any more than we know how to play authentic instruments. When Claudio introduced a dissonance he knew the effect he would achieve. But we cannot conceive what these surprises meant to his audience. Stunning? More than that. But to our ear now it is not so much. So you have to elaborate a little, emphasize, you know . . .? Put it this way. We have to go back into the past to meet Monteverdi. But the audience of his time was dragged into the future by him. There is a huge difference . . . '

As the weeks went by Petra formed the habit of going to the kitchen after her siesta time, where she'd brew up some of the tea she bought in the closed market at Campanillas. It was sold at a health food stall run by a German anarchist and his extraordinarily beautiful Spanish girlfriend. She was slight, small, but with long thin legs and a mass of curly, coarse dark hair which she wore pulled back into a ponytail when she was working. She had large eyes, the brown of mountain tarns, and a full generous mouth. Her largish nose gave her beauty character and strength it might otherwise have lacked. Petra fell in love with her as soon as she saw her. She fantasized that the German boyfriend would fall in love with her, and that out of the ensuing tangle the consummation she desired might come, but they turned out to be cliquy, part of alternative Campanillas, all into home-grown pot and hang-gliding off the mountains. They were suspicious of well-heeled interlopers.

Petra later learned that her name was Mari-Elena. In the meantime, and even after she knew her real name, Petra thought of her as the Parma Violet Lady. This came about as a result of her first visit to the stall. Having bought her tea and wanting desperately to prolong the visit, she glanced over the shelves behind Mari-Elena and picked out tubes of small pastilles wrapped in fine white paper printed in a lavender blue .They produced an instant recall of her childhood. Her English mother had found Parma violet pastilles in a tiny shop in Munich which specialized in *echt*-English products like Harrogate toffee, Barker and Dobson humbugs and so on. Was this Andalusian version as good? They turned out to be better – prepared from locally picked Parma violets, they were very fragrant and not at all like the cheap ersatz sweets bought by children in England under the same name. She bought a tube with her tea and whenever she went back the Parma Violet Lady reached her down another without waiting to be asked.

So, she had her tea, a fine greeny-black large-flaked Ceylon, and with it an almost daily impromptu lesson in Andalusian Spanish from Carmen and Paco.

Then, at five o'clock, if Querubín needed it she'd help him with his mail and business matters for an hour or so, reading letters, taking down his instructions and replies in a notebook, carefully reading them back to make sure she had the Spanish right, and then typing them up on the lap-top Amstrad ALT 286 PC he kept in what he called his salon. Fortunately the programme had a Spanish spell-check.

The salon was next to the music room and at the end of the block which had once been a Moorish fort. It was a large room, a rectangle rather than a square since there was no arcade outside it. The big windows looked straight out on to the space between the fountain and the pool and it was the sunniest, brightest room in the villa.

Petra was not sure she liked it. There was a huge soft suite of sofa and armchairs covered with a chintz that featured over-blown scarlet and black poppies on a white ground. Dwarfed by these there were also Sheraton high-back chairs and occasional tables. There was a baby grand, white. On it and on the tables photographs framed and signed carried fulsome praises of Querubín's interpretations. The Soltis. Leppard. Caballé. Los Angeles. Bream. Rolfe Johnson. Alfred Deller. Eliot Gardiner, and so on. Even Freddie Mercury. There were many paintings, but one that was striking. Melchor again but this time of the fountain outside, a strange picture making two sides of the square pool and about a quarter of the circular basin fill the picture. Two water-lilies bloomed, and the goldfish swam, but there were reflections too, summer clouds and a face which peered into the water from above.

When Petra had finished the correspondence Querubín could no longer manage because of his failing eyes, she returned to her rooms. There she studied scores, compared realizations of the same works, rejecting, accepting, questioning and endlessly memorizing, memorizing until she no longer had to see the notes in her mind's eye but, even in panic, would have them inside her head, part of herself. Over supper she would discuss, question again, argue until he tired.

This was a simple meal but increasingly often a long one as they became more at ease with each other. He would answer her queries about what she had read or what she was practising for the following day, but as time wore on he interspersed his answers with anecdotes about his career, the productions he had featured in, and so on. Often it was midnight before they went to their respective rooms, hers chill now as what passes for winter in Andalusia closed in, and often they were tipsy on the brownish rosé wine he always drank – a wine with no hangover.

Snow covered the mountains down to fifteen hundred metres and settled seriously on the Nevada twenty, thirty kilometres away to the east. In late December an occasional frost touched the garden and orchards for an hour before dawn but was gone before it could do any harm. With no heat to escape from she no longer felt the need to take a proper siesta: instead she drove about the mountains and valleys in her open cabriolet, discovered tiny villages, colossal views and later the swift rush of spring.

On almost her first trip, south and to the west towards Málaga, through mountains powdered with snow but whose lower slopes showed the first hint that the almonds might blossom, she parked on a watershed in a mountain meadow on the border between the two provinces. Grey hump-backs of rock broke dolphin-like through the green and tawny surf. Although the air was warm, rags of snow still loitered in their shade. Between and beyond, the sea, only twenty kilometres distant and fifteen hundred metres below her, filled the high horizon.

Rimmed in the foreground with bright bottle green, the more distant expanses merged from deep ultramarine to deep violets, with small patches of dark purple where puffballs of cloud, actually floating below her, cast their shadows. Furthest away of all a line of cumulus, at this distance a row of seed pearls, lay above a thin dark thread that seemed to mark precisely where sea and sky should merge. An optical illusion? She strained her eyes to make sense of it, even to be sure she wasn't imagining it, then: 'Goodness,' she said aloud. 'Africa!'

She was looking at Africa!

Week by week she felt she could cope more surely with and even exploit the magic land, and in much the same way she felt a growing confidence that Querubín too was an entity to be grasped; that maybe the project she was embarked on was realizable; that, and this was the way she put it to herself, albeit with a wry inward smile, she might yet be the Querubín of the twenty-first century. She knew she had a long way to go, knew there would be storms and worse ahead and perhaps emptinesses as huge as that which lay between her and the distant continent, but an inner toughness, forged out of guilt and loss denied, would carry her through.

One suppertime, after Carmen had cleared away the Manchego sheep's cheese but had left some bread, almonds, fat garlicky olives and a second jug of Vino de la Costa, Petra asked him when he first knew he could sing, really sing. There was a long moment of silence, and then he breathed out a sigh. Elbows on the table, he peered over clenched arthritic fingers into the candle flame.

'I have a problem with memory,' he began. 'The first thing I can recollect with certainty is singing the Te Deum in the choir of a big eighteenth-century church. The date was the twenty-fifth of February nineteen thirty-eight and I was fifteen and a half years old.'

'Let me get this right. Are you saying you have no memories of anything before you were that age?'

'At that time, that is right . . .'

'And now?'

'That is another story which I may explain one day. You asked me when I first knew I could sing. The date I gave you is the date on which I knew for certain that I could sing, that I sang.'

'Sorry.'

The church it happened in was, he said, built of grey stone, on a big scale, and, considering when it was built, very plain, free of extravagant baroque or rococo ornament. It was bitterly cold. Clouds of vapour rose above the black-robed Benedictine monks who filled the stalls. The occasion of the Te Deum, they later told him, was the defeat of the Republican army at Teruel, an event which signalled the certain success of Franco's rebellion against the Republic. By then it was clear that Britain, France and the USA would not intervene on the side of law and justice . . .

'I had, so they told me during the following days, been mute for the eighteen months I had spent there—'

'Where was this monastery?'

'Did I not tell you? The monastery of Santo Domingo de Silos, some fifty kilometres south-east from Burgos. Apparently when the Te Deum began, sung in the plainchant which has been sung there without a break since its foundation a thousand years ago, my mouth began to move with the first words: *We praise thee O God* . . .'

He sang them now, in Latin, in the same Gregorian plainchant. He rarely sang, not even in the lessons. His singing voice was thin now, flute-like, but perfect.

'Sounds broke forth with *All the earth doth worship thee: the father everlasting*; but it was with *To thee Cherubin and Seraphin continually do cry* that my voice came out pure, almost abrasive, and very clearly knowing the anthem's setting. You see I actually do remember this moment, the sudden surge of power flowing up from my lungs across my vocal chords, over my tongue.'

Because until then they had had no name for him but David, the monks added, in place of a family name, Querubín. Cherubim. And some of them, but not many since Benedictines tend to be sophisticated poeple, claimed a miracle had occurred.

'From that day, that moment, my memory functioned normally: now, with my seventieth birthday six months away, I can look back over fifty-three years and recall some things perfectly, others hazily, but most minutiae, unless I make a deliberate act of will to recall them, not at all, just like anyone else of my age. However my first fifteen years are a very different matter.'

'But surely the monks knew how you came to be there, or . . .' She was about to wonder aloud if in fact he had just turned up, knocked on their door. She knew from the histories of twentieth-century Spain she had read in preparation for her stay that stranger things than a lost boy with no memory doing just that had happened during those dreadful years. But he went on, still speaking slowly, not looking at her, but at the flame.

'A doctor from Granada, Jesús García Quintana, brought me to the monastery in September nineteen thirty-six. Apparently he had been coming to Santo Domingo for three weeks each summer over the previous five years, for a period of rest and contemplation. All he would say about me was that an old friend of his had brought me to him for treatment some weeks earlier, that I had no family at all who could look after me, that my injuries were psychological as well as physical. The doctor had somehow managed to get me through the chaos that reigned between Granada and Silos, but may have been killed on his return journey. At all events he never got back to Granada, and indeed was never seen again.'

'The injuries?' But already she knew, and he knew she knew. At last he looked at her, pale eyes a touch watery, a tremor on his lower lip, but a wry smile too.

'I had been castrated – a month or so earlier.'

The wound had been stitched up and dressed, presumably by Doctor García, and was healing well. However, he was in a deep trance-like fugue: he could not speak, he appeared not to hear. He performed necessary physical functions clumsily but well enough to survive. But eighteen months later he broke into song and they called him Querubín. The gift of speech also returned: normal educated Castilian. He also revealed himself to be a

48

likeable, well-educated lad with musical ability and a good grounding in English and French. He could play piano and guitar and he could sing . . . like an angel.

'But I could remember nothing at all of my life before that moment of song:

> To thee Cherubin and Seraphin continually do cry
> Holy, holy, holy, Lord God of Sabaoth
> Heaven and earth are full of the majesty of thy Glory.'

And again, like the light from the candle, the plainchant reached out to the dark corners of the room.

She could see he was tired and disturbed, though not immediately ready for bed. She switched the subject.

'Is it true, what I once read, that you first performed in a Barcelona night-club, singing torch songs in drag?'

The old man chuckled, dabbed his eyes with his napkin, reached for the jug. He topped up both glasses, but filled hers beyond the brim, so some spilled and she had to tell him to stop.

'Damned eyes,' he muttered, then chuckled again. 'Yes. That's perfectly true. And later in Montmartre.'

He explained how the monks hoped he would become one of them, remain in the monastery with its Romanesque cloister, continue to serve God and gratify their musical appetite.

'But as the years passed it became clear to me that I had no vocation, indeed no faith. I took no vows and gradually moved into the outer world, taking the bus to Burgos and so on, rediscovering what I had lost, but for the time being always returning to the monastery, which, was, after all, my home. At last, in nineteen forty-four, when I was, we supposed, twenty-one or twenty-two, I went to the abbot and declared my intention of going out into the world to study music and singing with a view to becoming a professional performer.'

They did their best for him: through connections they had always kept open with the music world (several of the more elderly monks had in fact been professional musicians before coming to Silos late in life) they got him a scholarship which paid for his fees at the Barcelona School of Music. They also found a sympathetic family who gave him bed and board.

Within a year he was earning enough guying popular female singers in the sleazier Barcelona night-clubs to pay his way on his own. However, since transvestism was illegal under Franco, it was a risky way of earning a living, and when the war was over he transferred to Paris and the Scola Cantorum, and later the Conservatoire.

'Not only torch songs. I did a wonderful Shirley Temple, very naughty, "The Good Ship Lollipop", you know? Doris Day and Judy Garland. My only regret was that Julie Andrews came along so much later – I could have *murdered* "The Hills are Alive", or "Doh, a Deer a Female Deer".'

Their glasses and the jug were empty, and still chuckling he stood. She took his arm and led him out into the chill night air, along the cloister by the pool, to the foot of the stone stairs that led to his bedroom. And there he paused, turned those pale eyes on her once more.

'But those were not my first performances in public, you know.'

'No?' She waited.

'The first time I sang in public was at my father's funeral. I was ten at the time.'

He began the climb, leaving her confused and feeling cheated. Incipient senility or some sort of joke? Had it all been fabrication, the story of the lost memory, the monks of Silos?

She turned away, walked between pool and fountain to her own rooms and somewhere a roosting dove cr-crr-crooed at her passing.

VIII

He lay in his bed and, prompted by the talk, the dream-like memory returned. He did not allow himself to follow it all through, but it was there, a huge presence in his mind, hovering like an unopened closet in a surrealist painting – a closet whose contents only the artist knows.

∽

Clouds of sweetly pungent incense drift between glossy marble columns, pale pink and glittery. Purple vestments sway among arum lilies, set the candle flames aflutter above the four gilded candlesticks at the corners of the catafalque, make them fume with the sweetness of beeswax.

The church is not big, though since it serves one of the capital's richest *barrios* it is filled with the worst the second counter-reformation could do in the way of religious 'art'. Our Lady of Lourdes figures prominently, She of Fatima is there too but still a side-show. A very recent addition, and it cost the bourgeois of the Salamanca *barrio* a lot of money, is not a statue but a painting. With large Murillo eyes raised to adore the figure of her Son on the Cross (not a day younger than her, from the look of him, and drastically foreshortened from below, so the feet are twice the size of the head, the wound in them bleeding like a menstruating slit). She is wearing a silvery dove-coloured satin creation (Poiret? Orry-Kelly?), finely pleated, cut a touch lower in the front than is usual in Madonnas; her snood is trimmed with fur.

What it cost demonstrates that the parishioners have acquired a work of art as good as any in the older churches. Unfortunately the building will be torched in 1936 and with it *Mary of the Sorrows*, an early pre-surrealist work by Salvador Dali.

From his choir stall David watches his family. They are sitting in the front row beyond the coffin which is draped in velvet

51

night, edged with gold. First, nearest the nave, usurping the place of the dead man, comes Miguel, his eldest brother, in his cadet's grey uniform but with a broad black arm-band. Well into his fifteenth year, he is a big lad, and already shows unmistakable signs of taking after his father: he has the same mousy-fair hair, cut now in military style very short up the sides and back to a thicker thatch on top, the same square reddish face with strong though not overly large aquiline nose, and firm, thin lips. His body is filling out: he will have his father's barrel chest, and already apes the swagger of his walk. He too is an insensitive bully.

The middle son, Jorge, a year younger and sitting between him and their mother, is very different. Already as tall as Miguel, he is a thin streak of a youth with black lanky hair parted in the middle. His eyebrows are thick and dark, his mouth large. He has the large strong hands of his father's side of the family, though attached to thin arms which seem always to make the sleeves of whatever jacket he wears appear too short. Today he is in a black suit and a black tie, since he was told not to wear his black cravat. At home he plays cello, believes himself to be as good as Casals or the young Tortelier, though as yet he has little gift for anything other than late-nineteenth-century salon music. While Miguel's bullying is insensitive, his is not, which means it is more efficient.

On the other side of his mother is her older sister, Aunt Ana. Tall, thin, with the face of an intellectual and sensitive horse, she clearly takes after her father, David's dead grandfather. There is a photograph of him in his mother's salon wearing Scottish tweeds, holding a Sherlock Holmes pipe, his baggy half-closed eyes separated by a wide long nose which droops over a mouth bent into a smile for the photographer, a smile which has not reached his eyes.

At his son-in-law's funeral his elder daughter wears a pale beige suit with mannish square shoulders. Not only has she refused to wear mourning, she has taken no part in the service, only bobbing, sitting, kneeling, standing when her sister's hand prompts her to. She refuses to cross herself or bow her head.

She is, David knows without understanding what it means, a professed atheist, a socialist, and perhaps worst of all is receiving instruction in Vienna from one of Freud's disciples. She is there because her much younger sister has begged her to come, and she arrived amazingly in time having travelled some of the way by aeroplane.

And in the middle of them all, on this side of the church, there is his mother: María Dolores . . . Dolí.

Madonna. Her black, close-cropped hair, above a heart-shaped face painted dead white with a dark slash of a mouth, is cased in a helmet of black magpie feathers iridescent with oily green. It supports a veil which reaches her chin. Just one feather, above her right ear, has a bright white bar. Not tall, not slim, she has the figure of a Tanagra Aphrodite, the Medici Venus, and the dress she has chosen to wear to her husband's funeral is emphatic. Like the cap it is black but watered silk, swirling, like the feathers, with evanescently discreet emerald and jade. In Querubín's memory she wears her sables open all through the day, even in the church, so the dress, and her figure, can be seen.

David guesses the clownish make-up is there for the same reason as a clown's: to hide the happiness she feels.

The service moves on, through the order of the requiem mass, to a homily in gratitude for the life of the departed. As he listens to the priest's unctuous recitation of the gifts Don Fernando Pérez y Mendizábal lavished on the church and the poor of the Salamanca *barrio* of Madrid. (The poor? There are none.) David decides to make the solo he has to sing an offering for the hitherto remote mother he adores. He would like to offer her diamonds, the way a nine- or ten-year-old boy often does, but he senses the gift of his voice will do.

'*Requiescat in Eternum.*'

He sings his heart out, makes the high notes silvery daggers, right up to a high C (the score reads A, but he knows he can get to the C, and the rise of a third will enchant rather than offend the ear), and the descending glissandos the plunge that places them in his father's heart. And the uplift of the 'amen' at the end, designed by the composer to offer comfort to the bereaved that their loved one has been received into a not too dismal purgatory, becomes a paean, a soaring cry of victory. Let María Dolores become María Victoria de los Angeles. Amen.

'You sang well.' A deep voice, made harsh by cigars and alcohol.

'Thank you, sir.'

'Perhaps a touch bright for such a sad occasion. But it was moving, very moving. I am sure your father, wherever he is, heard and was moved by it.'

The big man, his right hand makes the tall sherry glass which he holds by its base look like a fairy chalice, tweaks the boy's cheek with his left. He makes sure it hurts.

'It won't last for ever, you know.'

'Pardon, sir?'

'The voice. It won't last for ever.'

High above the boy the grey eyes, small behind baggy lids, grey like year-old ice, glitter dully, look down over the grey ridges and crevasses that crease his cheeks on either side of a craggy pitted nose to a fissure shaped like a shark's mouth. He turns away to speak to Father Jaime and his black back momentarily blocks from David's vision everything else in the big room, the salon of his uncle's house, and he shudders. Uncle Miguel, five years older than his father, has always filled him with a fear partly learned at his mother's knee. He is a banker, amongst other things, richer even than Papa, which means he is as rich as Croesus. He owns the Banco de Corpus Cristi, and, because his astute grandfather married the only daughter and child of a poverty-stricken aristo, he occasionally styles himself Marqués de Boltana, though not when to do so would upset the more republican of his associates.

The huge black back, above spats grey with black piping, recedes and David looks round for his mother. She is still standing near the double oak door, flanked by her two older sons on one side and supported by her tall sister on the other, receiving the condolences of late arrivals. A big brass bowl trimmed with a black moiré silk bow and filled with lilies brought by train from Seville stands on a marble pedestal between them and the door.

Further in, a long table covered with snowy linen trimmed with black crape is stacked with cold food: sea-bass in mayonnaise brought by night express from Pontevedra, a Scotch salmon in aspic, packed in crushed ice and flown from Harrods through Northolt and the new airfield at Barajas; two roast sucking piglets from Segovia, their torsos sliced, their heads and tails intact (especially David remembers the tiny tails: *this little piggy went to market*, his anglophile Mama used to say, in English, tweaking his infant toes); porcelain towers supporting shellfish: peachy Dublin Bay prawns, scarlet baby lobsters, phlegmy oysters, grey globules floating in bowls of silvery nacre, sliced lemons; tiny almond paste *petits fours* shaped and coloured like fruit or more fancifully like small coiled snakes; rich fruit cake, English style, soaked with brandy and served with crême Chantilly.

Waiters with trays loaded with glasses of manzanilla and oloroso sherries move through a funereal crowd spiced with occasional fancy-dress: an admiral in full fig, shoulders loaded with bullion; a monsignor in scarlet with a cross a Jew might kiss for the value of its gems; a small fat general, with dark hard eyes, who, David is amazed to hear, is a hero who rode a white horse into battle against the Moors. Francisco Franco y Bahamonde, a man with a future, or so they say.

David picks up a small plate, rimmed with gilt and laurel leaves, seeks and finds a *petit four* shaped and coloured like a strawberry, another like an apple and a third like a pear. If, he says to himself, she chooses the apple then she loves me best.

The last mourners are already picking their way down the buffet table. María Dolores turns to her eldest.

'I have had enough. Please go and tell your uncle we are leaving.' Then she sees her youngest, the offering he has brought. Her full carmine lips close to a tiny pout, then her tongue, a delightful and natural pink, flickers. 'David! How kind.'

She takes the apple.

Miguel returns. 'Uncle says you should stay a little longer.'

Behind the veil which is raised now but still curtains them her dark eyes narrow beneath the magpie feathers. She swallows the last of the almond paste and again her tongue flickers.

'Does he, indeed! Then if he will not send for them, Jorge and David may get our coats, and you will order the car.'

Miguel hesitates. They all do. A tiny movement of one foot, but it is real enough: she stamps.

'Do it.'

Across a sea of Aubusson her eyes meet those of her brother-in-law, and David shudders. Excitement and fear: war has been declared.

In bed that night the words echo in his inner ear, a harsh refrain: *Your father, wherever he is, heard and was moved by it*. But Father is dead in his huge heavy coffin, walled-up in the family mausoleum, a neo-baroque structure of peach-coloured marble and porphyry, purple and white, high on the slopes of the Necropolis del Este. When they arrived at the gate they were stopped by a picket of striking municipal workers, and for a terrible moment David thought they would be made to turn round and bring the cadaver back home. But Uncle Miguel had foreseen the danger and green-cloaked Guardia Civil, black moustaches beneath their shiny black hats, bussed in from the country at his expense, pushed the pickets to one side using the butts of their imported Mauser rifles to let the haughty cortège through. Cushioned in the spicy leather of the cream and black Hispano-Suiza with the sleak futuristic silver bird mounted on its radiator cap, Mama murmured *sotto voce* to his aunt: 'God willing this is the last time I cross a picket line,' to which Aunt Ana had replied: 'It has nothing at all to do with God.'

Walled up the monster was, as monsters should be, behind a slab so thick it took four men with crow-bars to shift it, men in black frock-coats, and top hats scarved in black, hired mourners who had to do the job because the workers were on strike. Shivering in the chill March wind, and from all the excitements and horrors, David watched them stack the wreaths and sheaves of flowers against it. Now, surely, we're safe from him. But eight hours later, exhausted by the strains and conflicting emotions of the day, he twists and turns in the darkness of his bed, and dreams, no, hallucinates how a great wind scatters the flowers, the earth shakes, the marble cracks, and . . . Stifling the scream, he swings his legs out of the bed, pell-mells down the corridor, knocks but does not wait for an answer.

The two women, his mother and his aunt, wearing long satin ivory-coloured night-dresses, are sitting on either side of the big bow-fronted dressing table: his aunt is smoking one of the sweet oval Turkish cigarettes she has brought from Vienna, his mother's long fingers hold a black chocolate filled with maraschino inches from her mouth. They comfort him with kisses and caresses, give him the chocolate and then another, and put him in the big soft bed. They stay up an hour or so longer, talking quietly about things he does not understand, lit by the warmth of a single lamp that glows in a curving flower-shaped glass shade, red and gold, above the mirrors. At last his aunt slips away, the lamp goes out and he feels his mother come into the bed beside him. In the darkness she smooths his forehead, then curls her cool arm around his chest.

'He's gone, you know. He won't come back.'

'I know.' He sighs hugely, with relief. Then: 'Mama?'

'David?'

'I wish you were not called María Dolores. It's such a sad name.'

'What would you have instead?'

'María Victoria de los Angeles.'

Wondering at the beauty of what he has said she allows her long fingers to caress his thighs and stomach and chest but always with the coarse cotton of his night-shirt between. I made this, she says to herself, but he can hear the words on her breath, close to his ear. This is mine. I made it. She pulls him closer and he responds out of the sleep he is sinking into, curls his back into her front. A deep instinct prompts her to pull off her night-dress, whose silky touch now irritates, and his night-shirt too. She rationalizes the resistance she feels: it will wake him from the sleep he needs, and she desists, contenting herself with the deep contentment she already feels.

IX

Petra took to attending the fiestas in Campanillas. This habit began with New Year's Eve, or rather day, for nothing happened until the church clock had begun its twelve strokes. A huge crowd had gathered in the tiny square all clutching bottles of cheap champagne, and paper bags each filled with twelve grapes. On the first stroke a small barrage of rockets and bangers cracked the air and pierced the night sky, and the grapes were consumed one by one with each succeeding clang. Carmen had told her about it: if you got through the lot before the final stroke you have a year of good luck ahead of you. And then still gagging on the grapes they swigged from bottles and glasses and a few feckless ones shook the bottles and sprayed their friends. In the middle of all this Petra spotted Mari-Elena, the woman from the health stall.

Her hair was no longer tied back and she had shed the nylon overall she wore at work. She was wearing a black cotton T-shirt with psychedelic swirls of appliquéd silver. It hugged her small neat bra-less breasts, in much the same way as her black leather mini-skirt held trim her boyish buttocks. She was very thin, but because she was small, not too thin. Her mane was now fluffed out on either side of her head in a haze of darkness. Petra followed her, the German boyfriend, and a boy of about seven who might have been their son, or, more probably, the offspring of an earlier liaison. The German's Spanish was not really good enough for someone who had lived with a Spanish family in Spain for eight years.

They crossed the main road, passed through open wrought-iron gates into a wide patio. It was roofed with a vine, and to the left there was a plastered breeze-block screen painted with a mural. It showed formalized peasants labouring in a broadly painted mountain landscape and was entitled, for reasons that were not clear, *El Precio de Libertad – The Price of Liberty*. The German pushed open a half-glazed door and heavy metal, until then a loud presence, rolled over them like a wave. There was an illuminated sign advertising Aguilar beer and the name of the bar: El Molino, the mill. Petra followed them in and as she did another small crowd of revellers followed her.

It was a big room beneath a high-beamed ceiling of rafters and cane, with swags of sacking slung beneath it. On the right was a pinball machine, then the bar which was conventional enough, and, in the far corner, 'babifut', bar-football. This bar area was separated from the rest of the room by a high wooden rail mounted between brick pillars. At the end nearest the door, next to a computer game, there was a huge screw of polished wood which might have been part of the mechanism of a mill.

Beyond it, in the main part, there were five islands of seats made out of breeze-blocks, stuccoed, whitewashed and cushioned, with glass-topped tables in each. Behind these there was a low stage with black curtaining on which stood a large, back projection television, and a set of amplifiers and speakers. To the left of the stage a pool table, and coming down the wall towards the door, a brick and stone open fireplace in which huge logs of olive wood slowly smouldered, but brightly enough to make the big room cosy.

But what made it were the paintings. These hung wherever there was room: large unframed oils or acrylic on canvas or hardboard. They were hard-edged and bright, depicting fantastic landscapes and magical people. They were not great art, in technique barely competent, but they had an unpretentious sincerity and innocence which spoke of a genuine inner world.

In the early hours of New Year's Day El Molino was where alternative Campanillas chose to celebrate – long hair, beards, beads, lots of leather, hardly anyone over thirty, and several small children scampering about in chase games. The noise was incredible. Apart from the sound system everyone was shouting, the television was on, and the computer game was squealing and banging.

Petra took one look at the bar and realized her chances of being served were slim. She moved down the side, past the fireplace and found a place to sit beneath a painting of a black lady in a clown's outfit skipping with a rainbow for a rope. Next to her a small man with long hair in ringlets smoked a huge joint. She looked around and saw that his was not the only one. The fumes filled the room – and the euphoria too. She knew she didn't need a drink: deep breathing was enough.

Yet presently a gentle-looking lad with a bushy sand-coloured moustache and spectacles came by with a tray and took her order for a *cuba libre* with gin. His courtesy in all the din and rush was almost touching; so too were the shy smiles that greeted her wherever she looked – there was even one from the Parma Violet Lady which stopped her heart.

She left when she had finished her drink and as soon as she was out in the frosty air felt a pang of loneliness that stayed with her as she drove home through the moonlight. It was still there when she woke in the morning. Monteverdi, Querubín, Carmen and Paco, Villa Melchor itself, wonderful though they all were, were not enough.

Almost a week later, when Petra was taking her tea in the kitchen, Carmen put in front of her a large cake in the shape of a thick ring. It was coated in a chestnut-brown glaze and covered with crystallized fruits: peach and apricot halves, cherries, slices of apple and pear, and even one of viridian kiwi-fruit. She cut a segment out, put it on a plate. Petra felt a sudden stab of nostalgia for lost innocence, for her childhood before her mother was killed, for a time when she was asked to cut the Epiphany cake, a brioche of sweetened dough, and found, if she were lucky, a tiny ceramic model of one of the Three Kings.

Her teeth jarred gently on something hard, she sucked off the crumb and took out what looked like a tiny urn.

'*¡Incensio!*' cried Carmen and clapped her hands. Petra remembered – gold, frankincense and myrrh. Carmen chattered on: tonight was *La fiesta de los Reyes*, the night of the Three Kings, when all the children of Campanillas would receive their presents. Perhaps Petra would like to go. Petra thought: Mari-Elena will be there because she has a child, a son.

'Of course, I'd love to. I must tell Querubín though.'

'And perhaps,' Carmen flew on, 'you could take us with you: we have presents for our grandchildren and the trunk of our car is not big enough . . .'

When they went to town on market day, Paco drove them there in a tired pale-blue Renault 4.

'Of course I will.'

But was the trunk of a small BMW that much bigger? Big enough but only just. Four packages were loaded in, all gift-wrapped in metallic coloured paper and tied with huge bows – one was a child's bicycle, another a big board game, the others she guessed were hand-held computer game systems.

They arrived in the village at six o'clock, in growing dusk, with a clammy cool drizzle falling. Petra parked behind the small square and together they humped the presents into the vestry to the side of the church where already a huge pile of similar packages almost filled the room, then Carmen hurried them up to the school near the top of the eastern side of the town. This was where the Three Kings were due to begin their progress through streets and alleys, ending up at the church where they would give their presents, first to the Baby Jesus and then to all the children of Campanillas.

They rode glossy mules and were just as they should be – decked out in flowing robes and cloaks, jewelled crowns, cotton-wool beards, with one properly blacked up as Balthazar. They had attendants who held the bits of the mules in one hand and sacks of boiled sweets in the other. Balthazar particularly was in need of an attendant since his mule was frisky and occasionally kicked.

Carmen sought out two of her older grandchildren, embraced them warmly, pushed sweets into their hands and their pockets.

Soon they were off, with a ragged fanfare from a small band and a cloud of children behind them, into the dimly lit alleys, drifting from one pool of light to another and as they went the low balconies filled, windows opened and more light fell on them all so their jewels glittered and the boiled sweets they tossed in the air every twenty yards or so shone like silver fishes.

Carmen, Paco and Petra followed for a short time then made their way back to the square and the church. The rain faded away, the sky cleared, stars pricked the dusky velvet of the deepening sky. The old people were soon surrounded by friends and relations of all ages, so Petra went alone up the steps between fruiting orange trees and had a look at the crib set just inside the big open doors of the church. It was real. Real people and above all a real baby, wide awake on the straw with shiny black eyes and gurgling with pleasure at all the attention – the surprise that they were real caught her out, moved her with its propriety.

The church bell began to ring, the procession was on its way back and she descended the steps again into the gathering crowd below. As she did a small group of adults and children lined up on the railing in front of the church. They wore ordinary clothes but clean, well-pressed and smart for the most part, and in amongst them she suddenly spotted the dark cloud of Mari-Elena's hair, the blondness of her son in front of her. The group was flanked by guitarists, their instruments be-ribboned in green and white, the colours of Andalusia, and behind them a couple of men shook and rapped a couple of similarly decorated tambourines.

With gusto and finesse, fine phrasing and acerbic boldness they sang three carols to welcome the Kings, praise the Infant, adore his Mother. Petra quickly picked out from the rest Mari-Elena's voice as particularly true and rhythmically driving, but also a high almost metallic treble, searing across the others in an occasional descant that could have been improvised . . . Under the spiky hair, and above a black leather jacket studded with silver, she recognized the goatherd who made the valley outside Villa Melchor ring with his mournful cries: 'Cabr-r-ra, cab-r-r-r-eeeeto.'

The Kings, with their Hamelin-like posse, pushed through the square, dismounted, climbed the steps, offered the baby their gifts, made their obeisances; thrones – big chairs with carved arms – were lifted out for them and the first parcels that had been left in the vestry throughout the day were brought out too.

The square filled with a thousand people, more, from great-grannies, grannies and a few grandads to tiny toddlers all waiting for the distribution to begin. Names were called, and the first little girls, dressed in their best, came shyly up the steps between the orange trees. Clearly it would take a long time. Petra sought out Carmen and Paco who told her they would either stay the night with family or someone would give them a lift back, no problem. She went to El Molino, and found it almost empty and dull with a football match on the big screen TV. She ordered a *cuba libre con ginebra* at the bar and took it to the seat she had used at New Year. The guy with the ginger moustache and spectacles brought her a wedge of Spanish omelette on a plate with a round of plain white bread. For free.

She finished the drink and the food quite quickly, headed for the door and as she did it opened and in they came: Mari-Elena, the German youth and the young boy clutching his gifts.

'*¡Hola!*'

'*¡Hola!*'

Struggling for the Spanish, Petra found what she wanted to say: 'You sing very well. I enjoyed your singing.'

'*Gracias.*'

'*De nada.*'

And passing in the narrow doorway, their thighs brushed. For Petra a lightning strike.

At Villa Melchor the garage door opened electronically, she drove the BMW into its slot, came out. The moon and stars were brilliant, a slight frost was just beginning to sparkle on the stones and the edges of the puddles. Way, way above, the snows shone with moon and starlight.

A stone moved in front of her, a pebble the size of a hand-grenade.

'It's a toad,' she said to herself. 'One of those really big ones.'

Squeamish, she hung back. Then she stooped over the humble brute which was a good eight centimetres in diameter. She whispered to it.

'You might get run over. When they come back.' She meant Paco and Carmen, brought home by friends.

She could not bear the thought of finding its squashed carcass in the morning. But nor could she think of lifting it out of danger. In the end she did and found its skin surprisingly dry and silky, the pressure of its toes like a kitten's in her palm. She carried it into the undergrowth away from the villa and released it. Then she had to find her way, over tumbled walls, to the back gate, conventionally fastened by lock and a key. It opened into a patio covered with vines. Beneath the vines five or six pinheads of phosphorescent light shone. Glow-worms. She unlocked the double stable-style outer door, pushed back the square wooden beam that secured the lower half. Warmth from the stove gusted around her. She realized that in spite of the familiar ache of being on her own she had had a lovely evening. The thought of it produced a tightness in her throat and her eyes pricked with tears.

X

The lessons continued, day by day, through the winter and into the spring. They worked on a variety of scores, mostly seventeenth century, occasionally early eighteenth, but weighted towards Monteverdi and his immediate Italian successors.

'The scores are incomplete, you know? Of course you do. The originals have a vocal line, and a bass line, that's all. No dynamics, no time signatures. So far we have been using modern realizations, often made for particular productions, usually by the man who conducted the performances, sometimes in collaboration with his performers. But now I think we should look at the originals, unedited, and see what we can make of them.'

He pulled a thin folio bound in soft leather from a shelf, placed it on the table next to a large magnifying glass, smoothed the leather with his palm, and peered up at her.

'There are pitfalls and we must do our best to avoid them. The first danger lies in the fact that we know the original material we have is pure Monteverdi and that any embellishment is supposition and not Monteverdi. And so we are weighted towards singing it straight, tinkering with it as little as possible. We keep the voices squeaky clean; ornament, dynamics, harmony and the rest as completely in keeping with what we know about seventeenth-century orthodoxy as we can for fear of betraying the master. And that is dull. Remember what old Goldsborough used to say . . .?'

She recalled he was the founder/conductor of what is now the English Chamber Orchestra and, after a moment, remembered the pronouncement Querubín was referring to.

'He said, "If it's dull it's not authentic.' "

'Right. So. We read the words. Analyse them, understand them, put them in context, interpret the character. These composers wanted their singers to interpret. Not just sing the dots. And more than interpret. Collaborate. There is no evidence at all that once a tempo was set it remained strict. The words made the tempi. Rubato, accelerando, rhythmic alteration, freedom – like in jazz and the best rock music . . . you like Queen? "Bohemian Rhapsody"? Freddie Mercury? Wonderful. What a tragedy. Monteverdi would have adored him . . .

'Listen. This is the secret. Commit yourself to the emotion. Commit yourself, like a swimmer taking a dive. All right?'

And so it seemed he was recommending the most adventurous, creative course but then when her post-baroque training led her into un-baroque excesses as a means of committing herself to the emotion, he not only seemed to contradict what he had said, but he came down hard as well.

'You are swelling into that long note. *Messa di voce*, crescendo, decrescendo. Now that is one thing that never happened in the baroque . . .'

'But you told me to be expressive. The way I sang that was expressive. It is what the words told me to do . . .'

'No, no, NO. It is what the stupid training you got tells you to do. All right for that, but not for this. You must see . . . both styles are artificial. How can I put this? We accept them, because we were brought up to them. The swellings, the moans and sighs, the swoops and glissandos of Romantic opera, especially late-Romantic opera, seem natural, correspond in some way to the sighs of a real lover in pain or facing up to consumption or whatall. But they are as conventional, as unnatural, as the baroque mode. And they are not appropriate to the baroque mode.'

'They are appropriate if the words and the emotion draw them out of me.'

She was learning to be stubborn, to speak up for herself, fight back. And not only to assert the rights of her personality against his, but because that way she could persuade him to elaborate, expound.

'No, NO. They are not appropriate. You know very well what I am saying. Very well.'

She waited. He sat at the portative organ and his fingers ran through phrases, trills and turns on the line she had been singing.

'Ornamentation. The ornaments that embellished the baroque line were not vocal gymnastics, though they may have been applauded as such – just as now the morons in the gallery at La Scala applaud a particularly throbby sob from Luciano or whomever. No. The fiorituras, the trills and all the rest of it, the whole gamuţ of tricks was there to express emotion, feeling, character, drama. And if you sing baroque and you wish to sing it expressively then it is in that repertoire of tricks you will find the means . . .'

'But will an audience of mainly rich ignorant people understand that? Will they not better respond to what they are used to? Will they not understand the emotion of a Solomon or Endymion if she sings like Mimi, or anyway Aida?'

She was being provocative, gender-swapping singers and parts, and Querubín knew it.

He put his elbows on the squealing keys, and his tired eyes grinned up at her.

'Yes. Maybe. And you weight each engagement, each production, each performance bearing in mind factors of that sort. And – ' the smile became kinder – 'the point I am making is that you should have the ability to do both. You already have the one, I am teaching you the other. And there is another factor too.'

'Yes?'

'Fashions change. When I started out on this . . . lark? Is that a good word? Why not? When I started out on this lark, the whole authentic movement was in its infancy. I fought crazy German conductors who remembered Bülow and Mahler. British and Americans, too. But now the pendulum has gone the other way. No conductor will engage you to sing Claudio or even Johann Sebastian these days, if you cannot sing baroque. Authentic baroque . . .'

And after all he made the word 'authentic' sound like something not altogether nice and she understood the importance of the lesson. When all is said and done singers, even the greatest divas of all time, are but servants . . . servants of the bums, the bums, that is, on the seats. And not only singers.

She was getting there, but it was a struggle.

'Good, good, GOOD. You are not singing the bar lines, which is excellent. But you are singing like a musicologist, not as a character. You're singing the score, the dots. Try again. The words, the drama, the character . . .'

'No, no, NO.' It was almost a scream, a squeal anyway. 'You're singing with your breath again, it's heavy and dough-like. Sing it *on* the breath, it must be lighter, clearer: an apparently effortless move from one important note to the next important note, to underline and to emphasize . . . Again. Light and quick. With great point and accuracy.'

He took a deep breath, clutched the panel at the end of the keyboard.

'The critics will say – she has had lessons. She has *studied voice*. If they do, then you are dead meat. You must learn to sing like an Italian – forehead, cheekbones are the sounding boards. Then chest and belly last of all. And then . . . don't think. Be. Be the person you are singing.'

Where had he learned an expression like 'dead meat'? she asked.

From an American conductor, he replied. Who wrote musicals.

'Look at the bass line. Unfigured. Horizontal, no chords, no harmony. Your interpretation of the vocal line, your embellishments will make the bass a figured bass . . . The bass line will become a figured bass because of what you will put above it. Again, again . . . Good, good. Quite good. Why did you stop?'

Head up, face flushed, one hand on her chest the other on the top of the organ, she was looking out of the window. Then she looked down at him, this little man with his clarinet voice, squealing like Till in *Till Eulenspiegel*, and her eyes narrowed in not hate exactly, not contempt, but filled with a momentary dislike that was intense.

'I just saw a swallow. It swooped over the pool. The first this year.' She looked at him. 'I think I did that rather well.'

'You did, dear. Very well. Quite well.'

'One advantage of being here,' she went on, 'is that one gets the migratory birds at least three months ahead of where I was brought up. In Bavaria. All right. What next?'

She had inherited her father's ability to put on a very German upper-class manner when she felt she needed to. Something he had kept for occasions when he felt somebody needed to be put down – trade, uppity foreigners, those sort of people . . . Querubín looked up at her, eyebrows raised in amazement, then pulled together in a frown. For a moment she thought he was going to pull the lid down over the organ's keyboard, and maybe lock it.

'Sorry,' she said.

He noted, even admired the way she weighted it – a statement, not a concession, and his fingers unravelled a slow arpeggio.

Then one day about the middle of February . . .

'The time has come to study one particular role, learn it, fix it, interpret it, know it. I have chosen for you Nerone, Nero, in Claudio's *L'incoronazione di Poppea*.'

In spite of the steel she was still tempering, her heart fluttered. This was truly straight in at the deep-end, sink or swim. But she kept her tremors and her thoughts to herself, merely nodded as if it were the most natural choice in the world, as if she were grateful he had made such a sensible decision.

XI

Meanwhile, outside the lessons the relationship remained on a tolerably even keel.

'How did you find this place?'

It was a fortnight or so after the Epiphany and some weeks before he decided to inflict on her the role of Nero: the candles, the big logs on the fire occasionally flaring to add flickering light and spicy perfume as oils of pomegranate sizzled out of sawn branches, the brown rosé wine in its fine glass jug, fresh almonds and pistachios.

'February nineteen eighty-one. I was in Madrid recording Spanish baroque cantatas.' The slight shy smile which always touched her because of its combination of inwardness and vulnerability breathed across the lines of his tired face, glowed in the cloudy eyes. 'My prejudice against liturgical music weakens when the music is a celebration and not devout. Frankly one cannot take much Spanish religious music seriously – most of it is far too jolly, don't you agree? Anyway. On the television in my hotel room I witnessed Tejero's attempt to hi-jack parliament. It had a terrible effect on me. That clown in his funny black shiny hat, with his big moustache, loosing off his pistol into the parliament ceiling. The representatives of the people crouching, as who wouldn't, behind their circular pews . . .

'I had palpitations, I could not be still, could not sleep. I knew I was on the edge of falling into fugue again . . . did I tell you I had had a serious mental illness a few years earlier? Almost a return to what happened when I was . . . fourteen? No? I must tell you about it, another time perhaps. But the possibility of falling back into the state I had been in at Santo Domingo was very real. And now, again, in nineteen eighty-one in Madrid I feared relapse a second time.

'Clearly the sort of scenes I had witnessed, the ceaseless commentaries on what was happening on the television and the radio, the speculation of renewed civil war when it became known that a senior general had his tanks out on the streets of Valencia in support of the coup, had . . . personal . . . resonances for me. Perhaps touched hidden memories of my late childhood, of the onset of civil war in nineteen thirty-six and of the months before . . .'

The old hands brushed down over his face, he shook his head, occasionally stubby fingers drummed on the polished wood. She wondered if he ought to go on, but he insisted.

'It gets better, you know? Coming here was, after all, a happy thing, yes?' And again that lost smile.

∽

The next day, when it became clear the King's courage and firmness had defeated the coup, he had felt a little better though still exhausted, not at all ready to get back to the recording studios. He made excuses by telephone and wandered out into streets already unaccountably familiar. He had not stayed in Madrid until 1957. But even then he had been immediately struck by this feeling that he had been there before, not just on a visit, but living there.

On that first occasion, in 1957, he decided to walk from his hotel to the Prado and did so without looking at a map or asking directions. He looked round the collection, and many times felt the hair rise on his neck and not just because of the beauty of the paintings. In front of *Las Meninas* he burst into tears, and ran into the Retiro.

'In those days it was displayed in a small room on its own with a mirror in front of it framed in the same ebony frame as the painting, and with an open window on to the side street. A plaque gave the title, the artist, and the following statement: 'The Greatest Work of Art in the World'. One looked at it and knew it was true. But that was not why I wept. For a moment I had felt her beside me, the warmth of her presence, the pressure of her hand in mine, just as I had when we looked at that painting the first time ever. When? When I was nine, ten? At what age would a mother who loved art think her son capable of beginning to appreciate such complexity, subtlety, emotion and truth?'

And indeed the tears were back again.

'Sometimes I really am nothing but a sentimental old fool. Is my glass empty?'

She filled it and her own.

'Back to nineteen eighty-one, February. A cold bright day, with a sky the blue *madrileños* call *velasqueño* and everyone walking about with silly uncontrollable grins on their faces, and cars flying improvised banners painted *Viva el Rey*. I was heading for the Prado again, when suddenly my sleeve was pulled. I looked round; there was no one near enough to have done it, but I realized that I was facing the entrance to El Casón, the annexe to the Prado which houses Spanish nineteenth-century painting. I had never been there before, so far as I knew. I felt . . . moved to see what it was like.

'At the back of the building three rooms had been set aside for a special exhibition of painters from the early twentieth century, not the moderns or imitators of the French school, but those painters who had learnt their craft in the nineteenth century and had been content to remain with nineteenth-century techniques, styles and content. And one of them was the painting that now hangs in my study. You know? The one of the fountain.'

She recalled how it depicted the square pool with the smaller round basin in the middle, waterlilies in bloom, dragonflies and goldfish, how one could make out the ghost of a reflected figure, upside down, peering into the pool from the other side, a face in darkness against the sky out of which it looked.

'I knew her instantly and the fountain too.'

The catalogue said that the artist was Gabriel Melchor (1872–1941). Querubín made enquiries, there and then, in El Casón itself. The director was able to tell him that Gabriel Melchor had been a very successful painter attached to the school of *sevilliano realismo*. Its members specialized in a wistful sort of hedonism expressed with tremendous technical virtuosity, especially in portraying reflected light.

He found out that between 1930 and 1939 Gabriel Melchor had lived in a villa in the mountains between Granada and Málaga. In 1939 he had gone into voluntary exile to Buenos Aires with his good friend the composer Manuel de Falla, and there he died – in 1941. Querubín went in search of this villa, for he was sure that there he would find clues to a past that had been only partially unlocked by the therapy he had undergone ten years earlier.

He recalled how the taxi, a large Mercedes from Granada, pulled up at wrought-iron gates. The words Villa Goya were twisted in serpentine iron across the top and they were fastened with a rusty chain and a huge padlock. The taxi-driver took hold of the chain.

'¿Si-i-i?'

Querubín nodded, and the young man, deep-tanned, thick black hair, with large hairy hands, short-sleeved shirt, gold ID bracelet, took hold of the chain and yanked it, brutally. It snapped. He then tried to heave open one of the gates but the hinges too were rusted through so the whole sagging structure swung away from him and clattered into the grass and brambles that had grown over the track.

He came back to the car with a broad grin on his face, but Querubín was already out. He had decided that he did not want this flashy oaf with him when he entered the domain which he already knew was his. The Land Registry in Granada town hall had shown it to be the property, under Gabriel Melchor's will, of one David Pérez Iglesias. It was the first time in forty-five years that he had seen his real name. As soon as he saw it an almost photographic image of the words written across the corner of an exercise book with the proud flourishes a ten-year-old might add seemed to interpose itself between his eyes and the ruled page of the heavy ledger he was studying.

'Wait here,' he said.

The driver shrugged, got back in the driver's seat. Before Querubín could get round the first corner he had lit a cigarette and the car radio was playing pop-flamenco.

'Tell me about it? About coming here, and finding it. You were the Prince in the *Sleeping Beauty*?'

'Too old. More like *Il ritorno d'Ulisse*. The end of my odyssey.'

'It must have been a strange, strange experience.'

'Overpowering. But a homecoming. Even though . . .'

'Yes?'

'Well, I have no idea for how long I, we, were here before. But I think it may not have been for much more than a month.'

'We?'

'My mother and I. Mama.'

ↄ

But first he had wandered slowly over the whole domain, his feet whispering through banks of dried leaves, tugged at by brambles and briars. The pool was empty of water, choked with garden debris: the fountain was cracked and the spring beneath it bubbled water into the overgrown terraces below. A whole colony of squealing martins, hundreds of them, with scores of wattle nests under the eaves, rocketed up and down the spaces between the wings of the villa. The orchards were impenetrable but filled with butterflies.

At last he pushed at a door and the lock burst the rotten wood in a cloud of musty powder. Tiny mouse claws skittered behind furniture shrouded in sheets and cobwebs. Curiosity got the better of one beady-eyed rodent who sat up on its haunches to wonder at this intrusive monster. Geckos too paused on the walls of stone stairs to eye him through vertical lids before slipping on padded toes into slits and crannies impossibly narrow for their asymmetrically bulging tummies.

The big shutters over the studio windows held him up for a moment until he remembered how to work the simple mechanism that simultaneously ratcheted long bolts down from the ceiling and up from the floor. He folded the shutters, first on one side then the other, then surrendered to a sneezing fit brought on by the dust he had disturbed. He paused to take in the once splendid prospect: the pool flanked by elegant simple colonnades, the wilderness beyond, and on the other side of the valley the fissured massif of the sierra. He turned, saw the packing cases, a blue envelope on top, his mother's guitar, the paintings on the walls and the canvases stacked beneath them.

The envelope was addressed to David Pérez Iglesias. There was a letter inside. He opened it and read it. He put it in his pocket and began to walk slowly round the big room, taking in the paintings Melchor had left on the walls: the one that now hung above Petra's head in the dining room; another of the same woman in the very act of pouring a stream of water from a shell on to the youth's bare back; the two of them in the pool embracing beneath a nearly full moon, with the silhouette of the same sierra behind them, black against a luminous night sky. There were other, smaller paintings, some merely fast sketches but radiating vitality, relating to the bigger canvases; some of still lives: fruit, food, wine and flowers.

'If you want to see them you'll find them in Granada, in the Museum of Fine Arts.'

On the end wall one big canvas was shrouded with a sheet. Querubín wondered why, and felt a tremor of angst as he reached to tweak it away: one does not throw a cover over a painting unless one has good reason.

A silent scream pitched at the limit of human hearing scythed across his brain and for a moment he knew he was on the edge of the abyss again. It required a psychic effort beyond any physical imagining to replace the shroud, but he managed, just. He stumbled almost blindly back down the stone stairs beneath the gaze of the geckos and into the sunlight.

'I vowed I would never look at it again, and I haven't. I am not even sure that I saw what I thought I saw. It's possible I hallucinated.'

Petra knew better than to press him to tell her why, or why, if its effect was so terrible, he had not simply arranged for it to be destroyed.

❧

The next day, at the end of her lesson, he gave her the letter Melchor had left for him. It was in its original blue envelope, faded on the outside, still quite bright inside. She fingered the thick paper, read the spidery sepia italic: *Señor Don David Pérez Iglesias.*

'I'll read it later.'

He nodded.

After lunch she took the envelope, her small bilingual dictionary, climbed into the car and drove into the mountains.

She felt she was on the edge of mysteries, of tremendous terrible things and she wanted space of her own in which to confront them. She drove forty kilometres to the east before she found she was winding down a track cut across almost precipitous slopes towards a tiny village clinging to a steep mountainside on which grew thousands of tiny vines. Again the sea lay beyond, promising though not this time yielding the other continent. From a distance the vines looked like insects with one long antenna, for that was how they had been pruned. The soil was stony, the slopes only a degree or so off the impossible, yet figs grew here and there between the vines; not like the giant tree back at what she already thought of as home, but hardly bigger than shrubs. The land was all tilled by hand, though occasionally a donkey dragged a plough or harrow across slopes too steep for the tiny motorized cultivators most farmers used.

She reached the village centre (it was called, in syllables strangely Greek, Polopos) just ahead of a big green van which had followed her impatiently for the last half-kilometre. It parked next to the BMW in front of the church's west door: handy that churches in the west look to the east for the resurrection since in this case the church had originally been a mosque looking towards Mecca. A tall strong man and a boy

77

climbed out, the man with a hand-held electric loud-hailer through which he bellowed the nature of his wares: cabbages, corsets, oranges, brassières, turnips, and huge flesh-coloured knickers. Petra escaped to a café on the edge of the village where she sat beneath a vast almond tree in full luxuriant bloom. She asked for wine – it arrived in a small earthenware jug. She guessed it came from the spidery vines. Under its influence the almond blossom took on mind-blowing properties, especially when a decrescent moon, a C-shaped nail-paring in the unblemished cerulean sky, appeared above it.

At last she drew the dry sheets of old paper from their blue envelope and carefully folded them out. Then she pulled her dictionary from her bag, and began.

XII

Dear David,

If you ever find this letter or this letter ever finds you, then I hope it will bring more happiness than pain.

I am certain that your closest relatives are dead. The elder of your two brothers, Miguel, was killed in the siege of Málaga in early February 1937 where he was a lieutenant in the so-called nationalist army. I have received information, possibly unreliable, that your second brother, Jorge, was arrested in Barcelona six months ago for spying on behalf of the nationalists. If that is the case his survival is unlikely.

And your Aunt Ana. She was an entirely admirable person, about eight years older than your mother, and I believe a surrogate mother to her. I knew her very well twenty years ago when I had a studio in Madrid and before she went to Vienna. In spite of the war I was able to make contact with her when I heard on the wireless that she had returned and was organizing an ambulance unit in Madrid. As one of Spain's first psychoanalysts she was a famous figure and the Republicans made much of her support. In spite of the war the telephone lines were kept open even across the front lines and I was able to telephone your mother's house in Madrid on the off-chance that Ana might be there. Amazingly I got through to her. I told her what had happened to you, and how my doctor and I had coped with the situation. And what had happened to your poor mother.

There followed several conversations during which she authorized me to go to Madrid as soon as it was in rebel hands and take over whatever I could on your behalf. Of course it took longer than she thought and it was not until the middle of April this year that I was able to make the journey. She also agreed with me that you are in good hands and that you should remain at Silos at least until this dreadful business is over.

Meanwhile she said she would leave in what is now your apartment in Calle Ayala all the documentation that would give you title to the property and your mother's fortune, and all the documents she could find that would explain to you who you are. She also asked me to take anything of value or beauty or even just interest, for everything there was rightfully yours and she did not want anything important of your mother's to fall into the hands of your uncle, the Marqués de Boltana, whom she referred to as Saturno. He, together with most of his side of your family, managed to flee Madrid. Ana herself left Madrid before it was cut off. She was killed at Teruel by a direct hit on the ambulance she was driving.

When the war finally ended three months ago I went to your mother's apartment and was able to collect all the documents Ana had left there. They filled three tea-chests. There was also a large library of books, many of which it would now be deemed a treasonable offence to own, punishable by death.

Dear David, I am leaving them all here because I have to go. I really do. And I do not have time to get in touch with you. Those silly monks who are looking after you do not have a telephone and I don't think I have time to write another letter. I am an old man, too old to face a trial and humiliation and prison and maybe worse, which is what will happen if I stay. Don Manuel de Falla is looking after me. I have done what I could. The car he has sent for me has just arrived and I must go now. It is all so terrible. I don't think I am going to be happy in Argentina. I don't think I am ever going to be happy again.

If you find this letter and I am still alive, bring me back if you can. If not, then please take over Villa Goya if you want to, make it your own and remember me.

     Kisses

      Gabriel Melchor

Petra folded the dry pages into their envelope, leant back in her white plastic chair and let her mind swim again with the huge luxuriance of the blossom and the magic of the moon which had moved a hand's breadth further on.

There was excitement, yes. But frustration too, a sense she had been cheated again. She sipped the wine, edgier, more metallic than the version Querubín drank. She knew that she was nowhere near the end, that Ariadne-like she had so far let out the first few turns only of the thread and that a labyrinth lay ahead of her.

There was a black Toyota Celica parked in front of the garage in such a way that she could not get the electronic up-and-over door to lift. She tried the big front door, found it unbarred, pushed it open, entered the cloister in front of the pool and wondered what to do next. A tall woman wearing a fringed dark leather jacket, jeans and calf-high boots emerged from the bottom of the stairs that led to Querubín's bedroom. She was carrying a thick case, heavy plastic, black.

'Hi, I'm Caridad Rocío Lorca. Querubín's doctor. You must be Petra Von Stürm. I know about you. How do you do?' The English was good, as good as Querubín's, but with a Berlitz mid-Atlantic accent. 'I need a word with you before I leave.'

They went into the dining room.

'He's all right, is he? I mean he didn't get ill . . .'

'While you were out? No.' The doctor, who had reddish dark hair, painted nails, not long but on some the lacquer was chipped, swung her case on to the round table and sat in Querubín's chair. 'But I think he did not want you to worry about what is wrong, so he asked me to come when he knew you would be out.'

'So what is wrong?' Petra pulled out one of the other chairs. Doctor Rocío moved hers closer to the smouldering logs in the fireplace. Why? She can't, Petra thought, be cold. Then from her bag the doctor pulled a pack of small cheroots, lit one, and tossed the match into the fireplace. Through the rest of their conversation she flicked dark grey ash into it.

'He's going blind.'

'I know.'

'But there is no physical reason for this. He has no cataract. He is not diabetic. Already he has seen a specialist in Granada and visited the eye hospital in Malaga. They have done tests. The cornea, the lenses, the optical nerves, all as far as they can see in reasonable order for a man of nearly seventy. But he can't see.'

'So?'

'It's psychological. Psychosomatic.' She drew on the cigarillo, puffed smoke but into the draught that sucked it up the chimney. 'I smoke,' she explained, 'and I do not believe this does me much harm. But I do not want to give you or anyone else an excuse to blame their terminal illnesses on me. I know why he is going blind, and I think you can help.'

'Certainly I'll do anything I ca—'

'Of course you will.' She swung back to the table and with the cigarillo clamped between her teeth and her eyes screwed up against the smoke, opened her big case, fumbled in it, extracted from it a wad of stapled sheets of closely typed paper, thrust them at Petra.

'I'm sorry but I am in a hurry. I had a call on this just before I left Querubín.' She held up a mobile phone, shook it, put it back in her case. 'About twenty years ago Querubín suffered a severe nervous breakdown. At that time he was treated by a German hypnotherapist with psychoanalytic training who extracted from him, under hypnosis, a series of, um, stories relating to Querubín's late childhood and early adolescence. Dr Kepler told him they were fantasies. Querubín needs to believe that they are not.'

'I don't understand . . .'

'Fantasies involving his relationship with his mother. Apart from being committed by his training to treating these stories as fantasies, Kepler drew attention to anomalies and inconsistencies, errors of fact. For instance this one,' she tapped the papers in front of her, 'this has an account of how he left Madrid on the thirteenth of July in nineteen thirty-six in the company of his mother and the poet Lorca. But the history books say Lorca left Madrid three days later. Prove them wrong and maybe Querubín will begin to believe his fantasies. Another describes how he and his mother visited a spa called Baños de Alhamilla. No such place exists.'

'But—'

With a swing of the cigarillo Doctor Rocío swept on.

'Whether or not they are fantasies is absolutely irrelevant. Querubín needs to believe they are not, that is the point. Now. There is a village called Alhamilla about thirty kilometres from here. You can get to it by turning left off the main Granada road at Padul . . .'

'I know it. There's a quicker way, up the valley.'

'Really? Already you know your way round better than I, and I have been here five years. Anyway. I must go now.'

'Hang on. Does he know you've given me this?'

'Yes. I told him he needs help from someone close to him and he agreed you should read it. So you can begin to understand the problem.' She tossed the butt of her cigarillo into the fire. 'Now pardon me, but I really do have to go.'

She closed her case and swung out into the cloister and through the big front door. Petra's BMW blocked her exit, and there followed a moment or two with both of them reversing and turning, going forward a metre or two and then back again, which, speeded up, would have looked like bumper cars at a fair.

Leaning across towards the doctor, Petra decided to assert herself.

'Just why are you in such a hurry?'

'Farmer up the road has a cow stuck in labour and the vet is up in the mountains with a shepherd. Of course they should stick to goats, but they'll never learn.'

Spewing gravel, Doctor Caridad Rocío Lorca's Celica sped down the track.

Petra went straight to her rooms, sat at the small desk, and stared at the sheaf of papers. First Melchor's letter, now this. She felt she was being urged into the labyrinth with more haste than was comfortable, but there was attraction too, lure, allure.

The papers were not bound, there was no cover, no introduction. The opening words, in English, stood at the top of the page.

∾

I am in a long but narrow room, ill-lit with unshaded bulbs of low wattage and it is filled with women, mostly young or middle-aged, though there are a few old ones in black. The lucky ones are sitting on collapsible wooden seats, the ones in the front are on the floor with their skirts pulled over their knees. At the back behind the seats there is standing room only and also down the sides of the hall. I am standing near the front on the side, with my back to the wall which is streaming with moisture . . .

∾

What was this? Irritated, as one sometimes is when told to read a book by an enthusiast and finds the opening tedious or confusing, she turned to the last page.

∾

But I feel the pulse and the sudden rush almost straight away, yet her fingers are all over me especially my buttocks and, 'Go on,' she cries. 'Go on, go on,' and I do and feel no lessening of the power in my loins. I go on and on until she cries out that it is sweet, so sweet, and then I let heaven fall about me.

Slowly peace descends and blesses us and in the boughs above us a nightingale begins to sing, or perhaps it sang all through and only now do I hear it.

Then the gun. Then the gun again.

'David?' She murmurs.

'Vikí. Mama.'

'No, not Vikí. Dolí. Because . . . David? I feel a little sad.'

'Please don't feel sad. Not now.'

84

'But I do.'

'Why?'

'We had such fun together. When you were a boy.'

Then an excited baying sound, some way below us, but not far, and getting nearer, near . . .

'Oh shit,' I say, and I reach for those stupid clothes.

∾

This seemed to her to be pornographic in its explicitness, maudlin too, and she found it difficult to relate it to the man and the artist she knew. She went back to the beginning and read the whole transcript through. When she reached the end again, she could not conceal from herself the relief she felt at the thought that it had to be fantasy. Just as Doctor Rocío had said, the middle section described how Querubín and his mother left Madrid on 13 July 1936, in the company of the poet Lorca, that is, three days earlier than he actually did. Relieved but troubled too. Make him believe these fantasies, whether or not they are true, had been the doctor's prescription. But how? To lie to him, to fabricate false evidence would be puerile and dangerously self-defeating if detected. However, she decided she would do what she could to find Baños de Alhamilla.

XIII

'You have read *Nerone* all through?'

'Yes.'

'Words and dots.'

'Yes.'

'Why do you think I chose this as the first major role we should study complete? Get by heart?'

'I have thought about that a lot.'

'And?'

The sky for once was grey, and a cold wind buffeted down the valley off the high plateaux to the north, the central *meseta* of Spain. Well, she thought, it would have to, wouldn't it? It was God, not John Ruskin, who invented the Pathetic Fallacy. She moved round the music room nervily, picking things up, scratching herself. Querubín sat in the green armchair with his mother's guitar across his knee.

'Nero,' she cried, '*Nerone* is a total shit. He murders, tortures, falls in love or lust with a woman not his wife, entraps his real wife in a plot against him, forces Seneca, his valued tutor and advisor to kill himself, and so on, and finally crowns his *inamorata* Empress of the World. You chose it because of all the castrato roles it is the one you judge most difficult for a woman to sing. Women, in your book, do not behave like this.'

'Something like that.' He cleared his throat. 'Let us start with the first exchange between Nero and Seneca: *La legge è per chi serve* . . . "Law is for those who serve, and if I wish I can abolish the old and enact the new . . ." The whole debate between them encapsulates the conflict between the Nietzschean superman and reason, between Dionysus and Apollo, which lies at the heart of the European soul . . .'

He unpeeled a broken chord from the guitar, looked towards her, but not at her.

'You are still there?'

'Yes. Can't you see me?'

'Not as well as I would like to.'

They struggled on for twenty minutes, but he was teaching her from memory and when memory failed him, he had to ask her to read the score and the text. It became a tedious business. At last he put aside the guitar, and sighed deeply.

'You talked with la señora?'

'The doctor? Yes.'

'And she gave you the transcripts?'

'Not all of them. Just the one about leaving Madrid and going to Granada. And the woods above the Alhambra.'

'And you are not shocked at my fantasies?'

'No.'

She looked down at him. He seemed suddenly frail in the armchair though it was not particularly big. Leaves now, not swallows, whirled down the colonnade behind him, pushed by the wind, and a spatter of raindrops hissed across the pool. She shifted the guitar, a string pulsed, and knelt beside him, took his hand.

'I would not be shocked if it had really happened. Perhaps less shocked.'

He turned his head towards her. Impossible to believe that those greenish-blueish eyes, though a touch cloudy, could not see her.

'Why not?'

'Because I did the same. I seduced my father. He slept with me. Several times.'

A moment or two of silence passed. He chewed his lip, clenched his knuckles as if to stop his hands from trembling.

'So,' he said at last. 'You too were the victim of fantasies. Did they also offer you therapy? Analysis?'

'Oh no.' She shook her head, struggled to keep the sob out of her voice. 'This was no fantasy. He made me pregnant. Procured an abortion. Then shot himself.'

Out of his darkness he placed his left hand on top of hers and they listened to the wind.

'Is that why you want to sing like a man, sing men's parts?'

'Perhaps. But that is not all. Not any man. Not any parts.

Yours. I heard you sing before . . . all that happened. I wanted to sing like you before . . .' Brusquely she stood up. 'Anyway. It is not I who am going blind. I can't, right now, do anything about when this poet Lorca you go on about in that transcript left Madrid in nineteen thirty-six. Is that the real Lorca? The famous one? Maybe I can though do something about this spa town that never existed. Do you have the transcript of that episode here?'

'It's in my desk in my study. The big drawer on the right. They are all there. That one begins: "I am in a small but light room with wooden walls . . ."'

∞

I am in a small but light room with wooden walls, tongue and grooved planks painted glossy white. The floor is made up of green and white tiles, ceramic tiles, patterned and laid in imitation of Moorish art. There is a bench against the back wall opposite the door and three clothes-pegs above it. A woman's clothes, mostly silks, the outer garments black, the inner ones white, very fine and with much fine intricate lace, hang from the pegs. On the bench lies a large white towelling robe, the sort with a hood.

I look up and see that it is not a room at all, but a cubicle, and that the walls are partitions not walls. High above them the ceiling is a dome of frosted glass, filled with light.

Noise? Yes. A high-pitched confusion of laughter and cries overlays a steady buzz of conversation and it echoes, has much resonance. There is also the sound of splashed and running water . . . gushing would be a better word. Smell? Rotten-egg gas, but not strong. The perfumes women wear, and the perfumes they emit.

I am wearing women's clothing. The clothing of an adult woman, though I am a youth, not much more than a boy. A very good-looking boy because I can see myself as if I am out of myself and looking at myself as well as being in myself. I have black hair, very glossy, cut short, but like a girl's, with two black half moons or scimitars of hair curling on to my cheeks. My eyes are greenish-blue, blue with greenish flecks. I am wearing make-up. My short-sleeved dress is ivory-coloured silk or cotton treated to look like silk and pleated, quite full in the skirt, and I am wearing a choker of small pearls, two strands, which matches it very well. Beneath it I am wearing a silk slip, and beneath that a combination brassière and corset with tabs carrying pink rubber suspenders. They have little wire hoops which squeeze over the pink rubber buttons to snare the tops of my silk stockings. Both of the cups of my brassière are filled with rolled-up woollen boy's socks and the whole flesh-coloured apparatus is laced up the back with a long white lace. My shoes are pretty, patent leather and matching the rest, heels quite high but they are no bother to me. I seem to be able to manage them. My feet are larger than they should be.

I pick up the towelling robe, and open the door, which has a simple cast-iron latch, the sort you lift on the inside using a button-handle, on the outside it has a handle you hold and a sort of leaf which you put your thumb on to lift the internal bar out of the notched piece of metal attached to the door jamb inside.

As I move out the noises intensify, and the temperature rises.

It is a large circular room, with a large circular pool in the middle. Everything is honey-coloured marble and veined. There is a haze of steam above water constantly renewed from the mouths of three stone lions sitting on its perimeter. There are perhaps as many as fifteen naked women in the pool. More lie or sit on marble couches around it. They are of all ages and all sizes, and I wonder at their variety, the variety of their phy-siques. Hair white, plastered over sweating or moist heads, and sparse so you can see the scalp beneath the streaks; hair full and young and very often covered in the only garment any of them wear, large but identical bathing hats made out of rubber, decorated with frilly and floppy petals. Faces lined and fissured; plump, rosy and triple chinned; neat and hard with eyes like agates. And their bosoms, their breasts! Droopy with teats as long as a cow's, but more wrinkled, that almost point downwards; huge, round, veined and very pink with spread brown nipples; tiny and pert with pink nipples that almost point to the glass dome. Backs broad and fat like a wrestler's, backs thin and long and grey; backs rosy and dimpled.

And how they all warble, and cry and sing-song and jargon and chat. I admire and love them all. It makes me happy to see how different they all are when divested of their uniform but fashionable clothes, and how relaxed they are with each other, all pretensions cast aside. It's their men who give them their social but unnatural statuses, slots, psychic corsets, and there are none of them here.

The sight of the multiplicity of naked female flesh stirs my sex, but the corset comes low enough to contain the possibility of embarrassment or even exposure.

And through them all, from the centre of the pool, comes my mother, her thighs pushing the blueish slightly effervescent water, her long fingers idly scooping the surface. *Madre*, I long to shout, to sing the word like a trumpet call, though I know that is the one thing I must not call her, for today I must always use her name, María Dolores or Dolí, or even Vikí which is my preferred nickname for her, for the most beautiful creature in that echoing hemisphere . . .

Her hair which is just like mine, though fuller, is slightly waved, and her face is like mine too, but finer and more delicate, her nose perfectly sculpted, her chin petite. Her neck is long and like ivory, her shoulders as delicate as a bird's. Behind the slight heaviness of her lids her almond eyes glitter with harmless demonry at the joke we are playing, and her angel lips lift at the corners, and I can almost feel the bubble of laughter she is suppressing. Her breasts are full considering the delicacy and petiteness of the rest of her but firm and soft, not floppy, with brownish well-defined nipples. Her backside is like that too with two lovely dimples just above and on either side of the natal cleft.

She has a narrow waist which I love to hold in my hands, trying to make fingers as well as thumbs meet, hands she says will be our downfall because like my feet they are too large.

Beneath her stomach which sags very slightly because, she says, of the four pregnancies, she has a glossy triangle of pubic hair, very neat, since she lets me trim it sometimes with the tiny scissors she uses for our nails, beaded now with droplets from the steam. Her firm thighs are rosy from the natural heat of the water, worthy pillars of the temple of delight they support, and the dimples in her knees also catch my throat with joy as she climbs the steps through the water towards me, *Vénus toute entière*, my Queen of Sheba. I hold out the bath-robe for her, fold her in it, as if she were a white dove and the robe her wings . . .

Now we are in the foyer of the baths, about to leave. Water gushes from a small lion's head set in the wall and into a semi-circular scalloped bowl. There is a simple metal cup chained to the wall. My mother makes me fill the cup and drink. I am taking the waters!

'Ma . . . Mareee-ah,' I cry. 'It is *horrible!*'

She raises her now re-pencilled eyebrows and her eyes harden. I know why: I have cried out in the way a boy of thirteen might, not at all like the young woman of twenty I am pretending to be. Her second cousin is what I am meant to be, on her mother's side of the family.

'Serafina, please!'

I remember that the name we have chosen for me is Serafina. *Cherubim and seraphim continually do cry.* The monks at Santo Domingo got it wrong when they called me Querubín.

We walk down steps out of the baths and into a street. I look back at the portico: stainless-steel letters in modernist sanserif spell out where we are: BAÑOS DE ALHAMILLA (GRANADA). It is not a street, but an avenue of young plane trees in new, fresh, green leaf through which bright warm sunlight dapples the pavement. Behind them the boardwalks, then a couple of hotels, a couple of pensions. In the distance mountains with snow on them. There is a stall on a trestle table selling herbs heaped in baskets. The labels tell you the ailments the herbs will cure: renal and cardiovascular diseases, cirrhosis, impotence.

'What's cirrhosis?' I ask.

'I don't exactly know,' she says. 'Something people who drink a lot of alcohol get, but just what it is I'm not sure.'

'Is it fatal?' I ask.

'Probably. If you get it badly.'

'Perhaps Saturno has it,' I suggest, hopefully. 'He drinks a lot. What's impotence?'

She giggles and I know I am forgiven my earlier mistake.

'I think it's when a man's thing doesn't get hard and stick up when he wants it to.'

'I don't think I need any of that then,' but this time I whisper. Nevertheless we begin to giggle and then splutter with laughter, and trying to control it makes the laughter hurt and people in the street stop and stare at us, as if we are mad.

Especially one, an old man I have seen quite often. He's staying at our hotel. He's quite tall, wears a high-crowned white hat with a turned down brim above a face which once must have been handsome, and still has dignity and poise. A craggy nose between good cheekbones defies the ruinations of age – the wobbly skin beneath his chin, the thin, flaccid lips. He's wearing his shirt collar attached, unusual in an older man, pushed up to make wings against his cheeks, and a silk cravat, scarlet and black, the colours (does he know, is it intentional?) of the Anarchists. But his pale yellow linen suit is silky and well-cut and he uses a cane with a gold ball for a handle. Indeed, in spite of his mottled hands and ancient face he is quite a dandy and I like him. He leans on the cane as he watches us laughing, and a slightly worried smile lengthens his mouth.

Later we play Contract Bridge in one of the hotel's public rooms. It is a nice room with mirrored walls made out of bevelled pieces of glass arranged in fan shapes, and a star-burst clock with no numbers on it. The furniture is all made from cane, like baskets, but painted green. In the centre there is a small hexagonal fountain with lights that change colour and a centrepiece that is a sculpture of a thin girl made out of shiny metal. She is leaning forwards with her arms thrust back behind her as if she is about to dive in, and is very smooth and shiny, almost angular. My mother is more beautiful than this statue.

This is the hand I pick up after my mother has dealt.

♠ 7 6 5
♡ K Q 9 8 7
♢ K 6 5
♣ K Q

She bids: 'One heart.'

'Pass.' On my right.

Now depending on her distribution her bid could mean she has anything from eleven to seventeen points. If it was possible for her to have a strong heart suit then the point count could be low. But since I have five hearts to the King, Queen, the chances are that she has four or five hearts to the Ace, Jack, and a high point count in other suits, especially spades. I have thirteen points, which, if she has seventeen, makes a total of thirty, and it looks good.

At this point, because I am after all only thirteen, and this is just the third time I have played Bridge properly with other people rather than dealing hands and playing them out with Mama, I begin to feel rather flustered. I look around – at our opponents. The man, fiftyish and fat, has a pin, an enamelled pin, in his buttonhole, a diagonal cross in black and white on a red background and each end of the cross has a bar coming off it. I have been quite fascinated by this since my mother, Vikí, I must remember to call her Vikí, has told me it is a sign of utter evil. How dare he wear it then, flaunt it? His wife is as ugly as he, and loaded with diamonds, in particular a brooch shaped in a bow which glitters on her black shrouded chest. She is thin and hard, not fat.

My doubts are resolved for I am sure I have felt the toe of my mother's shoe, under the table, caressing my knee, quite softly, quite gently, in what I can only believe is an encouraging way. Either she has the ace of diamonds or a void.

'Seven hearts,' I bid.

'Double,' says the wife, who holds the ace of diamonds.

'Redouble,' say I, guessing Mother to have the void in

diamonds and guessing that that was where she felt her strength lay. And I lay down my cards.

Mother, Vikí, gets through. She ruffs the diamond lead, draws trumps, then, since she has the ace of clubs, uses the king of clubs to get into my hand, plays off my winners, returns to her hand with the ace of clubs. On the strength of the thin hard woman's double she places her with the jack of spades and finesses her own ten. The rest is easy. She plays off the remaining winning spades (she has the Ace, King, Queen I placed her with), and is left with all winners. The opponents are furious. How could I possibly jump to a grand slam on the second bid?

'Because my mother, I mean Vikí, tickled my knee with her toe,' is not the answer I can give.

The man especially is very loud and very rude, and I have to struggle very hard not to punch him on the nose. In fact I really know I am going to lose my temper if I stay.

'Excuse me,' I say, 'but I am not going to sit here and listen to you saying these things. Vikí, come on,' and I pick up my little purse which is embroidered all over with shiny jet beads and I head off out, head held high, catching sight of my fragmented self in the mirrors. Now I am wearing a short black evening dress also covered in tiny shiny black beads and even more make-up than before.

But once I'm in the foyer, all brightly lit and with very big ferns and aspidistras, I realize that for some reason my mother has not followed me. I hang around for a minute, wishing she would come, feeling exposed, but at the same time knowing I will lose face if I go back into the lounge. The toilets. I want a pee anyway after all that excitement. I look around, push open the door marked *caballeros* and find myself looking at the dapper old man who was watching us outside the baths. He's standing in front of one of the urinals, but he hears me come in, and looks over his shoulder. He looks surprised, but not as surprised as he should. He shakes his wrinkled old willy, making no attempt to hide it from me, pushes it away, buttons up his trousers. I notice a small damp patch just below the lowest button, and cruelly I think: dirty old man. This is to shield me from the blow he gives me.

'David, I know your mother slightly. Twenty years ago I was commissioned by the man she later married to paint her portrait. At the time I was a close friend of your aunt Ana. I have not forgotten Dolí. I do not easily forget such beauty. Would you tell her that I would like a private word with her in the conservatory, in ten minutes' time? You can give her my card.' And he takes it out of his wallet and hands it to me. It has a name on it, and an address, and as I read it he continues: 'I will now go out into the foyer. I will knock on the door as soon as I am sure you can get out of here without being seen.'

No. I can't remember his name. I do not know why I cannot remember his name. Yes, I can. Don Gabriel. And the address was Villa Goya.

Now I am sitting up on our big double bed. I have no clothes on and I have my arms round my knees. I am waiting for my mother to come to bed. She is sitting at the dressing table in her night-gown and a silk flame-coloured kimono with an embroidered oriental cat, silver, grey and black, pouncing in a twisted jump down her back. She is removing her make-up with cotton-wool and vanishing cream. She has already re-moved my make-up for me, making her usual joke about the cream: 'See, it makes the girl vanish, and brings me back my lovely boy.'

'Nevertheless, straight to seven hearts was a bit . . . brisk,' is what she says now, and her eyes meet mine in the mirror. 'Not strictly Acol. Three would have been right, letting me make the decision.'

'But, Mama, you already had. You touched my knee.'

'I certainly did not.'

'Well, then it must have been Fatty. Why did he do that?'

'Sexual harrassment, quite common at, or rather under, the Bridge table,' says Mother.

'So, that's at least one man who thinks I'm a woman,' I crow.

'Serafina,' she says, 'let's hope so. But some men prefer boys.'

'Anyway, tomorrow let's tell them that I made the bid because he touched me.'

She looks at me with pity.

'But that would tell them that you were expecting a signal from me.' Her eyes return to the reflection of herself. 'So. What do you think of going to stay with Don Gabriel? He's a charmer, don't you think? Such a good painter though hardly *le dernièr cri*.'

'I wish you wouldn't use French expressions like that. It's awfully affected. It embarrasses me in front of other people. He told me he knew Aunt Ana, and painted you too, a long time ago. Is that true?'

'Yes.' She giggled. 'It was very romantic. When I was hardly older than you are now your father fell in love with me. He was very rich. I think he wanted to buy me, put me in a harem. He certainly did not want to marry me. But he was told that he had to and that he had to wait until I was sixteen. So he paid Don Gabriel to do a portrait of me. And while I was sitting or rather standing, for Don Gabriel painted me standing up, looking in a mirror, Don Gabriel fell in love with me too.' She giggled again, looked at me in her mirror. 'I used to flirt with my eyes, catching his in the looking-glass, while he tried to express his undying passion on canvas. The way you are flirting with me now.'

I grin at her, then turn away, jealous of all these earlier admirers. I think about the invitation: do I want to share the rest of the holiday and Mama as well with this grand but decayed old man? But I have to admit that the effort of being publicly a young woman of twenty which began as a joke has become a bit of a chore.

'I suppose it will be the end of dressing up, since he knows I'm a boy.'

'I'm afraid so. You like dressing up, don't you? You always have.'

'Yes, I do.' I look up at her with shy anticipation. 'But I prefer undressing.'

'Sometimes, David, I wonder about you.' She unwraps the kimono, teases me. 'Sometimes you really are rather naughty.'

She peels the night-dress over her head, and hesitates just long enough to be sure I am adoring her properly; then she lies beside me and turns off the light.

There are stars of street light cast through the half-closed shutters, strewn across the bed, and in them we play, play with each other, with tenderness, in the ways we have done before, but inventing new ways too. Later I curl up to sleep in her arms with the warmth of her breasts against my back, the whisper of her breath in my ear, and the damp mystery of her sex against the back of my upper thigh. She twines her fingers in mine close to my stomach, but later gently disengages them to hold my penis, which thickens in her palm again. I get my arm through the tangle of our bodies so my finger can find the sweetness hidden in her soft fur. Now we are one person again, more even than when I lay in the womb whose portal this is, and, home at last, I sleep, the perfect sleep of certain love.

XIV

'Alhamilla?'

'Yes.'

'There is a good bodega there, sells better Vino de la Costa than we get in Campanillas. Wait, I'll get you an empty *arrobia*.'

Petra followed Carmen into the kitchen, took from her the fourteen-litre, long-necked bottle contained in a heavy black plastic basket.

'It's in the village square, but if you can't find it just ask.'

The lid of the boot only just closed over the top, and Petra realized she would not be able to carry it full. No doubt someone in the bodega would help her.

She drove south-west, up into the mountains. It was sunny again, the air crystal clear after the rain. The road climbed with the river out of the valley and into high mountain meadow then crossed the watershed from which she had seen Africa. She paused at the top but only for a moment or so for the horizon was hidden by the storm clouds that had moved on. But in those few moments things became a touch clearer, aided by a sudden insight into herself.

First, she repeated aloud the thoughts that had been going through her mind on the way up. Fantasy, male fantasy. It had to be. Kepler was right. The baths like those paintings by Ingres, the reduction of his mother to a sex object with beads of moisture in her pubic hair . . . No wonder Baños de Alhamilla was not to be found on any map.

But was this not what she wanted to believe? And if so, why? What made her so ready to reject the possibility that these transcripts represented objective, historical truth? The answer was felt though not verbalized: if true they were a rebuke to her, a rebuke that could break her heart if she let it. If they were true then the love between Querubín and his mother had been one of joyful intimacy as well as passion – and perhaps the love she and her father had felt for each other could have been the same.

That it had not been so was her fault, at least in part. And so she drove on down, inwardly following a map of her own, a map which reiterated more forcefully than ever that the transcripts were simply wish-fulfilling fantasy, yet still feeling a troubled guilt because she knew that this was the way she wanted them to be.

She took a second road, barely more than a track, back to the north again, back over the watershed. This time it hairpinned down a wall of rock into a spectacular limestone gorge which presently widened into a valley and finally spilled both road and river out into a wide, tumbling, downy plain, leaving behind the north side of the mountains: great columns of fissured rock climbing above scree to huge ramparts. Over to the right, after a notable gap, the range continued but with lower spurs and crags between. The more distant mountains were lilac in the haze, but ice-glazed snow gleamed through on the highest slopes and peaks.

Now there were the almonds, thousands of small trees planted in geometric patterns across even the steepest slopes and, at the end of January, gorgeous in shades of dusty pink, pale lavender through to pure white like jagged bursts of foam. Below them came terraced orange groves filled with ripe fruit which the women picked and loaded into strengthened plastic bags almost too heavy to lift. The ground beneath was often sheeted with a light but brilliant yellow oxalis. The roadside was violets as big as pansies, galaxies of periwinkle, fumitory and spurges.

Presently the road followed the river again, and then the river itself quite suddenly began to broaden, filling out into a long lake which the road skirted, almonds and pine on one side, dressed boulders on the other.

Surrounded by groves of citrus and olive, but also with stands of eucalyptus, poplar and acacia, Alhamilla turned out to be a large village spread out on a hillside in concentric terraces of white cottages, many of them with upper stories merely roofed but not walled, where peppers and home-grown tobacco could be cured, and, in winter, hams. The pattern was broken by the Plaza Major in the middle, an irregular space bounded by the west door of the church, again once a mosque, a couple of bars, a *supermercado*, a shoe-shop or two, and a stone building with a big part-glazed door at the top of a small flight of steps. Florid lettering proclaimed the Bodega Sara García López.

Petra parked the BMW, went round to the boot and pulled out the empty *arrobia*, climbed the steps between commercial-sized food cans filled with geraniums and handsome feathery pelargoniums, some already recovering from the short winter and in bud, pushed open the door. A bell jangled.

She found herself in a small wood-panelled office, with a simple wooden table, old chairs, two calendars, one Coca-Cola, one with a topless girl advertising a Granada automobile-repair shop. Two old men in old grey suits but no ties, with the wizened faces of devoted drinkers, sat at the table and gave her a cheery if uncommitted Andalusian *"eno día"*. They had a brown terracotta jug in front of them covered by a bead-fringed serviette, and a couple of small straight-sided glasses part-filled with the brownish pink of the wine.

The woman who came bustling through a curtain of plastic strips was fiftyish, wore the usual black dress and white apron, had pulled her iron hair back in the usual bun. But her cheeks were like apples and her smile like sunshine.

'Come in, come in,' she called, grasped Petra by the arm, and led her back through the rustling curtain into a small medieval chapel or large tomb. It was very dark. Huge black barrels stood between stone columns eight feet high but with small spigots near the stone-flagged floor and small plastic cartons beneath them to catch the drips. On the other side were rows of filled *arrobias* like the one she had brought. The air was rank with the smell of wine and vinegar.

'At this time of year we have dry, medium dry and some still quite sweet. Taste them, come on, taste them.'

Holding three small straight-sided glasses in one hand she stooped and deftly half-filled them.

'The medium dry.'

Petra sipped, looked round for a wine-taster's spitoon, found none, swallowed.

'Lovely,' she said. Slightly metallic, slightly blackcurrantish, but to her taste a touch too sweet. Doña Sara waited for her to finish the sample before moving on to the next.

After tasting all three Petra settled for the dry. Standing close the woman chattered briskly with many gestures. She explained the virtues of the wine, but the liabilities too. The wine was alive, still fermenting. It could not be bottled, for if you added any sort of preservative or fermentation stop the flavour went. It was just not the same. The only thing that stopped it from going off was the carbon dioxide the fermentation produced. It acted as a seal between the wine and the carboy stopper. But if you corked it down it would blow the bottle or the cork.

The grapes were grown on the mountains to the south, actually overlooking the sea. That's why it was called El Vino de la Costa. Salt-laden winds after stormy weather had a lot to do with the flavour; and the sands of the Sahara which also got blown over the vines once or twice a year.

Doña Sara García took the empty *arrobia* away, and indicated which Petra should take in its place. She then called and one of the old men came in, helped her down the steps with it, put it in the boot for her. She went to the office to pay, astonishingly little. Then at her car again she recalled the real purpose of her visit and went back again. The woman had gone but the two old men were still there, with their glasses fuller than before.

'Excuse me, but could you tell me,' doing her best with the Spanish, 'how I can get to Baños de Alhamilla?'

Their old eyes, which had lit with curious smiles when she came back in, darkened, dropped back to their drinks. Then one of them cleared his throat, a sound like small stones slipping off a shovel, and gave a loud croak. '*Sa-r-r-r-a. Ven aquí.*'

She was back instantly, not from the cavern, but through another door, smiling, wiping her hands on an apron. Petra could see a kitchen beyond, caught the smell of freshly sliced potatoes simmering in olive oil.

'Could you tell me,' she repeated, 'how I can get to Baños de Alhamilla?'

The smile vanished. Silence settled round them for a moment like a shroud. Water, or wine, dripped beyond the doors.

'There is no Baños de Alhamilla, no Baños de Alhamilla anywhere near here. And there never was.'

And she went back to her cooking.

XV

'*Flagelli, flagelli, funi, funi, fochi, fochi . . .*'

'No, no, no . . . Again, you've lost the vowels. They're all German. For God's sake sing Italian.'

'*Flagelli, flagelli, funi, funi, fochi, fochi . . .*'

'Now you're too careful, you're losing the bite, the attack, think of the meaning: whip her, scourge her, SCALD her . . . in boiling oil. Again.'

'*Flagelli, flagelli, funi, funi, fochi, fochi . . .*'

'Go on, go on!'

'*Cavino cavino da costei il mandante mandante e i correi . . .*'

Drag out of her who ordered it, who helped her . . . Nerone's almost hysterical attack on Drusilla, whom he believes has attempted to kill Poppea. Act III, scene 3.

'*Prima ch'aspri tormenti . . .*'

First, the sharpest torments will make you feel my disdain, will persuade your obstinate spirit to confess your plotted treason . . . Petra heard the shrillness in her voice, knew the lesson had gone on long enough.

'Lips, tongue, teeth, get those consonants to the front of the mouth, "*tormenti, torrr*", you absolutely have to ROLL the "rrr" . . . Again, again.'

'. . . *di confessar gl'orditi tradimenti . . .*'

'You can sweep down on "*gl'orditi*", let us hear her scorn, her disdain . . .'

'*Di confessar gl'orditi tradimenti . . .*'

She managed the glissando but heard her voice swell a little. Had he noticed? Of course he had.

'Good, good. Well, better. But I can still hear a German frau in at the back there: Elektra or Salome even. So much to unlearn. Maybe it's too late. I should have had you ten years ago.'

He got up from the green velvet armchair, turned, laid the gilded guitar back on the seat. He used it to fill in a rudimentary continuo, a rumble on the bass string to keep her going.

'Come, it's one o'clock. Time to feed my fish.'

She found the tub of proprietary fish-food, put it in his hand, steered him by the elbow out of the music room and into the warm spring sunshine of the cloister, stood behind him while he fed crumbs shaped like tiny maggots on to the rippling surface of the water. Behind him, at the far end of the pool which sparkled in the late morning sun, portly old Paco in his battered panama raked gravel in front of the colonnade beneath the locked studio. Above, on the tiled red roof, the white doves cr-crooed and preened.

'Señor, I went to Alhamilla. They told me there that there never was such a place as Baños de Alhamilla. Lanjarón is the nearest spa. Twenty-eight kilometres away on the other side of the main road, in the Alpujarra.'

He was irritated, stamped a sandalled foot, brushed the fish-food off his palms, turned towards the patio windows that opened into his salon.

'There is,' he said, 'no hot-water spring at Lanjarón.'

'I know.'

She followed him, checking that he did not stumble. The little bald patch in the crown of his short white hair, on a level with her eyes, looked like an incipient tonsure.

'Señor. You have been here nearly ten years. And even before that, according to Dr Kepler's transcript of your dream-memory, you knew that you and your mother had visited a spa called Baños de Alhamilla. Did you never want to go there, check it out, see if it was as you had remembered it?'

'Of course,' his voice was testy now. 'It was one of the first things I did when I got here. And of course I got the same result as you. So then I began to check out those dream-memories, the transcripts Dr Kepler made of what I told him under hypnosis. A lot was right but so it would be. But some crucial things were wrong.'

The testiness was fading into weary despair. She waited.

'I bought histories of the period. Especially *The Spanish Civil War* by Hugh Thomas, a British historian. More reliable than most Spaniards. I found Kepler's transcripts contained several inaccuracies. Since my memories were very firmly rooted in the events of the time I was forced to concede again that Kepler was right. I made them up.'

He paused on the threshold of his room. The colonnade stopped short of the salon so there was no interruption to the light that flowed through the patio doors.

'It was a small place. Hardly more than one short avenue, with the baths at the top and a row of hotels. Ours was new. Or newish . . .' A puzzled look drifted over his cloudy eyes, and he rubbed his face with both hands, '. . . Or at any rate the interior was new, art deco, *modernismo*, you know?'

She followed him in, saw him safely settled in the upright armchair behind his desk. He looked up, towards but not at her.

'You don't believe them either.' It was a statement not a question. 'My dream-memories.'

She felt suddenly dizzy, sweat formed in her palms, her throat felt dry, but she forced herself to say it: 'Fathers abuse their daughters, sleep with them. Daughters,' and her pure voice fluked, choked, 'sometimes, as I did, seduce their fathers. Especially if there is madness in the air. But what sort of woman would knowingly seduce her son, her thirteen-year-old son? Not even Jocasta knew what she was doing.'

He opened a big drawer, pulled out a large folder, dropped it on the desk in front of him. A bowl of orange lilies, hot-house, bought by Carmen in the Campanillas market, shed a tiny cloud of yellow pollen.

'Read the rest. See for yourself what sort of woman my mother was.'

She looked at the folder, guessed there were fifty or so pages of typescript in it, felt a wave of revulsion at what they might contain.

'No.'

'Why not?'

'The woman in your dreams could be as much your invention as the things you make her do.'

He sighed.

'You remember Melchor's letter to me? Across the garden, in the library, you will find all my mother's books and papers; you can find there, if you want to, the real woman.'

She turned, looked out across the pool towards the four large black shuttered windows each framed by an arch of the colonnade. A wave of confused emotion flooded over her: frustration, a curiosity which she had to admit was not entirely wholesome, extreme irritation at her own indecision and, with it all, a spiritual fatigue. It receded and left one clear-headed percep-
tion: Querubín's voice was the product of a malicious injury followed by years of technical training built on a foundation of meticulous scholarship; but Querubín the artist, the interpreter, came from something far deeper. She knew enough now to understand that these roots lay entirely in the events that preceded his castration and that understanding Querubín the artist demanded an understanding of those events.

She sighed, looked back at him over her shoulder.

'Have *you* read those papers?'

He rubbed his eyes, did his best to focus them on the lean, dark silhouette placed against the light in a twisting posture which seemed to express departure, a setting-out. He too was deeply confused about who he was, who he had been. Decades of international stardom had been a defence against that confusion even while the confusion itself fed the artist. And then had come the discovery of Villa Goya and with it his identity, though not his past, and finally the busy-ness of gutting what was virtually a ruin and rebuilding it, moving in. But now . . . nothing. Except Petra. He had foreseen that she might be his future, a future that would survive his physical death. Now he realized she might also be a guide and escort into his past, the past freighted with guilt and horror but also, if his memories were real, with an almost unbearable brightness and joy stained now with an agonizing nostalgia. Indeed he needed a guide.

'I tried. But it was too . . . painful. It's all still much as Don Gabriel left it. Only the official documents which gave me a name and the properties that went with it have gone.'

'And you don't mind if I . . . have a look?'

'No.' He shrugged, spread his palms in a gesture theatrical enough to recall who he had been, declaimed in the voice of an operatic character who has decided to risk all for love: 'Search her out. Find her. Hunt her down. Bring her back.'

XVI

An hour, or nearly, to lunch. He leant back in the big chair, tried to compose himself, make himself comfortable, but he felt hungry: a distant aroma of chickpea, garlic, air-cured ham disturbed the nearer fragrances of flowers. Somewhere in the room there were oranges, but the effort of locating them, peeling one, and finding the right place to put the peel was beyond him. Hungry but tired too – the lessons were a strain anyway, and the conversation they had just had left him feeling drained in much the way he used to feel after a performance which had disappointed him. His hand came to rest on the folder. Petra had not, after all, taken it with her.

Remembering Dr Kepler, he sang through in his head the *Alleluia* from Mozart's motet *Exultate Jubilate*. At their first meeting Kepler had told him it was his favourite piece, his favourite of all Querubín's many recordings. Through it he heard the creak and crack of shutters opening on the other side of the pool. Petra had taken him at his word, had gone to the library. What would she find? What would she make of it? He pushed the questions away.

'Tell me,' Kepler had asked, head on one side. 'Was it really written for a castrato?'

'All the music I sing was written for castrati.'

'Tell me why that is, David. Tell me why.'

Now he recalled going there for that fatal last appointment. He was on a yellow bus, a number sixty his memory told him, which he had boarded close to his hotel. It was now heading through the suburb called Grünwald, towards the forest itself. He was on a bus partly because he preferred the private space it conferred: more private than a taxi; and partly, though this was largely paranoia for he was still a wealthy man, to save money.

He had come to Berlin four months earlier to record Handel's *Amadis di Gaula* with the large local band. The already elderly Austrian fascist (Querubín's description) was in charge and it had gone badly: in Querubín's opinion the old martinet had as much understanding of baroque as a run-of-the-mill film composer. In playback it sounded like the score to a Hollywood romance set in neo-Gothic Land. The sudden and inexplicable depressions that had troubled him for a year or more descended like a blanket at the end of each session, and then one morning he had come out of a fugue of which he had no memory, on the British side of Check-point Charlie, surrounded by anxious doctors and nurses. Apparently he had been trying to get to the Berlin State Opera House on the other side because there his musicality would be better understood.

He cancelled the recording, paid a large indemnity, and after he had seen a couple of consultants cancelled all his engagements for the next six months. He then set about seeking a cure. One consultant was insistent: a short regime of ECT would soon set him metaphorically on his feet. However, Querubín had recently read *One Flew over the Cuckoo's Nest*, and declined.

The other, a Freudian, on hearing that Querubín had been castrated in his early teens, and had no memory of anything up to the moment when he sang the word *Cherubim* (or *Seraphim*) in the monastery of Santo Domingo, advised that the root of all his mental troubles must lie in childhood. Which, since his memory was a complete blank, posed a problem. The answer lay with Dr Kepler, a psychiatrist who practised psychohypnotic therapy from his private clinic in the Grünwald Forst. Since he relied solely on what his patients produced under hypnosis he could not call himself a psychoanalyst; he did, however, subscribe to Freudian theory. And he was not cheap.

The bus dropped Querubín at the corner of Clay Allee and Königin Luise Strasse. Under a grey sky, the warm June drizzle little stronger than a haze and not enough to make him put up his umbrella, he followed the road into the forest. It was, he always felt, like entering the world of the Brothers Grimm: although much of the timber was less than twenty years old (the Berliners had used a lot of it for fuel during the Blockade) there was still plenty of beech amongst the newer birch, larch and spruce, with a thick undergrowth beneath it. There were deer, he had been told, foxes, wild pig, even perhaps a wolf or two; and certainly the thickets routinely yielded the dead bodies of missing persons, usually female.

Amongst the sinister trees and undergrowth, and laid out on a fairly strict grid system, strange houses stood, strange for often they were fancifully designed: Dr Kepler's for instance combined stark thirties modern with roofs tiled in glazed purple – good enough, if you were Hansel or Gretel, to eat. With pulse raised (it always was at this point) Querubín ran the electronically coded card Kepler had given him down the slit set in the gate post. The high but narrow wrought-iron gate clicked open.

He had been coming once a week for twelve weeks, and this was to be his last visit. During each session, after he had fallen into hypnotic trance, he apparently babbled out long re-creations of scenes from his late childhood and early adolescence which became more and more centred on his mother. He described these scenes partly from the point of view of a participant, partly as an observer of them. The erotic side of the relationship with his mother became steadily more explicit.

At the end of each session he was left with a visual dream memory, not a verbal one, elements of which he would be able to recall, more or less at will, for the next twenty years. He was also left with the transcripts which Kepler gave him, and Kepler's interpretation of them. He had accepted this readily – from a man who had assumed the authority of a Father and pocketed a very substantial fee he could hardly do otherwise. Now he recalled with a sort of sad shame just how ready his acceptance had been.

'Come into my office, David. We have finished with the studio, no more dreams, we're through with all that.'

Kepler was suddenly different. At every other meeting (perhaps not at the very first? Querubín could not quite recall how he had been then) he had been quiet, self-effacing, had quite quickly conducted the patient into a dimly lit room where everything, walls, ceiling, the leather couch and a chair, had been in varying shades of grey, a warm room, very warm,

110

blood-heat. Querubín had taken off all his clothes and lain on the couch under a light-weight, light-grey duvet and, after counting to ten in English forwards and backwards a few times, had fallen into a hypnotic trance. Just as it was with Petra, so too with Kepler: English was the language they had most in common.

Things were different on this last visit. Kepler now wore a red short-sleeved shirt and light-weight check trousers. He led Querubín into a very conventional office: carpets, glazed bookcases, filing cabinets, crimson velvet drapes. He waved Querubín into a buttoned leather chair that squeaked like a mouse farting if he moved, while he himself sat behind the sort of big antique desk that confers authority.

He then gave a lecture.

'Though there are no certainties in psychopathology I am satisfied that your condition has been very materially improved as a result of the course of hypnotherapy you have undergone and I have no reason to suppose that this improvement will not be maintained. You are now in possession, both in your own mind and through these transcripts of our sessions,' and he tapped a folder bound with red ribbon which sat like an invited guest at his elbow, 'of the material repressed to subconscious levels that was causing you to exhibit severe symptoms of psychosis. Not only have you brought these to light, you have also coped with, and learned to live with the content.'

He pursed his lips, blew out his cheeks, picked up a pen shaped like a plastic quill, tapped it on the blotter, then beamed one of the sunniest smiles Querubín had ever seen.

'There remains the question of how this material should be interpreted. In my opinion there is no doubt. The erotic material you produced under hypnosis is basically fantasy, albeit fantasy buttressed by circumstantial detail. These fantasies are probably rooted in and grew out of simpler, grosser fantasies formed during the actual period of your life in which they appear to have happened, that is between your father's death and your arrival at the monastery at Silos. It is likely that they were elaborated and embellished during the eighteen months preceding your recovery from fugue with catatonic symptoms, that is while you were in that catatonic state, but were repressed together with all earlier memories at the moment you recovered. Finally they emerge now, presented with the sophistication of an adult possessed of sensitivity and artistic talent. The sophistication of the presentation arises from the fact that you deeply wish them to be accepted as true by me, as well as by your waking self.

'The indications are that you underwent a serious psychic crisis originating in early infancy but grossly aggravated by your father's death, by feelings of rivalry directed against your elder siblings for your mother's affection, and by the close and probably over-affectionate attentions of your mother, especially towards the end of the period. The "normal" hatred of your father and lust for your mother, normal that is to say in families orientated along the lines that yours was, were present in a more than usually severe form. You felt an intolerable guilt for the hatred you felt towards your father, a guilt which was exacerbated by your father's early death and your initial feelings of triumph expressed in the way you sang at his funeral.

'On the other side you also felt intolerable guilt at the fantasies you created regarding the sexuality of your relationship with your mother. In their original form these fantasies were no doubt created against a background of reality, the background, in itself horrific and traumatic, of the months leading up to the outbreak of the Spanish Civil War. For these reasons they now reappear under hypnosis with all the trappings of circumstantial detail which surrounded their creation and which are now necessary to make them "real" and not fantasy. It is possible too that what you have read and learned of the period in recent years has also been incorporated to make these fantasies credible not only to you but to me as well.

'We come now to the circumstances of the crisis which you could not face even under hypnosis. You exhibited such distress that I terminated the session. One can only guess what happened. I would put forward the possibility that you needed to expiate the guilt arising from the vindictive hate you felt for your dead father and your lust for your mother and that the expiation you settled on was – self-inflicted castration. I believe your mother rejected this "gift". It is possible that once your physical recovery was assured it was she who had you sent to the monastery, and that you knew or sensed that it was her choice that you should go.'

By now Querubín was almost frying in the leather chair. The argument Kepler was putting forward was irrefutable, exact, perfect, correct. Sweat swamped him, dreadful angst, but also a sublime relief, the exquisitely perfect sensation of redemption achieved through confession and absolution.

'I believe that the re-emergence of these fantasies under hypnosis has already been shown to be therapeutic and will have lasting benign results. Through them you have external-ized deep emotions which formerly you rejected and suppres-sed, thus creating a permanent danger of retreat into psychotic trance or fugue. There is now every reason to hope that your condition has stabilized and that you will be able to resume the career which has been such an ornament to your profession, and a delight for all lovers of good music.'

Kepler leant back, made a church of his fingers beneath his chin and beamed seraphically once more.

Querubín forced himself to ask the unaskable.

'There is then no possibility that these dream-memories bear any resemblance to actual reality?'

'Oh yes. The circumstantial detail, the descriptions of where you lived and so on are very likely to be accurate. But the overt sexuality of your relationship with your mother is fantasy. Pure fantasy. I'm sure of it.'

His acceptance of Kepler's thesis carried him through the final decade of his career, during which he made more appearances, more recordings, and earned far more money than in any previous period. He was hailed as the greatest interpreter of baroque and early rococo music the world had seen and heard since 1792. He lectured and was given honorary doctorates. He put his name to good causes and was listed as their patron with only royalty above him. For his final appearance at the Met, in the role of Ulysses, tickets had been exchanged on the black market for up to twenty thousand dollars.

Then one day he walked or was led into El Casón. He discovered Melchor, Villa Goya, his real name, and the painting that described what had really happened to him in August 1936. Or did it? He had replaced the shroud, and had refused to return to the room in case he discovered that again he had hallucinated something that was not really there. He might go back. Whether or not he did could depend on what Petra discovered. But if he did it would be only when he was certain he was blind and ready to make the final expiation.

PART TWO

Dolí

XVII

Petra left the salon, walked slowly down the cloister, past the music room, through the angle, along the colonnade in front of the big front door and then the dining room. She paused in the open lobby, turned, looked back from this the shaded side of the villa, across the still water of the pool, towards the room she had left. The sun bouncing from the water almost hurt her eyes. An early midge or two cruised above it, the scouring swallows still sufficiently scanty to allow them to survive for much of their one-day allotted span. Although spring was well under way in the fields and on the hillsides, the flower beds were at their lowest ebb: only a few half-opened roses bloomed – the last of last year's or the first of this?

She pushed the big door open. The darkness in front of her, rendered all the more impenetrable by the blaze of sunshine reflected from water and warm stone that she had just left, repelled her. She allowed herself a moment or two during which the tea-chests and the bookcases, lit by the few thin bars of light that sidled past the shutters, became shapes rather than presences. She went to the nearest window, opened the casements inwards, then pushed the shutters out. She turned, discovered that diffused light had fallen across the portrait Melchor had painted some seventy-five years earlier.

'You can find there, if you want to, what sort of woman she was.'

Did she want to? She supposed so, for if not why was she there? She felt a lurch of panic. Did she need all this? Get away from it, wind up the thread of sanity and leave with the ball intact. Why not? Even the singing was going badly, always he shouted at her, called her a German frau. The whole project had gone sour, surely it had been ill-conceived from the start, prompted by psychological imperatives rather than based on any real ability she had.

She reached for the door handle but the portrait stood to the side of the door, guarded it. Suddenly she could not take her eyes off it: she was forced to explore it. She experienced, as had Melchor himself, the eroticism of the twisted torso, the glamour of the ankle above the raised foot, the way the full dark crimson skirt and the white blouse promised rather than concealed the adolescent perfection beneath, a promise stated in the creamy whiteness of the arms and above all in the slim turning neck and the top two vertebrae beneath, so subtly suggested with hints of lilac and blue. It lay too in the way a lock had drifted from the casually pinned up hair to suggest that the lot could come tumbling down . . .

Petra's preference for her own sex was real enough and she was not so blind to her desires as to deny that here was a girl with whom, across three-quarters of a century, she could fall in love as surely as she was in love with the Parma Violet Lady . . .

But there was more. She had been posed (or had she chosen the pose herself?) so that her face was turned away, like that of the Rokeby Venus, and could only be discerned in the mirror. Melchor was clearly, as clearly as Picasso was though in very different ways, deeply aware of the Spanish School, and not least of the importance of mirrors within it. You wish to observe someone in the same or even the next room without their knowledge, you look in a mirror. You wish to engage in eye contact with someone in the same room or the next without the knowledge of third parties, you use a mirror. You wish to layer with meanings a portrait you are painting, you use, or suggest, mirrors.

Was María Dolores Iglesias y Corazón observing her, or spying on her? Or had she caught the eye of the beholder in order to collude, secretly, in a journey into the past which was to be her future?

Petra shuddered, turned away, threw open the other three sets of windows and shutters; they creaked and banged, sent galaxies of glittering dust across the reflected sun, filled the room with a cool, indirect light. She turned, expecting to see the heaped books and files, papers and boxes made tawdry by the brightness. But they looked as pleased as she to be in daylight again, at last.

Where to begin? She circled the far end of the long table, picked up a book. It was bound in faded yellow end-papers with red lettering, now russet. The Spanish title presented no difficulties: *The Origin of the Family, Private Property and the State* by Frederick Engels. She knew it. Her father had owned a copy, but she had never read it. She looked at the fly-leaf: *Dolí Iglesias y Corazón, 3 Agusto 1932, El Rastro*. So. It had been bought by Querubín's mother in Madrid's flea market which had been and still is a place to buy subversive literature. Petra knew: she had been there during her language course in Madrid. The subversive stuff now was as likely to be *Mein Kampf* as Marx or Engels.

Dolí. Not Lola or Lolita. Like Molí – Querubín's cat. Clearly Dolí had been intellectually curious and for her time very up to date. As well as Marx and Engels, there were also Freud, Jung, and Fraser's *Golden Bough*, and the Spanish philosophers Unamuno and Ortega y Gasset. And the anarchist Peter Kropotkin's *Mutual Aid*. She paused for a moment, head up, caught by the odours of cooking: garlic, chickpeas in stock made from the bones of mountain-cured ham? It made her hungry – a sensation she had taught herself to value.

She moved along the shelves, found a complete set of the 1911 edition of the *Encyclopædia Britannica* in English. The name this time on the fly-leaf of *A–ANS* was Pablo Iglesias Frontera. Dolí's father? Querubín's grandfather? Probably. She crossed the fireplace and stood in front of the stacks on the other side, let her hand wander up the nape of her neck and into her cropped hair. No books now, just box-files, some stacked on their sides, most upright, all labelled. An archive.

She read some of the labels. They were cryptic, but not that cryptic: for example *M-D I y C Cartas 1.viii.33–31.xii.34*, written in a sloping, florid, but neat, almost legal, hand, must surely mean letters to or from or maybe to and from María Dolores Iglesias y Corazón, between those dates. She reached out, stayed, was suddenly aware of prickling in the throat, raised pulse, the symptoms of childhood trespass in both senses of the

word: she was doing something wrong, was in a place she had
no business to be.

This was ridiculous. He had sent her there. She pulled down
the file, carried it to the table, opened it, discovered a stack of
envelopes held in place by a spring clip, which she lifted. The
top envelope, cream, quality, a small stamp, Österreich, Vienna
postmark. She slipped out the letter, two sheets, closely written,
black ink faded to dark sepia, in the round hand that Spaniards
have been taught for a century: quite like the French but fancier
and less upright, nearer italic, the capitals with flourishes. It was
in Spanish, but, with her bilingual dictionary, none of it beyond
her.

16c Goldegg Gasse
Vienna
1.viii.1933

My dear Dolí,

Your letter did not in the least upset me, and it was silly of
you to imagine that it might. The only upsetting thing about it
was the unhappiness that you are obviously feeling, a distress
which I am sure you realize can become pathological. I am so
glad you felt able to write to me and I do hope you will continue
to do so whenever the wretchedness of your situation becomes
too much for you.

Now, with regard to your feelings for Miguel – in the first
place they are natural. Please do try to understand that. There is
nothing in nature to say that they should be condemned.
However, you are right to feel they should be constrained, but
not, dear Dolí, out of guilt, nor should they be repressed. Guilt
and repression are great evils. But, yes, clearly it is expedient
that they should be constrained. To allow them full rein will
bring trouble, serious, nasty trouble.

So here is what I advise: by all means revel in these feelings,
glory in his presence, feel proud of him, dote on him, enjoy
make-believe day-dreams . . . But no more. Don't repress your
feelings; in privacy give way to them, enjoy them, even while
knowing they must remain for ever unrequited except in fan-

tasy. And, dear Dolí, please, no guilt. There is nothing to feel guilty about.

I wish I could be with you and talk all this through so very much more deeply and carefully, using some of the techniques I am learning here. As you wrote in your letter, these are very turbulent times. Dolfuss has suppressed the Nazi party, but there is no likelihood of a return to constitutional government. Just as you fear *pistoleros* in Madrid, we have our gunmen, and my teacher, who is of course Jewish, says she will emigrate to England or the United States if things do not improve. And of course they will not. It is unbelievable how few people seem to understand that Europe is on the brink of civil war, not a war between rival empires, but a war between the classes, a class war.

I watch the newspapers for news from Spain, from Madrid, just now things seem a little quieter there, but it can only be the lull before the storm. That fool Azaña has clearly allowed a reaction to set in and it is only a matter of time before he will lose votes in the Cortés. Take care, Dolí. Don't try to get involved. Saturno will destroy you if you do. If . . . when things get really bad, I shall be, believe me, dear Dolí, back at your side so we can stand together as we have done in the past.

>   Kisses
>   Ana

Petra folded the dry sheets carefully along their creases and slipped them back into the envelope, then stood for a while, tapping her left thumb with it. She felt moved in several, contradictory ways. There was the guilt of the child in the larder, reaching for the jam jar and hearing a not too distant footstep. There was also excitement, a growing curiosity, though tinged with revulsion.

She remembered Melchor's letter. Ana was Dolí's older sister who had studied psychoanalysis with a disciple of Freud in Vienna, and who had died driving an ambulance at the battle of Teruel.

And Saturno? Again: Melchor's letter – Saturno was the sisters' name for Dolí's brother-in-law, the older brother of her husband. Naturally the Prado had been a place to go to during her stay in Madrid. Who could forget Goya's nightmarish *Saturn Devouring One of His Children*: a ghastly painting? Clearly Saturno, the Marqués de Boltana, was not nice. And Miguel? Who was he, this man Dolí was in love with, who was he that even presumably liberal, liberated Ana thought Dolí should not actually surrender herself to? He must surely be the oldest son, the first-born, killed at the siege of Malaga four years later.

So. Here, straight away (and again her palms sweated, her pulse thumped, the dryness returned to her throat) was evidence: if Dolí could fall in love, presumably unrequited love, with her oldest boy, what might not have happened a few years later? She could go to Querubín right now, wave this under his nose, read it to him, say: 'Look, you blind old fool, your mother desired your oldest brother, it says so here – probably she had a taste for all her sons and you were but the last of a line . . .' She could, but she would not. Quite simply it would not be enough: the Kepler version could comfortably accommodate Dolí's presumed preference for the older son as a stimulus to Querubín's 'fantasies'.

Instead she re-read the address on the outside of the envelope. *Dña Sra María Dolores Iglesias y Corazón, Calle de Ayala 29b, Salamanca, Madrid 1, Spania*. Well, that all meant something. Ayala she rememberd was only three blocks away from the private language school where she had tried to convert her Italian into Spitalian. Salamanca was not the university town but one of the richest *barrios* of Madrid, comparable, say, with Belgravia in London, Schwabing in Munich. She remembered it as a grid of high, late-nineteenth-century apartment blocks with very expensive shops at street level, the sort that specialize in oriental carpets or pre-Columbian artefacts from the Americas. There were restaurants too whose outdoor tables in summer were shielded from the traffic and the less than wealthy by moveable hedges of laurel – topiaried, it would seem, with nail-scissors. It gave a clue to Querubín's background. If this was where he was living when he was eleven years old then he was from the *haute*, seriously *haute bourgeoisie*. Which contrasted oddly not only with his mother's books but also with the tone of her sister's letter.

She checked the date again, put the file back on its shelf. If Querubín was approaching his seventieth birthday, then he was born in 1922. If he sang at his father's funeral when he was ten years old, then his father died in 1932, some months at least before this letter had been written. Her eyes ran up and down the shelves, across the books and files. Where next? Lucky dip or ponder the dates . . .

She lucky-dipped and found pages and pages of household accounts, together with envelopes filled with receipts. Interesting for some, perhaps, a historian researching the era would have a ball, but not likely to give insights into the woman who clearly haunted Querubín and was beginning to haunt her. She needed guidelines, she needed to know more, but how?

'Ask him,' came the answer.

A clatter of dishes outside. Lunch. As she passed the portrait Petra avoided Dolí's mirrored eyes.

XVIII

Petra waited until Carmen had settled Querubín into his chair, tucked his napkin under his chin, placed his hand over his soup spoon. Potage of chickpea cooked with bones from a mountain ham. Delicious, though she left the *tocinos*, small lumps of white pork fat, on the rim of her plate.

'I've been looking at the books your mother had in her library. There's some weird suff there. No, not weird. But odd for a rich woman living in the Calle Ayala to have. Marx, Engels, Kropotkin. Certainly she seems to have been an interesting woman. So far I've only looked at one letter. It was from your Aunt Ana in Vienna. It seems she was studying Freudian psychology. For the nineteen-thirties it all seems pretty high-powered stuff. But I really don't know how to go on. I also got bogged down in laundry bills, fuel bills, that sort of thing.'

She continued to deal with her soup for a minute or two more, then she put her spoon down.

'It's no good my just browsing randomly through all those papers. I have to know something of the context they came from. I'd like to know what sort of family your mother's was. After you got here, and established your identity as David Pérez Iglesias, you must have been able to find out a bit about all that, even if you still couldn't remember anything apart from what Dr Kepler had brought out.'

The old man pushed his soup plate away, sank back in his chair. As he began talking his fingers tore at a lump of bread, kneaded the crumb into small grey pellets. Presently Carmen brought in a plate of tiny grilled cutlets and a salad, cleared the bowls, tut-tutting at his since it was barely touched. Querubín seemed unaware of what had happened, but talked on, quietly, as if to himself, for ten minutes or more. Occasionally he chewed the nut of meat out of a cutlet and let the small bone drop to the floor for Molí to crack and crunch.

'They could hardly have been more different, the background

my mother came from and that of my father. And I did find out, from descendants of my uncle, some . . . things about them. She left a considerable personal fortune to which I was the sole heir. It was kept by the bank my father's family owned. The Banco de Corpus Cristi Internacional, no less. The man who runs it now is my cousin. I had to go to the bank, meet him . . . not quite ten years ago.'

∽

Banks are built to intimidate the meek and flatter the proud. Contemplating the façade of the Banco de Corpus Cristi, which had a small tower to itself on the Plaza de España, Querubín reflected that for those who are neither meek nor proud but simply hate banks they post uniformed paramilitaries on the steps armed with Beretta machine-pistols. In Spain they do, anyway.

He crossed the square in front of the inappropriately grandiose Cervantes Monument from which a marble Cervantes contemplates the Don and Sancho, half his size but cast in more durable bronze. On the way he plucked leaves from the not too healthy olives transplanted from La Mancha to flank the monument. He hoped that would act as a talisman as he entered, in Odyssean mode, the Halls of the Dead. Not precisely a Golden Bough, but they would do. He was about to meet, for the first time other than in dream, his ancestors and progenitors. A few flakes of snow, none bigger than a gnat, drifted out of a leaden sky and he shrugged off a memory of an earlier time.

He was expected. A mere flash of card to a flunkie and he was whisked across marble halls to the Director's personal lift. Housed behind art deco sliding doors, beneath a gilded half-moon clock, the actual elevator itself was reassuringly modern, electronic, computerized. 'Miss Otis regrets', but not for long. Within five seconds he was on the sixteenth floor, and there, as the doors opened in front of him, waiting with extended hand was . . .

Antonio Pérez y Mendizábal, Marqués de Boltana.

Handsome, robust, a well-kept fifty or so, he was still poised on a pinnacle of corseted good health. As Querubín crossed the threshold of the lift he took Querubín's hands, folded the older, slighter man in a close embrace, patted his back, made a kissing noise beneath Querubín's right ear, then held him at arm's length.

'David. Cousin David. How good it is to welcome you back into the Family Pérez.'

Beneath the odours of best cologne Querubín detected the self-secreted charismatic oil of the seriously rich and powerful. He was led across a half hectare or so of prime Aubusson, but on the way they paused in front of a full-length portrait, garishly lit. Wearing court clothes of the early nineteenth century, this man was lean and hungry. Done with broad unflattering brush-strokes against a background that had been barely sketched in so raw canvas still showed in places. Hungry yes, Querubín thought, but greedy too. Late Goya, not the best, but from the period when you paid him to insult you, because the cachet of being done by him was worth it.

'The first of our ancestors,' said Boltana, and he clutched Querubín's elbow. 'The first one, that is, to make real money. Not in the Americas, but the Philippines.'

He placed Querubín in a high-backed carved chair upholstered in lilac watered silk and sat himself behind the huge desk that filled the window at the end of the long, oak-lined room.

A person manifested, served coffee and best Spanish brandy with almond *langues de chat*. Eighteenth-century Limoges and English Georgian silver. The brandy balloons seemed almost ordinary. The brandy was not. Nor was the coffee. Colombian, grown above three thousand metres. Or so Boltana said.

'You must,' Boltana ventured, 'want to know all about our family.'

Querubín let the insulated silence lengthen between them, then he shifted, crossed his legs.

'Not really.' He wondered as he sometimes still did, even after all these years, in situations that were awkward, unfamiliar, how his speaking voice came across. Counter-tenors, male sopranos have normal masculine speaking voices. He did not. Somewhere between Dietrich and Caballé was how Freddie had described it.

'I have known who my father was for some months now and it's not really very difficult to find out about the Pérezs and the Mendizábals. They crop up in Spanish history and of course you are all often featured in ¡Hola!. I also read with interest the house history of your bank which you were kind enough to send me.' His forefinger nails scraped at the balls of his thumbs and he plunged in. 'It has been more difficult to find out anything about my mother's family.'

'They were nonentities. People of no importance.'

Querubín had outfaced the greatest conductors of his time. He would not be put down by a bank manager.

'Then I shall sign the necessary papers, and go.'

Since the necessary papers would put María Dolores's fortune safely in Querubín's hands, together with digests of how the bank had looked after it for nearly fifty years, Boltana realized that a swift reversal was in order. The unaudited and unchecked accounts had been a useful conduit through which large sums of not very clean money had been passed over the years and he needed Querubín to leave things as they were.

'That is to say as a family over many generations. Academics, liberal politicians, that sort of thing. But your grandfather, Pablo Iglesias Frontera, was an exceptional man, and your mother of course was not only very beautiful, but talented in many ways.'

'In what way was he exceptional?'

'He was an inventor of startling originality, but of course had no business sense at all. Also a dilettante of the arts: he was on intimate terms with many of the best minds of his generation. He was an anglophile – many liberals were in those days. And she, your mother, spoke English perfectly. She was a very good pianist . . . and so on. You must realize that I am merely recollecting what I have been told by my father, cousins, family friends.'

Querubín watched the snow outside thicken a little and swirl on a sudden gust of wind. He sipped the coffee. It was, he admitted to himself, perhaps the best cup of coffee he had ever tasted. He looked across the big desk and for a moment caught and held the banker's eyes: they were empty, expressionless above lips that still smiled.

'That such a girl should marry at the age of sixteen a man thirty years older than herself is odd, is it not? I am surprised they ever even met. I wonder how?'

'There is no secret about that.' Boltana was suave and expansive again. 'Your grandfather came up with a project which required research and development funds he did not have. An inexhaustible light bulb. His banker, a friend of our family, put him in touch with your father. During the negotiations he met your mother and fell in love with her. And she, presumably, with him.'

'What happened to the light bulb?'

'Your father bought the patent from your grandfather, but your grandfather retained the royalty rights. Those were the terms of the deal: it was not a loan but a sale. Your father then sold the patent to a light-bulb manufacturer.'

Boltana swivelled his big seat to an angle that left him not quite facing Querubín as full on as before. He continued, 'Who refused to develop it and was able to suppress its development elsewhere. There were at least four similar cases.'

Both men watched the snow which had now begun to tumble out of the sky. Since the room they were in was high and from their seats they could not see neighbouring buildings, it created the illusion that they were rising, levitating, rather than that the snow was falling. Querubín blinked, stamped a foot that was beginning to tingle.

'He had one asset left. My mother.'

'The marriage settlement was very generous. It included a large capital sum put in trust to become absolutely hers on your father's death. It has been well husbanded since your mother's death and it leaves you now a very wealthy man indeed.'

∽

Querubín pushed back his plate, leant back, let his head drop forward. Petra was shocked, felt a cold chill spread from her diaphragm.

'You mean your grandfather sold your mother to pay off a debt?'

'Yes. There was little else he could do under the circumstances. Don Fernando had him . . . what do the Americans say? . . . stitched up.'

'Your poor mother.'

'Well. Perhaps.'

'What do you mean?'

'She was young, not necessarily idealistic or romantic, young people generally are not. She may well have been a realist. Much older doting man for a husband, very wealthy. No doubt he gave her gifts and so on, generally turned her head. She doesn't look wretched in that portrait, does she? It was he who commissioned it. And finally in those days arranged marriages of that sort were common enough between business partners as well as imperial dynasties.'

'But later?'

'Yes. Later there was trouble. Both in the marriage and after. I'm sorry, I am very tired now. I don't want any more to eat.'

'You had better. Carmen will blame me for making you talk.'

'An apple, then.'

She reached out for one, put it in his hand. He caught her wrist, squeezed it, and she felt a sudden tremor of tenderness.

'What will you do now?' he asked.

'Go back to those files. I think I have a better idea of what I should be looking for. In fact I feel quite anxious to do just that.'

She stood up, pushed her napkin on to the table.

'No siesta, then.'

'Not for me, but you should rest.'

On his bed Querubín recalled the rest of that interview with his cousin, actually his second cousin.

～

'Your father too was a talented, imaginative man.' Boltana had been anxious to re-establish the Pérez family as people worth consideration.

'I have managed to find out two things about him,' Querubín said. 'First, he made a huge fortune out of buying land in the Canaries during the Cuban War. He developed tobacco culture there just when Spain was about to lose its cheapest source of the stuff. I suppose you could say that showed talent. Or imagination.'

He paused, forced Boltana to intervene.

'And?'

'Sixteen years after marrying my mother, he died of a stroke. He was in the company of a child prostitute at the time.' He leant forward, hands on his knees, caught again the wary look in Boltana's eyes. Boltana, on his side, saw anger. Querubín went on: 'What became of my mother? I mean, in the end. How did she die? How was it that I ended up in a monastery with no balls and no idea who I was?'

Boltana shifted with discomfort, almost as if he were plagued with piles. 'Frankly, David, nobody knows.'

'You must have some idea.'

'Why should I? I was six years old at the time. And our side of the family got away to Burgos almost as soon as the trouble started.'

And spent the next three years using their banking skills to raise foreign capital in Franco's support – Querubín had found out that much. Indeed, there was an allusion to them in Hugh Thomas. He waited.

'Of course, when it was all over my grandfather made enquiries.'

'Well?'

'Nothing certain. It seems possible . . . there are indications. Listen, David, you may not like this . . . '

'Come on.'

'Well, your mother had strange tastes, consorted with strange people. The last thing we know with any certainty is that just as the National Movement was getting under way she left Madrid in the company of a homosexual poet and an adolescent street girl who was probably her lesbian lover. We have no idea at all of where she left you nor who with. Nor of how you came to be at Silos.'

XIX

Ayala
Madrid
20 April 1932

Dearest Ana

It worked! Just a week ago Federico gave a lecture at the Residencia about New York and the poems he wrote there or after being there. He read many of them and they were wonderful, and there was a party after, which I got to, and I said to him, I am not a student and I have independent means (marvellous how quickly a rich young widow can master the language that describes her circumstances) and I said I want to support La Barraca, but not just with money, I want to come with you.

He is stockily built, wears fashionably floppy suits with 'Oxford Bags', has big eyes in a square face and huge eyebrows, and he is so intense! He radiates energy! You can't imagine. He asked me had I ever acted. I said: for sixteen years I was married to a man who thought I loved him, and he laughed and laughed, but will not give me a part because essentially it is is to be a student theatre! No, I am wrong. I have a part, but it will not be played on the stage. Ana, you cannot guess. I am to be a *dueña*! I am to sleep with the girl students, and shoo away the males! But also I am to help with the music.

We leave early in July, probably the eighth or ninth, and we'll be away for a fortnight or so. My boys of course will be in Santander by then for the summer, so that's all right. I shall probably join them when the tour is over.

Oh, I can't tell you how I am looking forward to it, to get away from this horrible apartment, and be with people I can talk to, be intimate with, understand. I feel ten years younger, no, more – sixteen. I am going to take up where I left off, start again, grow now into what I wanted to be then. But first I have to find out what that is.

I've taken up the guitar again, bought a fine Cordoban instrument which the shopkeeper swore is seventeenth century. Because Fernando did at least let me keep my piano neither my fingers nor my sense of music went to sleep during all those years and I find I am really doing quite well. I'm taking lessons from a lady called Juana Jiménez Morales, we're practising a couple of pieces by Sor, but she's also written lovely settings of some of the *Gypsy Ballads*, and some of Alberti's poems too, and we're trying to work them up into duets, both of us playing and taking it in turns to sing. She wants us to do them in public, but I'm not sure I'm ready for that yet. Anyway, she's a new friend, the first I hope of many, whom I really get on well with though I find her a bit wild, a bit of a gypsy at times, but that's probably because I'm still not used to freedom, freedom at last. She's in La Barraca too.

Your loving sister
Dolí

Ayala
Madrid
30 July 1932

Dearest Ana

It was marvellous, I can't tell you how marvellous. I never ever dreamt I could have such an adventure.

We were to assemble at the Residencia at seven in the morning and leave at eight. I took the tram, I always do, I think I might sell the Hispano-Suiza. I know it's beautiful but in these troubled times can give quite the wrong impression and anyway I have to have Manolo to drive the thing, and I find I really no longer like Manolo. Well, I never did, but now I think I shall have to get rid of him and Puri too.

Of course there were delays, caused mainly by the fact that almost all our student-artistes are bourgeois and consequently do not believe a day can actually start before ten o'clock. Nevertheless it was actually at ten that we set off.

What a convoy! A huge Chevrolet truck for the stage, scenery and props, four private cars, and for those who couldn't fit in the cars, what do you think? Two prison vans actually lent by the police who even supplied drivers. Federico was beside himself at the delays: we were billed to open at ten in the evening at El Burgo de Osma – a hundred and sixty kilometres away with the Guadarrama mountains in between, and he thought we'd never make it.

The Somosierra pass came at just about the halfway mark. We, that is Juana and I, shared a Ford with three other girls and the youth who drove, quite a crush I can tell you. We wheezed and rattled and finally boiled ourselves dry just five hundred metres from the top. No problem! One of the prison vans had also boiled and ditched its load so there were already six or so strapping lads in shirt sleeves, toiling up the hairpins on foot, and they pushed our chariot to the top. It was heavenly. Looking back over the hills and the campo we could see the walls of blue smoke where the workers were burning off the stubble, and in the furthest distance the haze over Madrid, but where we were the mountain air at fourteen hundred metres was heavenly, even though, at two in the afternoon, hot. We had a marvellous pic-nic, made a real *romería* of it, with cold omelette sandwiches, savoury pasties, peaches and water-melon, and a lot more wine than was good for us. Federico got very impatient, was sure we would never make it in time although we were already halfway and over the worst of the mountains. There were little blue flowers by the wayside, and eagles, I thought, but others said they were vultures . . .

Somosierra! Do you remember how you read Galdós to me, Napoleon driving his army through the snow and ice in a desperate bid to catch the English before they could embark at La Coruña? How you were on Napoleon's side and I on the English, and how I cried when Sir John Moore died . . .? Maybe now I shall go and see his tomb. There are so many things I can do now which I have only dreamed of for sixteen years.

Difficult on the tenth of July to think of snow and ice. We trundled on down the other side and presently left the main road to Burgos to head north-east for our destination, and the road was now dusty and hot, and a lot of the time climbed again as well as dropped. Nevertheless most of us reached El Burgo as early as five o'clock and the whole convoy was in by six. Some grumbled, saying why the early start, but nevertheless we were ready only just in time, setting up the stage in the main square, which was really very handsome for such a small town.

We started at exactly ten o'clock to a packed audience. Federico made a modest little speech explaining who we were, and then we were off. First Cervantes' *Cave of Salamanca* . . . you cannot imagine how rapt the audience was, not a movement or a whisper or a sigh, their lovely lined faces in chiaroscuro straight out of Velázquez . . .

∽

What was all this about? Petra, labouring with her dictionary at her elbow, skipped through eight more pages which described, almost day by day, how this motley crew of students and poets and hangers-on had trundled round the mountains north of Madrid performing Golden-Age Spanish drama to peasants in town squares and town halls. The final performance of the tour was given back at the Residencia in Madrid: Calderón's *Life is a Dream* in which Federico, whoever he was, himself played the part of the Shadow with great power and mystery. Afterwards there was, of course, a party.

∽

Juana and I had been practising her setting of Federico's *Son de Negros en Cuba* for weeks, and of course some wretched wag amongst Los Barracos had heard us at it and persuaded Juana, who then persuaded me to join her, into singing and playing our duet. I was terrified! But it went off terribly well, and they encored us, made us sing the other three numbers we had up to scratch, including one of Federico's *Gypsy Ballads*. And when we had finished he came up and gave us a kiss each and held our hands, and then went to the piano and sang it again, our setting, but transposed to the piano . . . just like that!

It was a lovely end to our adventure with Los Barracos but now something of a reaction has set in. They've all gone away, to the seaside, abroad, and Madrid is empty. And hot. But Juana has to stay here, I'm not quite sure why, and she wants me to stay with her. I think I might. I have used the telephone to check that my boys are all right in Santander. David sounded a little sad when I said I might stay on a bit longer, but the others were quite keen I should, which I thought was a touch hurtful. But I can't bear the cousins, and Saturno will be around, and I can't bear our apartment either. It's not mine. There's hardly anything of me in it. Only the piano really and a few books. So perhaps I shall stay with Juana for a bit. I call her Mad Juana, after the mad princess. Here's a photograph of us, taken in the afternoon before the disaster we had at Soria.

∽

The photograph, faded sepia now, a small Brownie snapshot, showed two women standing in what looked like a town square of no great distinction. The sun was shining full on their faces which had made the taller of the two wrinkle up her eyes, and the smaller lower her gaze. The taller had her arm round her companion's shoulder who in turn had her arm round the taller one's waist. Petra was just about certain Querubín's mother was the shorter one.

She had short-cropped dark hair with a fringe, rather heavy lids, highish cheekbones separated by a small straight nose and a mouth that looked full and a touch petulant: though Petra recognized that the apparent petulance could have been the result of being snapped when she did not fully want to be. Certainly there was nothing there to suggest that she was not the adult version, over double the age, of the adolescent girl in the portrait behind her. She was wearing a full summer dress with three-quarter sleeves, cut elegantly on the bias, not cheap, and suggesting a figure not at all fat, but certainly offering a very female sort of beauty, even comfort.

Mad Juana could not have been more different. She was tall, had long wavy hair emerging from what must have been a man's fedora worn rakishly on the back of her head, a dark linen jacket over a shirt whose collar stood high above that of the jacket in the style men of the time affected if they wished to be thought sporty. And, amazingly for Spain, even for America in the early thirties, she was wearing what looked like trousers, slacks. In short, Petra decided, a dyke, a butch dyke, the sort that gives or gave lesbians a bad name.

∽

'I've been reading letters your mother sent to your aunt Ana. Your mother seemed to have a good time after your father died. She went touring with a student theatre run by a man called Federico while you and your brothers stayed with relations by the seaside.'

'Federico? That was Lorca. Federico García Lorca.'

Petra was a touch put out. She did not know a lot about Lorca, but she had seen the Espert production of *Yerma* when it came to Munich, and had read, in parallel text, a selection of his poems. She knew he was probably the greatest of the many great Spanish poets and dramatists of the twentieth century. Since Dolí's letters had never actually used the word 'Lorca' she had not made the connection.

'Of course,' she said, after a moment or two. 'It was silly of me not to realize. And he was in the last of your dream-memories.'

He sighed.

'Yes. The one that has him arriving in Granada three days later than the historian Hugh Thomas says he did.' He gave a fatalistic shrug and sighed.

XX

Calle del Desengaño 15
Madrid
8 August 1932

Dearest Ana,

What about this address, then? Calle del Desengaño, the
street of the un-illusioned. Here is how it got its name. Two
gallants, back in the sixteenth century, met on a corner, ap-
proached a cowled lady, who, the district being then what it is
now, they presumed to be of easy virtue. They drew swords to
fight for her. But then she threw back her cowl and revealed a
death's head seething with worms. Both of them felt . . . un-
illusioned, and went back to the Plaza Mayor for a fino or two
more. I suspect, dear Ana, it is a moral fable about syphillis. See? I
am not the total innocent you sometimes take me for.

So. What is my situation, my way of life, what is this holiday
I am on which will last at least until the end of August when my
boys come home?

Mad Juana has a room here in what I think must be quite an
old building in spite of the modern additions and the new stucco
outside and so on. It is built round a square courtyard, open to the
sky, with an entrance to the street that was once high enough to
admit a man on a horse, and it still has a drinking trough filled
now with geraniums. Four stories with wooden balconies that
used to be the galleries that served as a corridor; but now there are
internal corridors. The ground-floor rooms which were once
stabling and kitchens are now workshops let to artisans who
make such things as window and door frames, repair damaged
furniture, and so on. Then there is a floor of largish rooms which
are partly let to an anarchist group who are running an adult
education centre: occasionally fascists try to set them on fire with
petrol in wine bottles but so far with little success. The remaining
two floors are sub-let by the Galician tenants.

There are all sorts here, but no prostitutes, the Galicians won't allow them: commercial travellers passing through; painters and poets, who stay a bit longer; and, when the university and colleges open again there will be students. There is a family of gypsies on the top floor who occasionally settle arguments by shooting out each other's light bulbs, but generally refrain from shooting each other.

And what is my friend's room like? Well, I am sitting at a plain table in the window writing this, with a corner of the late afternoon sun slanting across it. Being on the third floor, not the top, we have quite tall windows with rattly blinds and woven curtains, crimson and pale yellow; the floor is wood boards, but covered for the most part with a large but very worn oriental rug. The furniture represents her share of what her father left: he played and taught the flute, but died of drink. There are three dark mahogany carved chairs, a large sofa, and a small bed with an iron frame. I sleep on the sofa beneath a thin fringed tartan travelling rug which is all I need at this time of year. Incidentally I pay my way, no more, and also pay for the guitar lessons I continue to get for an hour or so each day. Juana is not sponging off me, far from it.

And how do we spend our time? Well, dear sister, do not be shocked, but first I have to admit that nothing much happens until eleven in the morning or even midday. One or other of us stirs around then to put a coffee pot on the small spirit stove which is our only cooking appliance. A cup of strong black coffee is enough to get us moving and the first thing we do is go round to Barco and the Café Nemesis for breakfast. Usually there are still rolls left or cold *churros*. By now it's one o'clock and we stroll down past the Telefónica into Gran Vía, maybe as far as La Puerta del Sol, and buy anything we might need, but this is very little as we always eat in bars or restaurants. Really we are just out to enjoy the sunshine before it gets too hot; the colours and the crowds. Then we turn back again into our own *barrio*, saunter up Barco to one of the cheaper restaurants at the far end.

∽

Petra remembered the Telefónica: a tall splendid building in art deco style which used to house the main Madrid telephone exchange. During the siege of Madrid the Republicans used it as an observation post for their artillery.

～

Sauntering up Barco in the early afternoon is not quite the degrading experience you might imagine. A few of the whores, painted like dolls, drape their bright mantillas and their bosoms over their small wrought-iron balconies aiming to catch the attention of a señorito hoping for a quick one before getting home to Mama or wife for lunch (you can imagine the excuses: 'Darling, a wild-cat strike on the trams . . . '), but for the most part they are in everyday clothes, or their mothers are, humping home their groceries. In this area there are still many donkeys and mules holding up the honking motors, there are gypsy ladies with withered babies on their arms selling carnations picked up from the floor of the flower market, and the lottery-ticket sellers not uttering the subdued mournful call they are allowed in Salamanca, but bellowing fit to make you jump out of your skin. Socialists, anarchists, Falangists and Jehovah's Witnesses all hawk or thrust on you their boring pamphlets, and occasionally scuffles break out. The Communists, you will be glad to hear, are more numerous than they were. I picked up a copy of *The Peasants' Revolt* the other day but have yet to find *The Origin of the Family*. Incidentally, Juana says that it is odd that you should be both a Freudian and a Marxist. Is it?

Where was I? On our way to the lunch from which we have just returned. At the end of Barco there is a Galician restaurant (these Galicians get in everywhere: what's wrong with Galicia that they all have to leave?) where the food is appalling but mercifully cheap, which means the company is good. We have a saucerful of chickpea soup, a dish of beans with occasional lumps of pork fat and black pudding in it, and a peach, but with as much bread and wine as we can eat and drink, and all for a peseta.

Petra remembered why Galicians leave Galicia: the inheritance laws forbid the breaking up of smallholdings between siblings, so only the oldest in any family stays put.

∽

The company? Poets, musicians, and political agitators. Painters and sculptors. And what do we talk about, rant on about as the heat-haze thickens, and the thunder growls above the high roof-tops and the swirling swifts? Well, today everyone is on about a plot the generals are putting together to do a *pronunciamento* and topple the government. Everyone seems to know about it, even that the leader is Pepe Sanjurjo, the Lion of the Rif, and that's why all the ladies of the street were out buying groceries; stocking up in case the shops and markets close. So presumably Don Manuel knows too, and is just waiting for them to show their hand before he locks them all up. Still, it does add to the excitement. I really don't know why we've always believed Madrid was a dull place as well as hot in July and August.

∽

Petra now had Querubín's copy of the *The Spanish Civil War* at her elbow. She leafed through it, found the right dates, the right place. The *pronunciamento* (a militarily led coup or attempted coup) actually came on 10 August. Don Manuel was clearly Manuel Azaña y Diaz, President of the Republic and Prime Minister.

∽

So. Back we come, having eaten too much bread and drunk too much wine, and Juana is having a doze and I am writing this letter. There is a flurry of shouts and cries from the gypsies above, and below the anarchists and their children who were chanting the alphabet are now on the seven times table. At five o'clock Juana will get up, and together we will have an hour or so playing our guitars, then one by one until ten o'clock her other students will arrive. Keeping myself to myself as far as I can I shall spend this period reading. Lorca, Ibañez, even dear old Galdós. And of course *The Peasants' Revolt*. And this evening we are going to a poetry reading where it's possible Machado and Alberti may turn up, though I suspect both are out of town – like anyone else of any real importance. That sounds a bit rattish, so maybe it's time I had a snooze too.

Anyway, that's how I'm spending my time now, and really it still is very, very pleasant. I'm making lots of friends and meeting people, and looking into the possibility of being involved in something musical or theatrical even after the boys are back.

Love from your affectionate sister
Dolí

XXI

Ayala
Madrid
12 August 1932

Dearest Ana,

Everything's gone a bit wrong. But first I must tell you that I am safe and undisturbed by the coup attempted the other day. You see, I was right, Don Manuel did know all about it. Apparently there was a bit of a tussle in Cibeles which he watched from a balcony in the War Ministry, smoking a cigarette! There's really not much likeable about that man, but you have to admire his coolness and control. Anyway everything's back to normal. I won't bore you with the details, I'm sure you know as much about it all from newspapers as I do, but it did give us plenty to gossip about, and everyone got a bit excited and drank even more than usual, and I suppose that's partly why what happened did happen.

Oh dear. I'm not sure if I can write all this down, even if I know the right words, but I think I must try.

Juana and I have always, almost from the very start, been very affectionate. We put our arms round each other, hug when excited or pleased about something, touch each other often, especially when she's teaching me guitar. Often we hold hands when out walking. Well, I like all this. It's something I've been starved of ever since Fernando got bored with me and the children got too old for cuddles, except little David, who's very shy anyway and keeps himself to himself.

And one thing we always do is kiss each other good night.

Well, on the night after the coup that wasn't, we came home a bit tipsy, got into our night-dresses, she got into her bed, and I went to give her my routine kiss. But she held on to me, and she tried to make it into, well, the sort of kiss Fernando used to give me when he was in love with me. And I let her for a moment, I suppose for a moment I quite liked it, but then she

143

went further, got her hand inside my night-dress, started stroking my breasts, and then my bottom, and, well, I just couldn't. I had to push her away and I'm afraid I slapped her. Which was silly, as well as wrong, because she's much bigger than me and she slapped me back, quite hard, over the ear, and then started calling me all sorts of unfair things like a tease and a flirt and where was the harm in doing what all our friends thought we were doing.

Anyway, although it was the middle of the night, quite near dawn actually, I gathered most of my things together and tried to go home. What I had forgotten was that there is a curfew. No one bothered much about it in Barco, but to get home I had to go past the Ministry of War and through Cibeles, which of course was filled with policemen and soldiers. And the result was I ended up in the new jail at the other end of town in Plaza de Moncloa. Because of all the arrests there was nowhere to put me and I had to sit in a corridor for most of the next day.

They didn't believe me, didn't believe who I was, thought my papers were stolen. But I kept on insisting, and finally it came out that I am Saturno's sister-in-law. I thought he was in Santander with my boys and his grandchildren, and a telephone call to him would get me out, but no, the day before, because of the coup that wasn't and the general uncertainty, he'd motored over the mountains to Burgos and caught the train to Madrid. So he came in person to say I am who I am.

Ana, he was furious. He didn't say much, but you know what he's like, he sat there like a block of black and grey ice in that car of his, the big black Mercedes-Benz. But worse was to follow. He insisted on coming up to the apartment with me. It was now about ten o'clock at night. I opened the front door with my key and of course instantly we both knew something was badly wrong. The place stank of tobacco smoke and oily cooking. People were singing in the dining room. As we walked past David's room we could see a naked couple copulating on his bed. There was a pool of red wine outside the kitchen which no one had bothered to wipe up. It was terrible. There were about twelve people living there, and they were having a high, a

144

very high old time of it: all ages from a couple of grannies, down to an extremely dirty babe in arms. And who were they? Brothers, sisters, uncles, aunts and cousins of Manolo and Puri.

Well, you know I never liked them. I always said they were a sly, conniving couple, but Fernando had them before he married me and they never seemed to do anything wrong, steal, or anything like that, and Puri's accounts were always immaculate. I should have got rid of them after Fernando died, but never got round to it what with la Barraca and one thing and another.

Saturno was, well, in a way, rather magnificent, he really is a tough old brute.

First of all he turned to me.

'Did you know about this?' he asked, in that gravelly voice of his.

'Of course not,' I replied. 'In fact I have not been here for nearly five weeks. I have been staying with a friend. I suppose they thought I was in Santander.'

Well, do you know what he did then? He locked the front door on the inside, pulled a pistol from his pocket and put it on the hall table by the telephone, where they could all see it, and then he cranked the phone and got the exchange to put him through to the Chief of Police who of course he meets almost every day at his club. The police vans were at the outside door within ten minutes. Oh, what a wailing, and a pleading, and a commotion there was then . . . almost I felt sorry for them, until I saw the mess they had left.

Saturno wanted me to go back to his place, said he'd send over some of his people in the morning to clear up, but I said no, I preferred to make my own arrangements, and he left. He didn't ask me why I had not been at home nor where I had been, which I thought odd. But then I remembered what Fernando used to say about him: he expects people to tell lies, so if he wants to know something he finds it out for himself.

I thought I'd just go to bed, I was worn out, not having slept properly for thirty-six hours, and I did fall asleep almost straight away. But I woke up at dawn, and just couldn't bear

145

what I could see and smell and so I started clearing it up all on my own. Then at about half-past nine there was a ring at the door, and . . . it was Juana. She was rather fine too. Quietly apologetic for the way she had behaved, and terribly worried about me. Apparently she called yesterday and saw what was happening, but of course had no idea where I was. She set about helping me with the mess, and really was very good with it, much more able to cope than I had been, knew which sort of brush and mop would do which sort of job, when to use soap, and when to use a nasty smelling white cleaning powder and so on.

Then, about one o'clock, Manolo returned. The police had kicked them all out and they'd stay out until I brought charges. He had come round to plead with me not to bring charges, but also (and the nerve of it!) to ask for his job back. I told him I'd think about the charges, but there was no chance at all of him working for me ever again. He tried to argue with me, and I got angry and he got surly and really I was very glad Juana was with me. And in the end he went, but not until he'd made obscure threats that he would get even with me, I'd see. Later I agreed with Juana that it would be better if she stayed for a night or two, or even until the boys come home.

So that's it. I'm absolutely exhausted, and now at last I'm going to bed. I'll post this in the morning.

Your affectionate sister

Dolí

PS. Morning. Last night Juana seduced me, no other word for it. I really rather enjoyed it. So. What do I do now?

∾

Petra verbally summarized these letters for Querubín.

'Don't you want to read the originals? Sorry. I'll read them to you if you want.'

'No.'

'Why not?'

'It's difficult to explain. Partly it's your voice. It's not her voice.'

'Which you still remember.'

'I think so.'

'I'm getting to like her.'

'Of course.'

'You were in love with her, weren't you? '

'Yes.'

'I think I may be too. Does that sound silly?'

'No. Not at all.'

XXII

Petra drew back for a week or so. The library had become spooky to her, she did not yet want to read any more of Kepler's transcriptions, did not feel ready to expose herself to the problem of establishing their authenticity or otherwise. She concentrated on her singing, on keeping herself fit, and Querubín also seemed content to let things ride. His blindness stabilized: through a sort of tunnel vision he could, he said, distinguish light, colour and blurred shapes. She drove him to an optician and a spectacle maker in Malaga and together they produced framed lenses that looked like two grey oysters stuck in front of his eyes. They should, the experts said, make all the difference, but they made little or none and he refused to wear them.

He was not, however, blind to the way their relationship was developing, and nor was she. For her he was the father she had destroyed reincarnated: the fact that he was not only old but castrated helped.

For him she was the child he could never have. But more than that she was the voice, the voice that would survive him in the way our children survive us all, carrying on not just our wretched little genes but what we have taught them, what we have helped them to be. He came most alive during their lessons, bullied her obsessively which she hated until she realized it was complimentary: he really believed he could do it, that he would live on in her.

Towards the end of February Carmen told her that Campanillas celebrated Carnival.

'You must wear a mask.'

'Really?'

Petra dressed as if for a party: black soft leather waistcoat over a black roll-top, leather trousers that matched the waistcoat; but she had no mask. She parked her car near the school, walked into the plaza beneath the floodlit church and realized Carmen had been right. It seemed that she was the only person showing her ordinary face. Many wore shop-bought shaped eye and nose masks with a satiny finish and tasselled fringes beneath, or jokey ones: Draculas, werewolves and so on. Some were of politicians – Felipe González she recognized but there were others she did not. Best of all were the ones who had used only face-paints with glitter and those little plastic stick-on jewels toyshops and kiosks sell. And of course most people had dressed to fit their masks.

Suddenly, spilling out of the town hall above the plaza there was a procession, a parade of what appeared to be groups, or teams, of eight to ten people each. One group was dressed up as traffic signs with red wigs and white faces, in another the men were all Columbus and the women all Statues of Liberty. There were nurses and doctors, professors, arabs, a group in red and black motley with face and nose masks to match, very Venetian, and a weird lot that included giant fruits and a sort of walking mouth with huge white teeth and a big red tongue.

Along with the rest of Campanillas she followed them to what had once been a cinema but was now a hall half-filled with collapsible chairs, all already occupied by the elderly or prudent. Petra took her place standing in a crush that was tight but friendly. Each of the teams which had made up the procession now came on to perform, singing apparently satirical songs to popular tunes, pop-flamenco, or rock, and dancing. The actual performances varied from the slightly embarrassing to something really stylish and witty. From her neighbours Petra gathered it was a competition and eventually the Columbus-Statue of Liberty lot won. They had a neat repeated routine that started with the men posing like the famous Barcelona statue of Columbus with his arm flung out to the West, and ended with them whirling the Liberties round in a mad fandango. In between they chanted *coplas* about everything under the sun from the ongoing corruption enquiry involving the prime minister's brother-in-law to the madness their mayor had shown in pulling up the trees in the plaza. The mayor himself, a young socialist politician on the first rung of the political ladder, took it in good part and presented them with a mountain-cured ham, a loaf as big as a car wheel and an *arrobia* of Costa.

All of which was fine; weird and fun, but it was not why Petra was there. Everywhere she sought to recognize the Parma Violet Lady: but amongst all the disguises and masks she finally despaired of spotting her. Her last chance had to be El Molino.

The big room, usually garishly lit, was in near darkness; the only light was from over the bar or glowing eerily from the computer game, the pin-ball machine, and flickering amongst the huge logs in the fireplace. There were a lot of people there, though it was not as full as it had been on the morning of New Year's day. There were clowns, blackamoors, princesses, fairies, wizards and witches. Others wore dark gauzes and muslins, leather, swishing cloaks and swaying plumes. The face-painting was fantastic, original, with much use made of stick-on jewels to simulate animals – cats, frogs, and insects. Liberated by the masks, the marijuana, and the traditions of Carnival, they sang, danced, shrieked and laughed in the characters they had assumed, the children as much as the grown-ups. Feeling more than ever out of it, Petra sought her usual place on the far side of the fireplace, near pool table, and waited, hoping.

Suddenly, and unbelievably, through the shadows came a shadow, her mane-like hair silvered in streaks, her face a purply black but with silver, emerald, and vermilion leaf or flame shapes painted over the purple. Her perfect trim and tiny body in a black lycra body-stocking with black muslin trailing from her arms and shoulders floated, it seemed, on to the glass top of the table in front of Petra. She then flung out a black arm behind her, palm upwards, and someone from the swaying shapes behind put in it a small plastic box filled with sticks of face-paint.

'Carnival,' she said, speaking German only slightly accented, 'and you have no mask.'

Her eyes were serious, it was an accusation, but a smile hovered in the corners of her angel lips.

She cupped Petra's chin in her cool left palm, and began to work, slowly and carefully, with her right. She took her time, nearly ten minutes, and Petra felt herself melt in a moment she wanted to prolong for ever. The physical closeness, so magically surpassing all fantasies, the firm dab of the paint sticks, and then a gentle rub with the ball of a thumb to spread the colour, the lips pursed in concentration apart from the occasional smile, the warmth of her breath, spiced with orange and tequila, and all the time the roar of the music. When she was almost finished she leant forward as if to put a finishing touch on Petra's temple. Her hair brushed Petra's cheek, and her breath whispered in Petra's ear but Petra could not hear. She covered her other ear with her hand, clamping out the climax of 'Bohemian Rhapsody', and this time she caught what the Parma Violet Lady said.

'You are in love with me.'

She felt her colour rise beneath the paint and in spite of it her expression must have betrayed her, for the Parma Violet Lady laughed, merrily but with gentleness.

'It's not something you can hide. There. You must promise not to look at your face until you get home. Promise?'

'I promise.' She caught the other woman's sparrow-wrist. 'Can I . . . can I . . . ?' She felt the sweat break out all over, a flood of embarrassment, but it was Carnival and anything goes when you're masked: 'Can I . . . hope?'

A frown, ever so slightly troubled, pulled the Parma Violet Lady's eyebrows in as she stood. She shrugged. 'Hope is free,' and she swung away into the storm of noise, the swirling, glittering shadows.

Petra kept the promise and refrained from looking in a mirror until she was back in her room in Villa Melchor.

Her first reaction was anger: a clown, a white-faced loon stared back at her. It was a trick, an unfair trick. But she was still looking in the mirror and her expression was now so comical-tragical that she had to laugh, and when she did the mask transformed and she understood the point of the white face, the dark eye sockets, lips apparently compressed into the clown's thin line of unrequited love.

XXIII

Ayala
Madrid
16 October 1932

Dearest Ana

A most dreadful thing has happened and I need your advice and help and comfort and support straight away. I need to talk to you, I need to have you with me.

I have been served with a court order. Yes. In the presence of two *alguaciles* a lawyer in a frock-coat and top hat pushed his way into my hall, handed me the thing, made me sign a document to show I had received it.

Whereas this, whereas that, the court in its wisdom has deemed the evidence placed before it by His Excellency Señor Don Miguel Pérez y Mendizábal, Marqués de Boltana, and by Manolo Díaz Ortega, lately servant in the household of Doña María Dolores Iglesias y Corazón, sufficient to promulgate the following blah-di-blah . . .

Apparently I have been neglecting my children. Of course the fact is the only time I did they were in the care of their cousins at Santander for the summer. And I have consorted with whores, and worse, entertained people of the utmost ill-repute, to wit a *lesbian* both at home and in a rooming house shared with anarchists and gypsies . . . and so on, and so on. In short it seems I have not shown myself to be a fit parent and guardian for the children of the illustrious but deceased Señor Don Fernando . . .

And so the court in its infinite wisdom has decided that the aforesaid Señor Don Miguel, being the elder brother of the deceased Señor Don Fernando . . . shall also be designated legal guardian, *in loco patris*, of the above-mentioned children, to wit . . . shall have control of their inheritance until they reach majority, and shall oversee their education and moral welfare, and will, with the help and assistance of the parochial priest

Father Jaime Portillo Ostos, supervize their religious upbring-
ing, and so on. And so on.

Well, you know what I'm like when I'm upset. It was silly of
me, I know, but I stormed straight round to his house in Conde
de Aranda, I couldn't take the Hispano-Suiza since I can't drive
it and I've sacked that thieving liar Manolo who can, so I walked
or ran. And I didn't stop to change, I was wearing a silk pyjama
suit and a lot of beads, and I suppose I drew some attention to
myself standing on his doorstep and howling. Anyway he was
of course at the bank in Plaza de España, so I went down to
Independencia where I hired a cab. It was only when we were
going through Cibeles that I realized I had no money to pay the
cabbie, so the first thing I had to do when I got to the Banco de
Corpus Cristi was persuade one of the tellers to pay up for me.

Of course my illustrious brother-in-law kept me waiting.
For an hour. Well, it gave me time to get my thoughts in order.
What I needed was a lawyer. Not a confrontation. Let someone
else do the arguing for me. So, I told them to tell him I didn't
want to see him after all, I made them give me a cheque so I
could take out some of my money, enough to pay back the teller
and get me round Madrid for the rest of the day. I went to
Desengaño, feeling pretty disillusioned myself, I can tell you,
and asked Juana if she knew any lawyers. When she found out
why I needed one she blew up. She was all for me getting all my
money from that awful bank and taking my boys somewhere
out of Don Miguel's reach – Paris, for instance. She said she'd
come too, look after me. Fortunately, I suppose, I insisted on
seeing a lawyer.

Well, she knew someone who knew someone who specialized in prosecuting fascist thugs, who she said would be just the
ticket since that was what my brother-in-law was. He turned out
to be quite a wise, sensible old man. He read through the writ or
whatever it is very carefully and told me really I had better go
along with it. Don Miguel had made no claim for actual
possession of my boys, as things stood they would stay with
me, the household would remain intact. But if I decided to fight
the thing the court would probably have them taken away while

it all remained *sub judice*, and if I lost then I'd never get them back. His advice to me was to go home, calm myself, get myself up like a respectable widow, and then go and see Don Miguel and find out what he wanted. He said he'd come with me if I wanted him to. I said no, it would be better if I handled it myself.

So, at the end of the day, I finally got to see Don Miguel, having gone to El Corte Inglés and got myself fitted out in black. And I did it properly. Long black dress, long black coat and a proper hat, not the flash things I wore to the funeral, and His Illustrious Excellency was kind and condescending enough to say he approved. Indeed, he was cool, evil charm all through, the way he always is. But quite firm. If I am to keep my boys then I must behave in the way the Pérez y Mendizábal family expects its widows to behave:

Item: Out of doors I must wear black at all times.

Item: I must conduct myself at all times with due and proper decorum.

Item: I must forswear the company of anarchists, poets, and homosexuals of both sexes (apparently Federico is queer: I didn't know that, did you?) and especially the company of Juana Jiménez Morales . . .

Actually I'm not too miserable about that. She's still a super friend, and we have had good laughs together and the music was lovely. But the sex seems to get in the way, and she makes too much of it. I'm not really inclined that way after all, and I haven't been able to hurt her by saying so.

And so on. I held out on one thing: I'm not having Manolo and Puri back. Saturno resisted – clearly he wants to have a spy in the household. But he backed off when he saw I was going to be a nuisance over that and we agreed I should have a woman coming in daily, but not living in, and she would have to be someone we both agreed to.

I'm not too bothered about religion. Neither Miguel nor Jorge shows any signs of being devout, and it's unlikely they'll catch the disease now. David is a bit of a worry though. He was offered a singing scholarship at the Instituto de San Isidro, largely and rather ironically because a canon from the cathedral was at the funeral and heard him sing. Well he's taken it up and of course it does mean he's exposed to several hours of the liturgy a week as well as to a lot of music. He seems to enjoy it all, and I'm pretty sure it is the singing and not the religion. He's still rather withdrawn and shy with me but I think he rather dotes on me. As for me, well, I dote on my eldest. I'm really proud of him now, in his uniform and all, he's growing into a fine strong man. And when I tease him about being a soldier he promises me he is a Republican soldier. He calls Pepe Sanjurjo a very rude name indeed which I shall not repeat.

I'm not so happy about Jorge. It's clear now that he is not going to be a great cellist or even a very good one. He likes the show of it all, the drama, but he doesn't practise seriously, just goes over and over again the lugubrious pieces his teacher finds for him. He's also got rather a nasty streak. What would your new science make of this? Apparently when they were on the beach at Santander an out-of-work fisherman, presumably starving, came along the sands trying to sell his fisherman's knife, and Jorge bought it. It has a horrid, thin, crescent-shaped blade which folds into a grooved handle of whalebone. It's very sharp. Jorge says it was designed for beheading fish, gutting and scaling them. Well, the other day we found mice in the pantry. Jorge went out and bought a trap, the sort that catches them alive. And I found him cutting one up with this knife, but actually cutting it up while it was still living. Is this normal? 'As flies to wanton boys, are we to the gods, they kill us for their sport.' Is he just a wanton boy? Or is there something more to worry about? I must say, though, that he, too, like Miguel, is growing into a very fine figure of a young man, though more romantic with his long black hair. Poor David. In many ways he's the nicest of the three, but . . . well, you know how it was. I wanted a girl.

Well, dear sister, you see that as I write this long letter, and it's taken me a day or two, I'm calming down a bit, coming to terms with it all. I'll survive. Thanks to you and your good sense all those years ago I've got my money and they can't take that from me. I've only got to hold on until the two older ones are grown up and David can spare me, say seven or eight years, and then I really will be able to do what I like. I tell you, Ana, though I shall miss my new friends, and for the time being anyway I shall have to be very careful, no clandestine slipping out to the cafés in the evenings, no number eight tram to the Resi. I'm allowed books, so long as I keep unsuitable matter in my private room and do not let the boys see it. Which is just as well. You know what, Ana? Now I'm calmer about it all, and the first anger has faded, and dear me, but I was angry, very angry, do you know what really frightens me? The boredom. Resentful bitter boredom. With the boys out for most of the day I shall die of boredom, so if you can't come and see me, then write, and write, and write again. Please?

Your loving sister

Dolí

XXIV

> *'Conducete, conducete costei*
> *al carnefice omai . . .'*

The voice rang out across the pool slicing the warm air like a
steel bolt fired from a cross-bow, then died. A long silence, or
rather a murmur of voices from the music room, then the tinkle
of the clavichord as Querubín elaborated whatever point he was
making about Petra's phrasing.

Then it came again: *'Conducete, conducete . . .'* but swiftly
broken off.

Dr Caridad Rocío Lorca, recently admitted by Carmen but
told to wait until the music lesson had finished, walked as quietly
as she could down the colonnade, through the right angle, and
then sidled up to the open windows of the music room. Looking
out through the arches in front of her she watched the newly
arrived red-rumped swallows skim the pool for water and
midges, allowed her eyes to climb the pine-clad mountain beyond the red-tiled roof opposite, up to the visual ridge and the
blue beyond.

> *'Take her to the executioner who awaits her,*
> *Make him discover some long and bitter agony*
> *to exacerbate the timely death*
> *of this monster . . .'*

'You still fail to make me believe you are an emperor, a
psychopath, a BRRRRUTE. Can I believe that when Poppea is
pregnant you will kick her to death? Can I believe that you, a
woman, can ever do the things men do?' Suddenly something
snapped, and the old man stormed on. 'There's no way I can
do it. There's no way you can do it. Your sex is wrong; your men-
tality is wrong; you're modern, you're soaked in your training
as a German Romantic singer. You've got a young voice, but
it's too late. It's too late for you emotionally. It's too late in
history for you, and it's too late for me because I cannot train
you.'

The voice was high, quavering, manic; in it the doctor detected the timbre of despair.

Presently the door from the music room to the colonnade opened and Petra crossed it, stood framed in the archway, with newly opened roses about her knees and waist. Then she turned on her heel, strode up the colonnade to the smaller pool and out on to the terrace beyond. From the upthrust of her head, her swinging gait, the doctor guessed she was both tearful and angry. She followed, found her standing between two palms. Thirty feet above her new yellow florets had formed in grape-like bunches. Petra knew she was there and turned, welcoming her brusquely. Her face was pale and hard but her lip trembled and so did her voice.

'He's a bastard. You know that? You heard what's going on. Three days now. Just that one passage. He makes me repeat it again and again and again. I must have sung it a hundred times, more.'

Caridad came up to the first palm, put her hand on the friable husky trunk. Petra's hard beauty, made vulnerable, takeable by her distress, mesmerized her.

The singer continued, 'What's wrong with him, then?'

The physician answered, 'The past. Isn't that what's wrong with all of us?'

Petra turned, ran down the steps and into the orchard, pushed on down, brushing with her thighs fresh spurges that already, in March, bloomed handsomely round the fountain's overflow, through the blue borages, poppies and daisies that had come after the fumitory and violets, and took a small leap across a soggy irrigation ditch. Crickets, like the bi-planes that circled King Kong, whirred round her shoulders and head, zoomed haphazardly away between the shrubs and trees. Caridad followed her.

'He says . . .' and Petra stooped to ease a sharply cased seed from the heel of her espadrille. 'He says it's the most manly moment in the role of Nerone. And if I am to sing Nerone as if I were a man, that is the bit I have to get right.'

Caridad stood back and waited. She realized she was in the presence of the deep obsessive frustration a performing artist feels when something will not go right. But at the same time her professional eye noted how Petra's white singlet had dropped forward to reveal breasts small and mutilated. Inwardly she sighed and wondered at the distress we inflict on ourselves, let alone on others.

'If I get that right, he says, then the rest will come . . . But it's an excuse. He's punishing himself, and me too, and I'm fed up with it, fed up with it all. I've done everything I can. I fought to get here. But I should have realized: he's never trained a female before, only falsetti and counter-tenors . . .'

In a twisting, slow movement which brought her knees to the side she sank into a tangle of green grass and flowering vetches, a pose similar to Copenhagen's mermaid. Caridad recognized that it was a gesture, studied and perfected to the point where it could be used almost (but never completely) unconsciously, but to express genuine, as well as pretend, feeling. She hunkered in front of the mermaid and put her hands for a moment on her shoulders.

'He's very, very unhappy.'

'I know.'

'Have you read any more of those transcripts?'

'No. He gave them to me but I can't. Is that phone thing of yours going to go off?'

'No.' Caridad pulled the mobile phone from her bag and slipped a button. 'There. Why haven't you read them?'

'Because, because . . .' Head up she twisted away. 'I know this sounds ungrateful, judgemental, that sort of thing, but the two I have read are so, I don't know, self-consciously erotic, like passages from an erotic novel, classy, I grant you . . . I just can't accept the possibility they describe real experiences. And that's what you, and he want me to do, isn't it? And I suppose Kepler knew what he was on about, I mean, he was a dedicated professional, all that sort of thing. Yes?'

'Listen. In all probability Freud himself got it all wrong. Those bourgeois women of Vienna who came to his couch with tales of being seduced or raped by their fathers: he told them they were fantasizing, expressing their suppressed desires. Stupid man.'

Petra's pale northern eyes met the doctor's across the short space between them, held them for a moment, then a shudder shook her almost bare shoulders, and again she swung away.

'They were not fantasies? They were real?'

'Do you find that hard to accept?'

'Not at all.' She still kept her face turned from the doctor's. 'But probably they were not raped. Probably they all seduced their fathers. I did.'

The Andalusian afternoon was poised to bloom like a flower around them: its noises and silence gave substance to the warm but motionless air. Caridad thought: true or false? Whichever, she has her problems too. But I must remember, she said to herself, that Querubín is the patient I am treating.

'I think Querubín is at risk. Of suicide.'

'I don't understand. Surely . . .' Petra sighed, a deep, hurt sound. 'Surely the way to live with a dreadful truth is to turn it into a fantasy?'

'No. Querubín's dream-memories, resurrected under hypnosis, are all he has left of what was the most wonderful, perfect period of his life. By misrepresenting them as the guilt-ridden fantasies of early adolescence, albeit artistically embellished later, Kepler has destroyed their true meaning, dirtied them, corrupted them.'

'If it was all so wonderful why did he castrate himself, why did he suppress the memory, why escape into a catatonic state for eighteen months?'

'I don't think,' the doctor replied, 'it was like that at all. I don't think that that was what drove him into fugue.'

'What then?'

'I don't know. I wish we could find out.' She stood, brushed grass from her denims, picked up her bag. 'I ought to go. He's expecting me.'

Petra looked up at her, eyes squinted against the glare of the blue depths beyond the doctor's head.

'Are they really so wonderful, those dreams of his?'

'Yes. Read them. Read them all, get the whole picture.'

PART THREE

The Transcripts:
Madrid, 1935–1936

XXV

The bath is a very big bath, enamelled cast-iron, white, but with its rounded corners supported on black claw and ball feet that stand on chequered black and white marble slabs. It has big brass taps with porcelain insets that say 'Hot' and 'Cold' in English. Round the overflow outlet scrolled letters baked into the enamel read: Armitage Shanks, Stoke, England, 1885.

Since my father died my mother has insisted that it is wasteful to fill it with hot water every time each of us has a bath, we should share each other's hot water. She says this is what she and her family used to do before she married our father.

I remember now, as I sit in the bath with water up to my chest, water fragrant with the aromatic oils she has added to it, for it was she who bathed in it first, I remember in the way you often remember the same thing when a circumstance repeats itself how Miguel, the older of my two brothers, objected, 'But you were poor, and we are not.'

Mother said: 'It has nothing to do with poverty. Reasonable thrift is a virtue when practised by the rich, a necessity when practised by the poor. And needless waste is vicious at any time.'

And Jorge, my other brother, said: 'I think she makes us follow each other through the bath so she can look at us, see us with no clothes on. That's the real reason isn't it, Mother? And sometimes it also happens that we get to see you with no clothes on. You like that too.'

Mother was very upset when he said this. She went flaming red and ran to her room and stayed there for an hour. I could hear her sighing heavily and perhaps weeping, or nearly weeping, but I think there was more anger in it than anything else.

Yes, I am remembering a particular incident, but, as I said, when I get into the bath these memories usually come back anyway, like a sort of mental tick. I am now watching myself in the bath, my back pink from the heat and I think a little chubbier than I will be at Baños de Alhamilla, and my genitals are smaller. It must be a year or so earlier. I am playing with a big square lump of green soap which has a relief of a baby in a nappy moulded into one side and the word 'Fairy' on the other: like the bath, it is English. Mother always makes a fetish out of English things, but just now everyone does since it is the Silver Jubilee year of His Majesty King George V and Queen Mary. It gives our shopkeepers a chance to fill their windows with crowns and similar gewgaws and sell English things, while really they are saying: give us back our own Alfonso XIII.

I am trying to blow big bubbles by making a ring with thumb and forefinger tips touching and breathing on the membrane of soap, with its swirling colours, until it balloons and bursts or detaches itself for a brief moment of independent life, floating through the steam before popping in a little haze of droplets on one of the taps. Tiring of this I take a face flannel beneath which I can trap air and then, holding the corners, drag it down to the bottom between my knees. I imagine it is a diving bell, and there is a crew inside the pocket of air: diving bells and the like have been featured in the second monthly supplement of my children's encyclopaedia, a subscription to which was this year's Epiphany present from Aunt Ana.

I let one corner of the flannel free and the air floats up. The bath is so deep that there is a measurable moment before it breaks the surface, like, and I giggle to myself at the thought, a fart. There is a boy in the choir at the Instituto who can fart the broken chord of G major, but will only do so if we pay him a peseta. Each. That can be a lot of pesetas. But if he is flat we make him give them all back.

'What are you grinning at?'

Her voice, like the movement which brought her back without my noticing, is gentle, amused.

I look round and up. She is still pink and fresh from the bath she left only moments before I climbed into it, is wearing a white bathrobe open low enough for me to see the beginning of the gap between her breasts. She also has a towel wrapped like a turban over her hair. It frames and accentuates the perfection of her heart-shaped face.

'Nothing, Mama, honestly, nothing.'

'"Honestly" means it was naughty. Never mind. Young boys of your age are allowed naughty thoughts. Come on, I'm going to wash your hair.'

She swings in a cork-topped stool and sits on it, briskly pushes up the sleeves of her gown and takes the soap from me.

'Wet your hair.'

I slip down on my back, grasp my nose with a theatrical gesture between thumb and forefinger, and let my head drop beneath the water. In the rosy darkness of closed eyes and with the bubbly roar of the water in my ears I realize that my stomach and genitals are close to the surface of the sudsy water, and that my penis which is small, but larger than it was, and my little balls in their neat sack, loose because of the hot water, must be clearly visible to her. I feel pleased, and blow a bubble or two of air out of my mouth before swinging up.

'Naughty again!'

But why? She is brushing water off the front of her wrap and then seizes a towel to dab the upper slopes of her breasts, so I am to understand I am naughty because I splashed her.

'Cover your eyes.'

I find the flannel, squeeze it out, fold it neatly using my raised knees as a table; when I have made a satisfactory rectangle out of it, three folds thick, I place it across my eyes and hold it there, with my elbows pressed to my sides and my head forward so my forehead almost touches my knees. She scrubs the hard edges of the soap into my scalp and follows with her finger ends, a hard and rough massage, and I sense she is enjoying the roughness of it, and the control she has, without actually hurting me, and I am pleased, and I wonder about how she must have looked at me when I lay back in the bath to wet my hair.

Without modern shampoos it's a long process: two washes, then several rinses, the first on my back again, then I take the flannel once more as she fills a china jug with a careful mixture from both taps and sluices me with it again and again, the water sliding through my hair, over my back and forwards over my collar-bones. At last she pulls the hair through clenched thumb and finger, making it squeak, here and here, and then there, until she is satisfied all is indeed squeaky clean.

'Right. Out you come.'

I stand and she slices the water off my sides and torso and thighs with the soft palms of her hands, then holds out a huge hot white towel and I climb out of the bath and into it.

'Along to my room with you. You're not perfect yet, you know.'

A little later I am sitting cross-legged on her big wide bed, the towel she wrapped me in has slipped and I am sitting half in it and half on it. The room is filled with a warm soft light, and is itself very warm, though I sense that outside snow is falling on already frosty streets. She is kneeling behind me but very close. Her knees are clamped against the sides of my upper thighs, I can feel her breasts against my shoulder-blades, her tummy and perhaps even her pubis against my back and my buttocks. Within my towel and her bathrobe we are naked within a nest, a nest within a nest. With cotton wool wound on to a cocktail stick she is probing the wax out of my ear. Already she has cut my nails; toenails and fingernails.

I wince, and she folds herself closer around me.

'There. Nearly over. Now the other one.'

I am aware that my penis is now very erect, more erect than I can ever remember it being before, the glans rosy and moist pushing through the foreskin, and all tingly warm. I push the towelling over it and hope she will not see me do it. But she does.

'Why hide it?' she murmurs. 'There's nothing wrong with it, you know. It's perfectly natural, nothing to be ashamed of. There.' She puts aside the cotton wool stick, and I feel her chin on my shoulder. She parts the towelling and takes my erect penis between her thumb and forefinger, and though it's done gently I am very conscious of pressure. And pleasure, as she eases the foreskin down and then up again.

'What a fine little man he is.' And I feel the warmth of her breath on my cheek.

A door clicks open and a draft of cold air surges through the apartment.

She arches back from me, snatches her robe around her, and, equally quickly though without knowing quite why, I cover myself as well as I can with the towel. Her bedroom door, which she had left unlatched, swings brusquely wide.

Miguel in his cadet's uniform under a long black fur coat that glistens with icy drops stands there, and the little red tassel swings across his forehead. Ariel, his huge Irish wolfhound, her grey shaggy head held well above his waist, her grey pelt also jewelled with snow, sniffs and points. She looks at us, and her eyes glow red in the light, then her heavy head drops, her long tongue droops out and she pants – she has felt the heat of the house.

'Lecture cancelled,' Miguel says. 'The tram-drivers are on strike protesting against the sentences on the miners. And they're smashing up every taxi they see on the streets. What the hell are you two up to?' But like Pilate he does not stay for an answer, moves off to the kitchen where sliced mountain ham, bread and Rioja wine have been left out for him. Ariel's claws clatter on the marble floors.

Mother holds me close for a moment, kisses me warmly on the cheek and then more teasingly under my ear, murmurs, 'Go to your own room now.' But she has had a fright, and I know why. What would Miguel have seen had he come in five minutes later?

XXVI

We are in the kitchen, which is not a large room, nor very well equipped compared with the rest of the apartment. There is a cast-iron range which houses a coal fire that frequently goes out or burns too hot and changes the room into a Turkish bath. It includes a small oven and a hob. There is also a two-ring electric hob which Doña Pili refuses to touch since her sister had one and it electrocuted her when she went to warm up hot chocolate after washing the kitchen floor. A huge Frigidaire stands in the corner by the window – it has a big concave door, cream enamel, opened by a handle which could grace an American car. The window opens to the floor and has a balcony, no more than a ledge, abutting on to a fire escape which takes three turns to reach the wide square service area below.

It's not much of a kitchen because we Spanish, especially the rich townees, eat at home out of contingency rather than choice. We eat pre-prepared food from delicatessens, snack simply off hams, dried sausages and cheeses, crunch an apple or suck an orange. This is not because we do not set a high value on splendid meals, quite the reverse. We leave such important matters to the professionals, and even when, or most particularly when, we are entertaining our friends we eat out or, as on the occasion of the wake following my father's funeral, buy in.

I am finishing a rich but clear broth laced with sherry, and she is chopping cooked quail eggs into a salad of crisp lettuce, tomato, olives, onion rings as evanescent as the haloes that sometimes surround the moon. There is a round loaf of hard-crusted bread, the crumb dry and floury and as white as a choir-boy's surplice. Our local baker is a Salamantino . . . from the city of Salamanca. And to finish there is a caramel egg-custard prepared by Doña Pili before she returned home.

The whole block is centrally heated from a huge furnace in the basement. One of my delights, it happens once a month through the winter, is to watch when the huge cart drawn by two mules arrives to tip a load of Asturian coal down a chute and into the cavern beneath us. What shouting and pushing and beating there is to persuade the mules to back the cart up over the kerb of the pavement! What a screaming clatter when the men, blackened like Moors, heave up the front end of the cart enough to make the coal slip and slide and then rush! What great clouds of dust! I love it best in sunlight because it is then the black dust glitters. And Alfonso, our concierge, prances and curses and threatens until the Moors have got out their big brushes and swept every last rock and pebble of coal down the chute. But they never sweep up the dust; they leave him, still cursing, to do it himself.

And today I hear the shouts again. Together we rush to the other side of the apartment, out on to the salon balcony which looks on to the street, and look down, and, holding hands tight clasped, revel in the tiny drama, the frosty air burning our cheeks, the railway smell of the coal filling our nostrils.

Back in the baking kitchen I sit at the table and put my face in my hands. She reaches across from the other side of the table and takes my hands in hers.

'David, what's the matter?'

'I want to be like this for ever.'

She withdraws her hands, and I sense that she is standing now, is taking a turn or two about the kitchen.

'For ever,' she says at last, 'is a long time. But . . . I have a plan. Come on, come on out from behind those nasty old hands and listen.'

I look up at her. Her face is radiant with promise but doubting a little too. I cannot tell you what she is to me at this moment. All right. She is the mother I longed for but never properly had. Why not? Because she had two older sons she doted on. Because she longed to get back to the intellectual life, not just reading, but meeting people, being part of things, which was just opening in front of her when her awful marriage came along. And most of all because I was not a girl. She wanted a girl, had miscarried a girl fifteen months before I was born. So she never was, until a year or so ago, much of a mother to me. Now . . .

Now, she is not only a mother, she is a friend, the very best of friends. We have been having marvellous times together since I was ill and during this long convalescence. We play together. A few days ago she said she has forgotten how to play, I must teach her again. I said, let's pretend. Pretend what? she asked. Pretend that the devil, like a roaring lion roaming about seeking whom he may devour, has got into the apartment. What shall we do? Oh, I know what we shall do, she cried. We shall hide, hide in the big wardrobe in the hall. And taking my hand she made us run down the passage to this wardrobe we have just inside the front door. It's Castilian. That is to say, it is huge, heavy, black, the doors carved in relief with arabesques and monsters, harpies with fish-tails, and acanthus fronds. It houses all the coats of our family, hanging from runners beneath a shelf where the hats are kept, and above a raised floor on which there is a great clutter of shoes and boots. It smells of stale wool, damp fur, and leather that has had carnal knowledge of feet.

She hauled open the big doors, grasped my elbow, pushed my behind, bundled me in, tumbled in behind me and drew the door as shut as she could from inside, pushed past me, and burrowed through boots and shoes to the far end. I followed her.

'Are we safe here from the roaring lion?' she whispered.

'I should think so.'

'For how long will he be out there?'

A coded question for how long shall we stay here.

'Not easy to say.' An intellectual's answer, the sort of phrase my mother's friends use. 'Ten minutes?'

'Longer than that. I mean, we should not take risks. How shall we pass the time?'

'You could tell me stories.'

'Certainly I could. But I'd rather you told me a story.'

I was very conscious of the darkness and the horror of all those coats and boots, but also of her so close in the darkness, part touching me, but not overtly, just because I was there. Oh, how I love that sort of undemanding closeness. Not that I don't love the demanding closeness too.

'All right, but you first. We'll take turns.'

'Hrrm.' She cleared her throat and her fingers, laced with mine in the dark, tightened: 'Here goes. Once upon a time . . . once upon a time there was a wolf who was good even though the sheep treated him very badly. And . . . and, let me see, there was a bad prince, a beautiful witch, and a pirate with a strong sense of honour. Goodness, what's that?'

Her fingers tightened even more and she folded her other arm round my shoulder.

The front door had clicked open in response to someone who had a key. We heard footsteps, boots, heavy and clattering, and another noise too, a skittering of claws on the polished surfaces.

'Mama! It's me, Miguel.' Dry laugh. 'Cadet Ensign Miguel Pérez Iglesias at your service.' And he stamped his boots, just outside the big wardrobe.

'He mustn't find us here.' I felt the touch of her lips in the dark like the fluttering of butterfly wings against my ear.

We heard the brute Ariel snuffling against the door, then she whined.

'Come on, you silly bitch. There's nothing there.'

The steps again, and the claws as he checked out the apartment for a second time. Long silence. Then the boots but no claws, and the front door opened, then clicked shut again and we heard the wards of the lock slide back.

'Pooof.' My mother let out a long sigh. 'Come on, let's get out before they come back.'

On our hands and knees, pushing back over the boots and shoes, the hems of furs and rubberized raincoats brushing our backs, I followed her backside to the door. She pushed it open and . . .

Ariel bayed and howled, straining at the leash Miguel had left her on, the other end of which was tied to the antlered coat-stand by the front door. Mama ducked back in.

'David, David, what are we going to do?'

I peeped out, round her back. The great long snout, the grey head with red tongue and liver-coloured jaws, white teeth like scimitars, snapped at my face which I withdrew. She couldn't reach us. Quite. I pushed Mama back.

'Ariel. It's me. David. Now shut up. You stupid animal, it's me. You know me.'

I pushed the door open wide, and managed to get my feet on to the cold floor, just out of her reach. Did I tell you? We were both only in our night-things: the apartment was so hot, we never bothered to get dressed unless we were expecting someone. And I scampered up the passage. Ariel launched herself behind me, pulled over the hat-and-coat-stand which clattered and banged behind her on marble and wood panelling, upsetting the odd occasional-table and chair on its way. I got to the kitchen with her snapping at the hem of my night-shirt, her breath literally hot on my heels, but fortunately the coat-stand snagged, the antlers caught in the open doorway to my mother's sitting room/library, the base on the door jamb of the dining room. I wrenched open the Frigidaire door and dragged out a loop of black puddings, turned to offer them to the brute and saw that Mama was right there behind the bitch smashing her big long back and shaggy grey haunches with a riding boot. With blood sausage at one end and a beating at the other, Ariel sank her stomach to the floor, flapped her tail and whined in pleasure and defeat combined.

Back in her room Mama read aloud from the note Miguel had left on the Sheraton table she uses for visiting cards and so on.

Mother

     All available troops, and that includes ME, have been called to Madrid. The official reason is to protect lives and property when the election result is declared against likely riots if the National Front win. But also in anticipation of a Coup if it goes the other way. Look after Ariel for me. It's some time since she ate, so give her some food.

     Where are you? You should not be out at this time, especially since you have been so ill.

       Your affectionate son
        Miguel

174

XXVII

'. . . I have a plan. Come on, come on out from behind those nasty old hands and listen. You are now just about completely recovered and next Monday you should go back to the Instituto. But if I tell you how, we should be able to persuade silly old Dr Perlimplín that you are still in a very bad way, and give you a note to get you off for another four weeks.'

'And after that?'

'We'll think of something.'

She cranks the handle on the telephone and gets through to the doctor's nurse/receptionist who promises he will be round shortly after four o'clock. No, his name is not really Perlimplín. Perlimplín is a comic character in a play by Lorca, and is the name my mother gives him. It is a little like his real name, which I cannot recall, possibly never really knew.

'We have an hour or so then to get this right.'

She makes me get into my own bed, piles up pillows behind me, then goes to her room and comes back with the make-up she still has from when she travelled with La Barraca, an episode in her life she loves to remember. This was the travelling student theatre Lorca created in the early thirties; she went with them on their first tour the year my father died. And very slowly and carefully she paints me a grey face with brown-purple shadows round my eyes, and pale cracked lips. Then very subtly she rouges my back and chest.

It works? Yes, it works. Perlimplín is an old man whose breath smells of the brandy that rounded off his lunch and the cigar that went with it. He wears a morning coat, and striped trousers, and a huge Homburg hat in which he keeps his stethoscope. He has eye-glasses, pince-nez, which keep falling off because his nose has swollen too much for them to grip properly.

He does not think the rash is scarlet fever, though it might be: more probably it is a heat rash caused by prolonged fever and sweating. I should stay off school until it has gone and until my strength has been built up and, meanwhile, I should have daily doses of brewer's malt with added cod-liver oil and an iron tonic. When the weather gets warmer I should be taken to a spa, one which has hot sulphurated water which will ease the congestion in my chest: there is a new spa near Alhamilla in Granada that he has had good reports of . . .

I am a little nervous, but mainly exhilarated, even exalted. We are part of a huge crowd, pressed up tight in it. I clutch Mama's arm with both hands, scared to let go in case she is carried away. This is the first time it has really come home to me that I am as tall as she, possibly heavier, certainly stronger, and that in this situation I am looking after her. For the first time! Some of the exhilaration I feel comes from my sudden awareness of this, that I can offer her the sort of care, as well as love and fun we already share, that she has given me over the last three years.

She pulls her arm brusquely away so she can raise it in a clenched fist salute above the black glossy feathers in her hat. She always wears black on the rare occasions we go out, but this time she has wound a red silk scarf round the slender column of her neck and fastened it with a diamond pin. She thrusts her slender black-gloved fist in the air in unison with the thirty thousand around us, all crammed into the Puerta del Sol, and together we chant in a great swelling roar: '*Amnisteeee-a, Amnisteeee-a, Amnisteeee-a, Amnisteeee-a.*' With my arm round her waist, my palm can feel her flat stomach and sense how her diaphragm hardens and relaxes, hardens and relaxes beneath the black satin as she shouts. I raise my other arm, look round to make sure I am getting it right, and raise it, clenched like hers. She looks round at me, our faces are only inches apart and now I am if anything a touch taller than her. Her face is flushed, and her eyes sparkle, and she pauses long enough to plant a kiss as near to my mouth as she can get. For once she is wearing no, or very little make-up, and this pleases me too. She is younger without it. If we go on like this, me growing and she getting younger, we will soon be the same. '*Amnisteeee-a, Amnisteeee-a, Amnisteeee-a, Amnisteeee-a.*'

A tall, bulky figure, with glasses, appears on the balcony of the big building in front of us. He is smoking a cigarette through a holder. He raises it, nods once or twice, and goes back indoors. A promise? Many in the crowd think so and they begin to disperse.

'Who was that?' I ask as we allow ourselves to be carried along towards Cibeles with its white marble statue of Cybele, the Earth Goddess. The sky is leaden above it, pricked with tiny dry snowflakes.

'Don Manuel Azaña, the new prime minister. Prime minister yet again.'

'He did not look like a socialist to me.' I have ideas preconceived for me by Mama about how a socialist should look.

When we turn the corner into Ayala, my mother's hand tightens on mine, and . . .

'Oh shit,' she murmurs, and speedily removes the pin, unwinds the scarf, and lowers the bobbled black veil, a cobweb with dead flies in it, over her eyes. 'Saturno.'

I recognize, fifty yards ahead of us, parked outside the street door to our block, my uncle's big black Mercedes-Benz.

'Quick.' She drags me back round the corner. 'Did he see us?'

'I don't think he's in it. Only the chauffeur.'

'That creep Alfonso must have let him in.'

She looks down the street we are now in, picks out the green cross and twisted serpent sign of a pharmacist, bundles us along towards it.

When we get up to our apartment she has a big brown paper bag filled with medicaments including Radio Malt and Parrish's Iron Tonic. Uncle Miguel looks up from the ottoman in the main sitting room. His fissured, ancient, evil face lours above his stiff winged collar.

'You should not be out at times like these. Nor in weather like this.'

'David, go to your room, straight back to bed. Of course not, señor. But I had to get the medicine the doctor prescribed, and I did not want to leave him on his own.'

'I have been here an hour.'

'The pharmacist did not have one of the items and had to send his boy down to his other shop on Velázquez to get it.'

'Shut the door. I want to speak to you.'

I sit shivering in my bed, partly with fear: suddenly, in this awful presence, I feel myself to be, after all, just a boy, partly because some of my symptoms have returned after our outing. I sit there for half an hour or more. I can hear their voices, sometimes raised in anger, his rasping like heavy furniture dragged across a stone floor, hers like a silver trumpet, or an oboe in wartime. At last he leaves and she comes in, sits on the bed, takes both my hands in hers. She is shaking too, and pale now rather than flushed.

'David, we have some fences to mend. Your rotten brother told him that we were out when he called in on his way from Toledo to the Don Juan barracks a week ago. I managed to get round that, but only just. And there's worse. He says we are too intimate, closer to each other than is healthy between a mother and an adolescent boy. He fears I will make a milk-sop, a *maricón* out of you. But how could he have got this idea, where did he get it from? I pleaded with him to tell me but he would not.'

I tell her what I said when I went to confession the day we fell ill, and to my great relief, she dissolves in peals of laughter, part reaction I suppose to the events of the morning. Then: 'David, my love, we can scotch this one, it's not a problem . . .'

'Father, I have sinned. I have felt unworthy anger towards my mother.'

'Why, my son? Has she been embracing you more than you feel she should?'

'Oh no, Father. Quite the reverse.'

'My son, I do not understand you.'

'She no longer embraces me at all. She says I have reached an age when a mother should make a man of me by denying all softness and physical affection. When she said this I was angry with her and shouted and stamped.'

'Like a spoiled little boy?'

'Father, that's just what she called me. How did you know . . . ?'

XXVIII

I know, I know. You want me to go back, fill in what I have left out. The first confession to Father Jaime. The onset of the influenza. You want me to go back two . . . three weeks? I . . . Yes. Yes. I can tell you. I can bring it back, I will remember.

Thirtieth January 1936. I can see the date in the mounted calendar thing on my mother's desk. It is about ten centimetres high, framed in wood, and the face is divided into four sections, day of the week, day of the month, the month, the year. There are little knobs on the sides which you turn to make the figures and words change. So, so long as my mother has remembered to change all the knobs, it is Saturday, the thirtieth of January, 1936. I am wrapped in a big silky green eiderdown, I am sweating like a pig, or so Mother says, though I didn't know pigs were noted for sweating, and I feel very poorly. I have just taken two aspirin tablets which hopefully will abate the fever. In spite of my fever, caused by the influenza, I have just been to confession so I may attend Mass tomorrow, according to Saturno's stern instructions.

Juana has called. Since she is wearing trousers, a long black cloak, and her high-crowned, deeply brimmed trilby, I hope her arrival has not been detected by any spies my uncle may have placed around us. I am quite thrilled by this duplicity, but still disturbed by the confessional I have returned from.

'Have you, my son, entertained evil thoughts at all about your own body?'

'No, Father.'

'Have you entertained evil thoughts about anyone else's body?'

'Yes, Father.'

'So what were they?'

'I wanted to see my brother Jorge run over by a tram.'

180

Pause. I imagine Father Jaime Portillo's face behind the grille, the black hair Mama believes to be dyed, the thin white face with black brows she says he trims, the thin long nose always a bit pink at the end. Some say it's drink, but she says it's constipation which is also the cause of his bad breath which sometimes stinks of shit. The hands that feel cold and clammy when he offers you them to shake (she says: never trust a man who offers you both hands; she also says: never trust a priest) and which forever twist and twine in and out of each other like a basketful of blind sun-starved worms, the sort that infest your gut and will eat you to the bare bone when you're dead . . . it's the fever getting at me, makes me see them thus.

'I think you know the sort of evil thought I mean.' His voice rasps with irritation. 'Do you ever desire to hold another person close, hold her tight, rub yourself against her?'

Incest, I mean incense, and churchy dust hit my inflamed throat, and I succumb to a horrendous coughing fit. With irritation very manifest in his voice he repeats:

'Do you ever desire to hold another person tight and rub yourself against her?'

'Yes, Father. Often.'

'A girl?'

'Not exactly, Father.'

'Older than a girl?'

'I think so, Father.'

'Does this . . . woman, invite you, tempt you to act thus?'

'Yes, Father, often.'

Another long pause as he thinks this through. I am educated all day at the Instituto de San Isidro where there are no women. I am taken in a taxi to and from the Instituto. The woman who comes in daily to clean for us and prepare our food and do the shopping, whom Mama insists we should call Doña Pili, is tall, gawky, bony, a little simple, and well over forty.

'My son. I think . . . considering your situation, and the trust placed in me by your uncle to supervise very closely your spiritual growth, I must ask you the name of the female in question.'

I feel a terrible headache coming on. Again the influenza. Do you know what the word means? Mama told me yesterday: it comes from the medieval Italian for 'influence of the stars'. As soon as I began to develop the symptoms she looked it all up in the big green encyclopaedia that belonged to her father. 'Someone with influenza,' she remarked, 'may therefore be described, like unfortunate lovers, as star-crossed.'

'Father, are you allowed to do that? Ask me to name names in the confessional?'

'You will apologize for the impertinence which has earned you ten Hail Marys.'

'Sorry, Father. I did not mean to be impertinent.'

'And since you will tell me when I ask you outside the confessional, you might as well tell me now, tell me who this woman is who tempts you to sinful embraces.'

'I do not think they are sinful, Father. The lady in question is my mother.'

A pause again, then:

'My son, you will let me decide for you what is sinful and what is not . . .'

'Yes, Father.'

But judgement on the matter is withheld. He goes on to ask me yet again if I play with my penis, and I say that I do not, but forbear to add that my mother does. Finally:

'Please do not forget to remind your mother, whom I do not see here often enough, to vote for Gil Robles and the CEDA on the sixteenth of February. *In nomine Patris et Filii et Spiritus Sancti, te absolvo . . .'*

Whoopee. If I die of pneumonia tonight I go straight to heaven.

And now I shiver and sweat under the draped window close to the big black ridged radiator whose top looks like the back of a dinosaur and is too hot to touch, and wait for Juana to go, but she is overflowing with news and enthusiasm. And anxiety.

'The Hounds of Hell, where are they?'

'Don't worry. Miguel is at the Spanish Infantry Officers'

School at Toledo, and Jorge is in Barcelona studying cello and whores.'

'Good, now listen.' Reassured, Juana continues, crowing. 'Even the anarchists have joined us now . . .'

'The anarchists . . . part of the Popular Front?' My mother is incredulous. 'They are going to vote, in a bourgeois election? I don't believe it. Why?'

'Azaña has promised amnesty to political prisoners once the Popular Front has won.'

'Pah!' My mother is angry and disgusted. 'Don Manuel knows everyone has their price, and he has found the right price for anarchist leaders in jail. Once he's in power again he'll find other ways of betraying the cause. And, no doubt, of putting them back in jail.'

'You were never so troubled about the anarchists in the past. You claimed you were a Marxist, a Communist. And the CP is at the heart of the Popular Front.'

'I am a Communist. A Communist of the old school. Not of this new lot who call themselves Communists. They are the tools of the Comintern, of that Bulgarian Dimitrov and Stalin of Russia. If Marx were alive he'd be trumpeting against them, mark my words. Alliance with Social Democrats, even Catholics! And now the anarchists too! I don't believe it.'

'But, Dolí, it's the only way to get this lot out of power. Surely anything is worth that.'

'No. The only thing that is worth anything is the world revolution, and that can only follow the emergence of a world market and the apparent triumph of capitalism, which will then implode under its own inner contradictions creating the conditions necessary for real revolution. It is the inexorable flow of history that will create the revolution, and petty bourgeois alliances against the bosses simply muddy the flow, are boulders that make it eddy and swirl. Stalin and these so-called Communists in Russia are no more than a boulder. They'll be swept away, will be forgotten when the real revolution comes.'

A long silence falls between them and I begin to shudder

convulsively, and the middle of my back feels icy in spite of the heat around me.

'So,' says Juana, with sardonic finality, 'we are all to sit back and do nothing?'

'No. We do what we can to raise the consciousness of the proletariat, the only revolutionary class, through praxis rather than mere posturing and shouting from parliamentary soapboxes, and we exploit the inner contradictions. People like us, renegades from the bourgeoisie, déclassé artists, bohemians, intellectuals, must strive to undermine the system from within.' Her voice is cracked and harsh and I look at her. Sweat glistens on her forehead and she is very pale. I realize she too is under the influence of the stars.

Juana is angry. 'Fat lot of praxis in your life, Dolí,' she says, almost it's a snarl. 'Wrapped up here in this hothouse with all the food you want and garments enough to clothe a family three times the size. The food that bitch of Miguel's eats would feed three Asturian children. Your trouble is you read too much, do too little. If you were out on the streets where the real struggle is you'd realize what shit most of these books are.' She gestures at the shelves that line my mother's private sitting room.

'That's not fair and you know it!' Mama flings her head back, her eyes wide and staring beneath hair wild and streaked with sweat. Under her chin, her long white throat glows in the light of a room lit by only one large tasselled standard light. Phlegm rises, her voice crackles. 'You know I can't go out, you know I can't risk losing my boys, especially my David, you know all that. I am *marginalized*, but so are you, and so is every other artistical, intellectualized *coño* in this town and every other town. Don't imagine you are doing out there anything more important than what I can manage within this apartment.'

'If the Popular Front wins,' Juana contrived to remain cool, 'with a proper mandate for change, then laws will be passed to stop men controlling the lives of women in the way that fat arse in the bank controls yours. Anyway, I came to ask you if you'd like to spend the last few days before the election at the PSOE headquarters. We're desperate for helpers, just to do simple things like keeping a check on which streets have been pamphleted, stapling up copy from the printers, oh, all sorts. But I can see it was a wasted journey. I'll let myself out. Leave you to get on with the real business of undermining the system from within.'

Almost before she's gone my mother is on her knees in front of me, her arms about my waist, her head in my chest, and she is sobbing, 'Oh what a mess, my little David, what a mess. And I feel so ill, and you're ill too, what shall we do, what shall we do?'

'Undermine the system from within?' I croak, my hand in the damp hair on the back of her neck, then moving down below the top of her dress to the wetness between her shoulderblades. I have no idea what I mean by what I have said, but I feel it's a phrase that pleases her, will cheer her up. She pulls back and looks up into my face, her eyes wild, her cheeks streaked with mascara, her full painted lips trembling between her haggard cheeks.

'Why not, my little David, my last little boy? Why shouldn't we?'

She stands up, takes both my hands in hers and pulls me.

'We'll go to bed, and even if we don't start the revolution we'll kick the system in the balls.' She stands back. 'Go on, you get into bed, my bed, while I get the medicine.'

I drop the eiderdown which belongs on my own bed, and stand but it's like banging my head on a door, except that the pain stays, does not go away, a ferocious headache, like the ones I have been suffering in the last few months. I stagger and she takes my arm.

'Are you all right? Can you manage?'

'I can manage.'

But the room rocks and swings as if I am in the basket of a hot-air balloon in a gale, and when I am out in the passage the walls billow at me like the sails of a ship. My knees hit the marble floor so forcefully that electric pain shoots up from them as I lean forward and retch and retch again, vomiting up everything, it seems, I have eaten for a week. She's kneeling beside me, one arm round my back, the other holding my forehead.

'Oh my poor boy, my poor darling, my poor boy.'

At last it's over, and I feel a little better, not much, but at least the building seems stable again, and she takes me to the bathroom where she sponges my face, makes me change my night-shirt for a warm clean one from the big airing cupboard with its double mahogany doors. The new night-shirt is flannel and has red and white stripes.

I am in her bed, looking up at her, as she feeds yellow fluid from a squeegee with a red rubber bulb on to a lump of sugar.

'Tincture of quinine,' she says. 'Very bitter, but the sugar will help.'

'Ugh, it's foul.' I splutter, my gorge rises again, but I hold on.

'That's for the fever. Now this for the vomiting. Dr Collis Browne.'

'Oh good.'

Two spoonfuls of a dark reddish-brown syrup. I've had this laudanum- and alcohol-based medicine before and I like it, the warmth it brings to the stomach, the pleasant sleep which follows, often with good dreams.

She also takes the Dr Collis Browne in a larger dose and gets into bed beside me. She is wearing a silk, beige-coloured night-dress, and she has washed her face, taken off her make-up. For a time I feel her gentle caresses moving over my chest and legs, and then I fall into a deep sleep.

No doubt for a time the medicaments work, but I am too deeply under the influence of the stars to make any sort of real recovery, and the next few days are a mixture of dream and nightmare, illusion and reality, further doses of quinine and Dr Collis Browne. They include a visit from the doctor, Perlimplín, I've already told you about him, how we fooled him later; he prods and pokes me, places his cold stethoscope all over my chest and back, taps me, makes me cough, and finally prescribes some big yellow tablets, called, I think, M and B. Can that be right? With this new sulphur-based medicament I begin a slow recovery.

But it is what happened between, this confusion of dream and reality that I feel I must tell you about now, for it is coming back to me.

I remember her taking the thermometer from my mouth, looking at it, then holding it closer to the light.

'Oh, my God.'

Then she rushes over to a table where for some days or hours, I don't know, the big green book lies open, presumably at the entry for *Influenza*. The syllables *HUR* to *ITA* throb now in my mind. Then I hear her moving about the apartment. She comes back with a small white rubber sheet which fills me with revulsion and horror, but she makes me lift my body in stages so she can slide it beneath me. Then she peels off my night-shirt which is now striped blue and white. Then she goes again, but the horror remains. I don't know why. Perhaps I do. Do you want me to tell you now?

I am small, an infant. Two? Nearly three? I am in a big cot and I have pushed back the covers and I am squatting to . . . defecate. I produce a neat tidy coil on . . . a white rubber sheet. The coil smells good, and looks good. Good enough . . . to eat? I am very happy and I wish to give this thing I have made to the person I love and fear most in the world. I call out, 'Papa, Papa.' He comes into the room, sees what I have given him. He pulls me out of the cot and slaps my face and then the back of my legs. My mother comes in and screams at him, and he hits her too, so she falls to the ground . . . Weeks before this his father died and we saw the body in its coffin. I wish my father into that coffin too.

Because of this memory I can no longer tolerate the smell of the rubber sheet my mother has left me on. She comes back with an enamelled bowl from the kitchen filled with tepid water. She looks again at the encyclopaedia, and then begins to sponge me, slowly, gently, she pats me dry, and I feel cooler. She jiggles out the rubber sheet and the nightmare recedes.

She is beside me in the big bed. I feel better but now it is her body, naked like mine, which feels too hot. The bed is filled with odours: fresh sweat, distant diarrhoea, and sweet musky ones that are magic. She sighs, moans and gives little cries and she is very restless. I want to soothe her, make her happy, make her better. In the darkness my hand slips over the curve of her waist, across her stomach and up to her breast. It's full and soft, and I feel endlessly happy to have it in my hand. I find the nipple, which thickens between my finger and thumb, and I feel my penis also thickening and hardening. She takes my wrist and moves my hand down to her sex and holds my hand over it, firmly, not allowing me to pull back. My fingers slip through the silky pelt and one of them finds the moist folds of flesh hidden amongst them. Her grip on my hand tightens, and she makes my hand and fingers move, caress her. For a time she seems calmer, but then she becomes more agitated. She twists on to her back, keeping my hand where it is, and cries out:

'Oh my God!'

Then. 'Why not?'

Finally and with a deep throaty call of a laugh, a bugle call blown by a dragon or a pythoness. 'From within!'

She hoists herself upright, turns me on to my back, straddles me, and attempts to feed my penis into her sex. For a moment I am frightened, she senses this, pulls back then takes me into her mouth in a caress that transforms my whole body into something radiant and gloriously happy, the feelings beating out in waves. Then again she straddles me, and this time finds what she wants, rocking herself on me.

There is no physical climax for me. I am too young, or too ill, or both. Perhaps there is for her. Certainly there is a rush of joy, of triumph which may be physical, is certainly spiritual. Spiritual? Yes. By that word I mean a leap beyond mere feelings. She throws back her head and shouts, no sings once more like a high trumpet: '¡LIBERTAD!'

You are German. It is not a word that translates easily, even into French. Leave it in Spanish.

Then her head drops, and what little light there is glistens on the sweat that sheets her breasts above me, her torso and her arms. She smiles then, I know she does, because also she giggles.

188

María Victoria de los Angeles. Vikí.

Me? I am happy at last. I know now that I am the he she loves, the only he she loves.

∽

'*Che si tarda* . . .   Attack, attack it. Make the consonants like barbed wire.'

But it was the guitar, his mother's guitar that he attacked, swung cracked nails across the strings in violent discord, and through it Petra drilled her voice:

'*Che si tarda, o ministri* . . . Why so slow, my servants, why so slow to put her to the test of a thousand deaths . . . *provi costei mille morti* . . . ¡BASTA, señor!' And she struck the lid of the clavichord with her clenched fist.

The echo of her shout, overlaying the jangle of keyboard strings and the interrupted chord on the guitar, filled the stone cube for a second or so and then died. His head came up, his body remained twisted and bent over the gilded sound-box. She looked down at him, at the tired sightless eyes, the wrinkled skin, the knotted knuckles still poised over the strings and fell to her knees in front of him.

'Why, Querubín? Why always the horrors? The ugly threats, the screamed denunciations, the sadism of it? Why won't you ask me to sing the love scenes too, Nero's part in the love duets?'

'A girl can sing those parts. I need to be sure you can sing like a man. Sound as if you can do the things men do.'

She got up, swung away, turned on him.

'That's not true.' She gathered herself together. 'In the first place I shall find it more difficult to sound like a man in those love passages than in this stuff, and you know it. But there's more to it than that. I heard you sing Nerone. I heard you sing the role at Glyndebourne in England . . .' She took a deep breath, pressed her hand into her diaphragm and sang, '*Per capirti negl'occhi, il sol* . . . *to arrive in your eyes the sun has diminished itself, to be harboured in your breast the dawn leaves the sky*. I know now why my heart melted when you sang that, why every woman in the audience felt you were singing it for her.'

Without changing his position at all he had somehow become a statue of himself, frozen where he sat, but his sad, distressed eyes filled and spilled. She sat back on her heels in front of him, lifted the guitar out of his lap, took his hands.

'You really loved her. Fantasy or not. You really loved her and she loved you. Always I think as a mother and son, a son and a mother. That's what matters. It's the other business or what you made of it that's destroying you, making you hate yourself. We can all hate, I can sing hate. But love has to be learned, taught. She taught you love, real love, not just sex. Help me to sing love. Help me to love. Teach me.'

But he shook his head.

'You need someone to sing with.'

PART FOUR

L'incoronazione di Poppea

XXIX

Every shop, every bar and bank in Campanillas had Him. Every wallet and handbag, every classroom and every home. Either framed hugely in glossy colour or on a small card tucked behind a glass on a shelf, He was always there: a lean sinuous body, a touch bigger than life-size, the perfection of male beauty and baroque carving, but with the slashes in the rib-cage leaking blood, the tendons and sinews caught in a wrenching spasm, the head crowned with thorns slumped at last. *La Expiración del Señor*, the Last Breath.

'On the Friday two weeks before Good Friday,' said Carmen, 'He is brought out and carried round the town *con mucho pulvo*.'

'*Pulvo*?' Petra did not know the word.

'*Fuegos artificiales*,' Paco explained. Fireworks.

'Is He very important, then?'

Carmen clattered away at speed and with much enthusiasm. Once a year the image of the dying Christ which stood behind the altar of the parochial church was paraded around the streets. It was the most moving, tremendous, splendid experience, not equalled anywhere in Spain and so not anywhere in the whole world either.

'Listen,' she said, and caught the hem of the top Petra was wearing in her claw-like hand. 'Some time ago the bishop decided the candle smoke had made Him look like a Moor. He was to be taken to Granada. But we put farm carts across the road and manned them with pitch-forks and shot-guns – we would fight to keep Him in the town to . . . well, our own last breaths. So cleaners had to come from Granada. You must go. And if you like you can take us too.'

Always she liked to arrive in Campanillas in Petra's smart BMW, preferably with the roof down so she could wave to her gossips.

Petra was not so sure. She had been brought up a Roman Catholic though her mother had remained Church of England.

With her father's suicide she had rejected it with the distaste with which one cleans dog-shit from a shoe. Since then she had felt only angry hatred for the Nazarene, especially when He was trundled out of his charnel-house to justify killing – Croats, Moslems or whoever it was happened to be sitting on a bit of land you thought should be yours. But she guessed that like New Year, Epiphany and Carnival this would be an occasion when the Parma Violet Lady would be out and about, so she agreed to take them.

They arrived at about half-past five, to find that the square had been closed off. She could not get to her usual place near the school but had to park well below it. The spaces at each end of the square were already filling up with a crowd in its funeral best. The men wore dark suits, caps, berets, hats, even ties – which in Campanillas was not usual. Not even the bank clerks wore ties to work, not even the head-teacher. The women with pretensions wore tailored black suits (oddly sexy for the occasion since the skirts were fashionably short and slit at the back to reveal black nylons with seams) and black veils. Even the young ones were in their cleanest newest jeans and sweaters of sombre hue. And of course the older ladies, like Carmen, wore the black they always wore, but the best black.

Yet there was a difference. There was more jewellery about, and the women had taken a different sort of care with their make-up: Petra had seen a couple of Campanillas funerals leaving the church and she felt that for the Last Breath they had dressed more theatrically than they did for the real thing.

She used the back alleys to get to the area at the top, below the town hall, and then squeezed her way through almost to the front. The space between the two sets of barriers, maybe eighty metres downhill and sixty across, was almost empty of people and the seven or eight men who were there wore builders' helmets. It was filled with racks and racks and racks of fireworks packed in plain brown card. There were only two sorts: thunder-flashes and whizz-bang rockets. Thousands of them. Every bar and bank and shop had run lotteries to raise the money; every individual and certainly every business, and anybody with pretensions to be somebody in a town of some-bodies had contributed. There was the diaspora too. For a hundred and fifty years Campanillas had exported the labour its own fields could not support to Barcelona, Madrid, Bilbao and all of Spanish America. And every exile carried a picture of the Image in his wallet or purse, every home had its framed photograph, and they all sent money for the Friday two weeks before Good Friday.

The big church bell had been tolling – the way it did for a funeral. It stopped. The church clock began its pre-hour chime. The big doors of the church opened and two robed altar boys carrying big lanterned candles appeared beneath the orange trees. Then the clock struck, the first stroke of six, and there He was. Twelve feet high on his cross, borne by four strong lads in white shirts and pressed jeans, and . . .

They all went off at once. Fast fuses linked each rack and almost instantly the whole scene was blotted out with flash-filled smoke; the noise settled into a steady unbroken roar that made the ground shake. Petra felt her lungs and liver were shaking inside her too. The barrage continued for a full five minutes before the smoke cleared and they brought Him down the steps into the square with María Dolores, the Sorrowing Mother, high up between her candles, behind him. Then the next lot went off, nearer Petra this time, from the unused racks at the top of the square between her and Them.

They passed just below her so their heads were almost on a level with hers and she felt her reservations crumble. This was nothing to do with the New Testament – this crowned sacrifice and the sorrowing woman, his Mother maybe, but she looked hardly a day older. Out in the fields beneath the olives and the orange trees the beans and lentils were already in pod, being picked. Next week they'd plough them in, organic nitrates for the barley and maize that would follow. Most smallholders raised three, sometimes four crops a year off their land, as well as the olives and oranges, and without the artificial fertilizers and plastic sheeting they use on the coast. Just good husbandry, the sacrificed King, and the Goddess who mourns her Son and Lover.

Each street and alley had its own firework display, vying with each other in elaboration and beauty – giant Catherine wheels, miniature castles, fountains of light. They had all been set up hours before and left untended or only partially watched over, waiting for Her and Him to arrive. And if there was a single naughty boy in Campanillas who felt the urge to set them off prematurely he suppressed it.

Petra fell in with the procession, followed its slow, halting, serpentine course through the recent apartment blocks, then the drab municipal tenements. As dusk changed to night they moved up the hill and into the poorer part of the village. Here the houses were smaller, never more than two storeys and often only one, their edges and corners rounded with decades of whitewash. At the top she knew there was a chapel, dedicated to St Sebastian, but really it was the mosque. And there, dressed in black, small face white, was the Parma Violet Lady on the steps of the chapel, with her little choir standing round her. The Slain Christ stopped beneath her, but it was for the Mother, sorrowing in purple with the silver crescent at her feet that she sang her *saeta*.

It began with a long drawn-out cry, something between a wail and a scream: '*Madre, María Ma-a-a-adre . . .*' and went on, a long outpouring of soaring melody, interspersed with throaty cries of pain. She was, Petra realized, both possessed and quite obviously and consciously performing: the emotion was real but so was the art. At last the voice spiralled down and ended on a sigh. Silence lay over the procession like a mantle, but then she raised her head again and the little choir around her moved closer, cleared their throats. This time it was the *Stabat Mater* in a modern setting, bluesy, rhythmic.

Petra turned away, walked down the hill, past the nougat and toy stalls, the man selling spiced pork kebabs, and found her car. As she unlocked the door the sky lit up with a huge sunburst of bright lilac-coloured stars.

*

Next day she had to pick up Carmen and Paco who had stayed the night with Paco's sister. But first, with heart beating, a sheen of embarrassment on her brow and the determination of someone who knows she could be about to make a fool of herself but no longer cares, she climbed the steps into the small municipal market and made her way to the health stall.

Mari-Elena saw her coming, looked over her shoulder from the scales where she was measuring out two hundred grains of camomile for a French ex-pat. She smiled, a touch shyly.

'¿Té Ceilán?' she asked.

'No. Something else. Like you, I sing. I am training to be an opera singer. With David Querubín. You know?'

'Of course. We all know about Querubín. And you.'

'And I would like you to sing with me. I need to practise . . . a duet, and I have no one . . .' She felt her colour rise, her mouth dry up.

Mari-Elena tipped the dried daisies into a thin plastic bag, tied a knot, took money, gave change, frowning slightly all the time. Then she shrugged.

'Why not? If you think I'm good enough.'

'*Pur ti miro, pur ti godo,*
  pur ti stringo, pur t'annodo . . .'

'Stop. Put your hand in front of your ear, like this, listen to your voice, blend, blend, we've got to get the blend right.'

The very last love duet, the only time in the sequence they were attempting when they actually sang together, rather than in turns.

'Again, just the second line, hold the "o" of "stringo" and listen to it and listen to my entry.' Petra spread a chord across Mari-Elena's Spanish guitar.

'*Pur ti stringooooo, pur t'annodo . . .*'

'I don't like it.'

'You don't like it?' Mari-Elena was nonplussed. 'What don't you like?'

She was standing on the far side of a round table with a

brown fringed moquette cover. She looked down at Petra, dark eyes serious, wanting to get it right.

'Tell me again what it means,' she asked.

'"Now I behold you, now I enjoy you, now I press you, now I am knotted to you, no more pain, no more darkness, oh my life, oh my treasure, I am yours, I am yours, you alone are my soul, my idol, yes, my heart, my love, my life, yes."'

Mari-Elena bit her lip. It was not just a translation Petra had given her: there was confession too, declaration.

Petra drew breath and went on, 'And I'm afraid we sound just . . . pretty.'

To each other they spoke German. Wilf, Mari-Elena's boyfriend of three years' standing, was lazy about learning Spanish, so she had learnt German.

'So. Let's start by giving those *fioriituras* on "miro" and "godo" the full works. Go for a full-throated throb on "godo". And I think we should beef up the tempo a bit, what do you say? Give it some urgency.'

'*Pur ti miro, pur ti godo . . .*'

It was all going so much more easily than Petra had expected. They worked in Mari-Elena's apartment during the siesta hours – Wilf was up in the mountains teaching hang-gliding to Germans on holiday; Emilio, her seven-year-old boy, stayed at school and would not be home until shortly before five.

The apartment was small, an *ático* on the top floor of a small four-storey block behind the square: it was clean, sparsely furnished, airy and light, with terrazzo flooring. There was a small stack of Lego in one corner, pushed, she guessed, out of the way moments before she arrived, and a kid's Red Indian outfit. The basic smell of Spain indoors – a blend of eggs and potatoes cooked in olive oil, mountain ham and garlic, all overlaid with furniture polish and eau de cologne – was present but not cloyingly so. The only signs that this was not an entirely typical young married household were a poster-sized photograph of a hang-glider set against the snow-clad peaks of the Sierra Nevada, and the pots of marijuana on the tiny balcony. The very domesticity of it all was a good thing: it undercut the passionate nature of the music they were singing, gave an everyday context to the passion she felt for Mari-Elena's tiny waist, her long fingers, her bird-like bones, above all for the air of transient lightness she always carried with her.

Petra had decided she did not want Querubín to know, to be part of it. She wanted to surprise him, present him with a finished performance of the last pages of Monteverdi's *L'incoronazione di Poppea*, though she had said nothing yet of this to Mari-Elena: just that she needed someone to sing with, to help her master the part of Nerone.

Presently they took a break. Mari-Elena went into the tiny kitchen, busied herself with a small two-tiered espresso coffee jug, first emptying the grounds from the previous brew into a bin, then grinding beans in a rackety electric grinder. Standing behind her, Petra closed her thin waist between her palms. Mari-Elena shrugged and moved to the side to fill the bottom half of the coffee-maker with water from the tap.

'Not now,' she said. 'Not yet.'

She turned, saw Petra's confusion, distress.

'It's all right. I don't mind. Just . . . not yet.' She bit her lip again, gave a brusque sigh, sought for something to defuse the situation. 'It must be lovely to live in Villa Goya.'

'Yes . . . Querubín calls it Villa Melchor. It's . . . it is lovely.'

'I went there once. Your housekeeper, Tía Carmen, she's a sort of aunt of mine, or second cousin, something like that. She showed us round.' Mari-Elena laughed. 'She was so proud of it all. She kept saying it's like the Alhambra but better.'

'Is it?'

'Is it what?'

'Like the Alhambra?'

The coffee's gurgle died into a hiss and a puff of steam. Mari-Elena shut off the flame, turned, looked up at Petra.

'Just how long have you been living here?'

'Six, seven months.'

'And you haven't been to the Alhambra?'

'No.'

'That is crazy. Really dumb.'

XXX

'I think I should go to the Alhambra. Don't you?'

Querubín put down his fork and reached out an unsteady hand for his glass. He sipped the wine, sucked in his lips.

'Some more Casera, please.'

She topped his glass up from the icy lemonade bottle.

'It gets a touch tart by this time of year, don't you think? All the sugars are fermented out, and of course that means it's stronger too.' Again he drank. 'That's better.'

'The Alhambra, señor. It's worth a visit? You must have been there.'

Querubín made the silence a long one, gazing at her, she presumed sightlessly, across the arc of the round table that separated them. Then without speaking he picked up his fork again and with a finger pushed on to it a piece of the grilled hake which Carmen had de-boned and cut up for him.

'No,' he said at last. 'I have not been there, not that I remember.'

Petra felt a sudden coldness as if a ghost had passed, and then an irritating wave of embarrassment. But why should she feel embarrassed? She recalled the last of the transcriptions, the first she had read, how it ended in the woods above the Alhambra, how, because the gate to the palace itself was guarded with rebel soldiers, he and his mother had gone into the woods and there made love. All right, so on that occasion he had not actually gone to the Alhambra, but it was surely reasonable to suppose that he had been there in the last ten years or so since coming to Villa Melchor. She pushed on relentlessly, less inclined than ever to be crossed by him.

'I understand the best time to go is between half-past one and two in the afternoon.'

'Yes?'

'Because the coach parties with foreign tourists go there in the morning, while the Spanish tourists and locals prefer to visit in the late afternoon or evening.'

'Ah. I see where we are heading.' He fumbled more flakes of fish on to his fork. 'You want to cut short our lesson. Tomorrow?'

'Well. Cancel it, actually. Because before I go there I'd like to visit a good bookshop in Granada. Can you recommend one?'

She joined the queue of cars climbing the long steep hill beneath the huge dark ilexes to the free car-park at the top and, because Mari-Elena had warned her about them, refused the blandishments of the gypsies who claimed there were no parking spaces higher up. There were of course plenty, the big car-park was emptying at that time of day faster than it was filling, she was even able to park in the shade. She slipped back her driving seat to give herself more room to eat and read and then delved into a paper bag for the meal she had bought in a sandwich shop outside the Librería Urbana: a small loaf shaped like an American football filled with omelette, an apple and a tin of Diet Coke. It all made a not unwelcome change from Carmen's cuisine. Then she considered the books she had bought, still wrapped in the thin paper printed with the bookshop's name.

Tales of the Alhambra by Washington Irving, which had claimed her attention because of the fine reproductions of nineteenth-century engravings, a modern guide in German with good colour photographs and two books by an English author called Ian Gibson. One of these *En Granada, Su Granada* was in Spanish and was a guide to Granada and the Alhambra done for devotees of the poet Lorca, the other a big biography of the poet but in English. Those, she decided, would have to wait; as she began to work her way through her lunch it was the Irving and the conventional guide she peeled free from their wrappings.

Fortified with some knowledge but a little overwhelmed by the superlatives – should this place really be numbered among the wonders of the world, did it really surpass the Parthenon for harmony and perfection? – she passed through the tourists' entrance to the palace half an hour later, and found herself a touch underwhelmed by the first room or two. From them an angle took her into the Hall of the Ambassadors – a large room, perfectly square, the walls completely covered with tiles and stucco miraculously carved into endlessly intricate intertwining patterns. Three walls were broken with arched belvederes that looked across a quite daunting chasm to the Albaicín and the Sacramonte beyond, where the gypsies used to live in caves. These casements filled the room with reflected sunlight . . .

Querubín was bereft without her – at first he could not believe how lost, deserted, almost betrayed he felt. Of course she had been away before for a day, half a day, missed a lesson or two, because of a cold or a tender throat which both agreed should not be strained. On one occasion they had not spoken to each other for nearly two days after he had called her a German frau once too often and with sarcasm sharper than usual. But apart from these exceptions she had spent most of every day with him, through to midnight and beyond, only leaving him in the afternoons when he slept.

There had been no break in the routine for five weeks – not since the evening she had gone to Campanillas for the fireworks. And now, without her, he began to experience for the first time the extent of his blindness: he simply had not realized how much he had come to depend on her to get from one room to another, to find his mother's guitar, to put a glass where his hand would find it without knocking it over, to feed his goldfish without strewing the paving with crumbs or, worse still, taking a stumble. But it was more than that, much more. She gave his life meaning, a purpose.

He stayed in bed, as the morning wore on, marvelling at the vacuity of the noises he could hear – the splash of the fountain, the crrrooo-ing of the doves, even the purring of his cat, all bass-lines and harmonies to the sound that normally floated above them and gave them meaning: Petra warming up with scales, arpeggios and snatches of song. Carmen came and went. Testily he told her he did not want breakfast nor lunch, and that he would get up when he felt ready to.

*

In the Court of Myrtles there were six big chairs, thrones really, their frames made out of four semi-circles, two set on top of two, supporting slung backs and seats of thick leather, three on each side of the entrance to the court. Two Japanese ladies who had been sitting there for three minutes until their tour moved relentlessly on stood up.

Am I allowed? Petra asked herself and looked around before sinking into the wide seat. She smoothed her palms down her thighs to her knees over the full light-weight Indian cotton dress she was wearing, midnight green but scattered with small bright flowers. Why had she put on a dress when normally she wore jeans or leggings? To counter the promise of heat? Or, remembering the few images of the place she held in her mind, had she sensed a propriety in dressing thus? At all events she was not the only person there in skirts for presently nearly seven feet of African darkness folded himself into the seat not next to her, but discreetly leaving the one in the middle empty. And he was wearing a full-length white Morrocan *djellabah*.

She glanced behind, up and around. Behind her and above a dado of tiles, deep bottle-green, terracotta, white and jade, another frieze of carved stucco, pale peach in colour, proclaimed again and again in flowing calligraphy that there is no conqueror but God. In front a row of high semi-circular arches, also finely decorated, were supported on slender marble columns above striated polished flags, a soft bluish grey. Beyond the arches hot spring sunlight lay like a lover on the water in which carp, black and gold, slowly swirled. She sighed at the loveliness of it all, felt a generous surge of gratitude as well as longing for Mari-Elena. She had wanted her to come too but she was chained to her stall in Campanillas market. Petra did feel niggled, though, that Querubín had not thought to encourage her to come here, oh, almost as soon as she arrived, for she sensed it was a place she would want to return to, perhaps month after month, certainly as the seasons changed.

Presently the tall African reassembled his huge height and, with a swish of his skirts, moved off down the side of the long rectangular pool. He made a slight obeisance to her as he passed and she noted the haze of silky hair on his chin, carefully trimmed, caught a hint of his fragrances – sandalwood and spices overlaying male richness. He walked, she realized, as if he owned the place.

That, Petra said to herself, is how I should walk when I am Nero. She followed his progress, how he paused above the pool, then the way he moved into the cloister again and the whiteness of his robe became pale bluish violet before he disappeared. But can I? She pulled in her stomach, straightened her back, lifted her chin. Of course I can. The world is my oyster – and I am the pearl.

His eyes were, he supposed, open. He lowered and raised the lids, consciously noting how the main movement was in the upper lids, then he blinked quickly, then more slowly. Gradually he sensed there was a difference – open shut, grey black, but the difference inconsiderable, negligible: he was blind. At last. The strangest of realities now hit him as he pushed his feet out from under the thin duvet and on to the floor: he knew how they looked, behind the darkness in his eyes still shot with occasional passing meteors his brain could 'visualize' them – long toes twisted, greyish and yellow, the left ankle more swollen than the right, the nails vertically ridged and brittle, a bunion behind the left big toe, but this visualization was shadowy, ghostly, insubstantial. Enough though. For just as his feet were totally familiar to him, so was the route he had to follow, and so was the memory of where he had to go.

He paused at the door and the short but steep stone stairs dropped below him. There was something he needed, something he had forgotten. He moved back into his bedroom, and with hardly a fumble found the bottom drawer in a big chest. The smell of camphor, sharpened by his blindness, assaulted his nostrils as he felt about for silk. He hoped that what he pulled free from the rest included red.

And Petra? He comforted himself with the thought that he had taught her all he knew and it was up to her now. And he pushed aside the other thought that said that was a lie, but it came back, so he added, if she were that serious about the whole business she'd be here now. But he felt the lack of her, the space she had made by her absence, and pushed on to her at least some of the blame for what he had in mind.

Why, Petra asked herself, stretching her legs and sandalled feet so her toes actually caught the heat of direct sunlight in the Court of Myrtles, why *Poppea*? Why is it his favourite? Because they get away with it. Nerone and Poppea. It's love and duty, but this time love wins and duty is out of the window. Never mind, maybe Monteverdi didn't write *Pur ti miro* at the very end. It's the opera as we have it which is on Nero's side, and Poppea's. An emperor falls in love with the loveliest, cleverest woman in the world. They're both married to other people and his old tutor, boring old Seneca, tells him he's wrong. So he tells Seneca to top himself, he gets shot of the spouses, and Poppea ascends the throne and the three continents of the world, Europe, Asia and Africa, bow before her.

Ascendi, ascendi . . . In her head Petra could hear Poppea's triumph as Nerone tells her to ascend the throne. María Dolores, Dolí, Vikí, the girl in the portrait, she was Poppea, she had defied every taboo and . . . Petra shuddered.

She stood up, pushed Querubín and the rest away, and walked through sunlight, into shade, then out into sunlight again. She wandered slowly through the Court of Lions and all the other courts and gardens relishing the constantly shifting interplay of interiors and exteriors, of water still and water running, of roses freshly out, plumbago in bud, cherry blossom and old walls curtained with wistaria, the apartment Irving had rented, the baths below where eunuchs had filled cisterns with steaming fragrant water and women had bathed together to music played by blind musicians.

And as she moved through it all she felt her spirit lighten, and then, to her acute embarrassment, her eyes began to fill. It was, she decided, the scale that made it perfect, always domestic, always a place to live in (and die violently there too, if the sultan believed you had been up to something with one of his wives);

there was no self-conscious grandeur, no desire to impress, for there had never been anyone to impress – the outside world stopped in the Hall of the Ambassadors. From there on in it was simply a place to live in: but perfect.

And yes, OK, it's better than the Parthenon, and she accepted its repose and inner rhythm.

Outside a screen wall punctuated with towers including the one still haunted by the princess who loved her father the sultan too much to elope with a Christian prince, even though her two older sisters had done so, led her to the old stone bridge that spans the ravine between the Alhambra and the Generalife or summer palace. She climbed through more gardens, past more pools and fountains, in and out of pavilions airy and small, less decorated, even more intimate. The usual route finally brought her into a fine avenue of cypress and arched oleander not yet in bloom. Above her the hillside climbed through thickly planted beeches and elms, tall and slender because they were planted so closely. Inevitably a nightingale began to sing, a long chain of melody winding down from the boughs above.

Petra shuddered and remembered. This wood was the wood, it could not have been anywhere else. And suddenly she felt panic, she did not know why, but it was at that moment Querubín began to climb the stone stairs which would complete his Via Dolorosa.

XXXI

I am in a long but narrow room, ill-lit with unshaded bulbs of low wattage and it is filled with women, mostly young or middle-aged, though there are a few old ones in black. The lucky ones are sitting on collapsible wooden seats, the ones in the front are on the floor with their skirts pulled over their knees. At the back behind the seats there is standing room only and also down the sides of the hall. I am standing near the front but on the side, with my back to the wall which is streaming with moisture. It is very, very hot, and nearly all of us are fanning ourselves with pamphlets, news-sheets, and, especially the older ones, fans.

At the front there is a slightly raised dais with a trestle table, and behind it six women amongst whom is my mother, still, as always when in Madrid, dressed in black, but again with the red scarf wound high round her neck. This time it is fastened with a small brass safety pin, not a diamond. She asked me to fix it for her before we left the apartment.

Me? Yes, I am in woman's clothing again. A long cotton chemise, dark grey, over a full black cotton skirt, tennis shoes, no socks or stockings. My legs smart a little because she made me shave them before we left. Next to me is Mother's friend Mad Juana. She is wearing her usual mannish clothes which this time include a leather helmet of the sort aeroplane pilots wear, and large round goggles pushed up on her forehead.

A woman is speaking. She is beautiful, with high cheekbones and large eyes, five or ten years older than my mother, her black hair already lightly streaked with grey pulled back in a bun. Oddly, she has the same first name. She is coming to the end of her speech, her voice is like a trumpet, and like a trumpet it can be lyrical as well as abrasive.

'Comrades. The assassination of Comrade Lieutenant Pepe Castillo yesterday was an act of despicable barbarity not least because it has widowed a woman who was first a bride less than a month ago. Nevertheless the execution last night of that arch-enemy of freedom and the working class, the most excellent (said with terrible scorn) Deputy Calvo Sotelo, carried out more as reprisal than an act of justice, was ill-judged and is also to be condemned. Ill-judged because it will provoke a crisis we are not yet ready to meet, a crisis that will be upon us perhaps as soon as tomorrow. Indeed even as I speak it may be that the generals are on the march. So, ill-judged and to be condemned.

'Sisters, this fatal act of reprisal is precisely an example of the individualism which could destroy our movement even now as we approach the threshold of revolution and triumph. However strong the temptation may be to break ranks in conspiratorial acts of terrorism, driven as we may be by feelings almost uncontrol-lable, we must resist it. And discipline, the iron discipline which will overcome the enormous forces of evil that are marshalled against us, can only come from the Party. Comrade sisters, join the Party if you can, travel with us if you would prefer, but above all let us remain united and ready and willing not just to die for the Cause but to serve it in the ways your democratically elected leaders will indicate. Heroism, yes. Sacrifice, yes. Force and violence where they are the only way forward. But above all Unity. Solidarity. Obedience. Discipline. Long live the Republic, Long live the Party. Long live Spain's Union of General Workers.'

Storms of applause, many fists are raised to echo her farewell salute, an attempt in some sections, which includes Mad Juana, to sing the Internationale, but all dies quite quickly as this stormy passionate lady leaves the dais and the hall by a side door. There have, I have to say, been some boos and jeers too.

'She has four meetings to address this evening,' Juana shouts in my ear, 'and I wish I could be at every single one of them.'

But now my mother is on her feet, and the hall falls still again, and I feel a surge of emotion: admiration that this small beautiful lady should have the strength and the conviction to place herself in this situation, tremendous pride that she is my mother and my friend and my lover, and an awful tender anxiety that she might bruise herself or be bruised by what might well become a confrontation.

'Sisters,' she says, and her fine gentle voice immediately suggests song, the sweet song of reason, after the passion of the lady who went before. 'The work we are taking on today and in the coming months is nothing less than Social Revolution. And I do not believe that this can be carried out by a central government, or a ruling party. It requires the knowledge, the brains, the willing collaboration of a mass of local and specialized forces, none of which alone can cope with the diversity of problems such a revolution implies. If we sweep away that collaboration and trust and bow only to the ukases of party dictators we will destroy all the independent forces, which already exist, for progress to a better world, each in its own way expert in the areas they were born to cope with. Trades unionists, teachers, scientists, artists, co-operatives of producers and distributors will never serve us, serve the whole of humanity in the fullest way they can, if they are dominated, as they have been in Russia, by the bureaucratic organs of the Party. The Russian way will undo the Revolution, render its realization impossible . . .'

And at that moment the big double door at the back of the hall is burst open by a phalanx of ruffians in blue shirts and black breeches. One lobs a smoking bottle into the air which crashes spreading flames that catch the skirts of an older woman who has been less nimble than her sisters in getting away from it. Others, three or four, loose off pistols, for the most part into the ceiling where a bullet smashes a light bulb. And through them, and then through the scattering screaming women, comes an unmistakable and familiar sight: Ariel, baying in short deep howls, leaping across upturned seats, and panting madly. Miraculously, considering the confusion and the noise, she has picked me out almost straight away and is soon pawing my chest and licking my face in excited recognition.

Then fighting his way through from the back of the hall comes her legal owner, my brother Miguel, and it is horribly apparent that in spite of the clothes and make-up I am wearing Ariel has betrayed me. Miguel's face twists with fury and pain. He levels his pistol, fires, and the top of a woman's head which rises between us explodes in a spray of bone, hair, blood and brain, much of it slashed across my shoulder and face. The deflected bullet smashes into the wall above me, Ariel drops to a cringing crouch, and her baying becomes a whine.

'Dolí, Mama,' I scream, desperate now to get to her before he can do either of us any harm, and Juana turns me towards the dais and herds me towards it and the other door. I glance over my shoulder, though, in time to see Miguel collapse beneath blows struck by two of the women nearest to him, one of whom I know works in the vegetable market and can lift a sack of potatoes more readily than most men. They are beating him with the collapsible chairs which are folding up like traps in front of the Falangists. The noise is indescribable. Screams, the chanting of rival hymns: 'History is on our side . . . '; 'Tomorrow belongs to me'; 'Arise battalions and conquer;' 'Arise ye starvelings from your slumber . . . ' The smashing of furniture, cries of pain, and still, occasionally, shots.

Pushing and shoving, both with and against the tide, for at least as many women want to get down into the front line as are trying to get out into the street, we at last manage to link up with Mama and spill outside into the heat which sits on the pavement like a fat cat.

'Juana, *querida*,' my mother cries, as we storm down the sidewalk, 'I am done for. Unless you can get us back to the apartment and then to Atocha railway station . . .'

We swing round a corner, and there, parked where she left it, is Juana's motor-cycle, a British Norton with side-car. Juana buttons the leather strap beneath her chin, pulls down her goggles. Mama and I, first Mama, then me, but that won't work, first me and then Mama perched on my knees, pile into the side-car. Juana rises in the saddle and kicks down, kicks down again and again, her strong bottom and thundery thigh close to my face. At last the engine fires and roars as she twists the handgrips which are high and spread like the horns of a bull. The cobbles beneath us judder like bullets fired from below, a tram-driver frantically sounds his bull-roarer and rings his bell and we shoot beneath the curved prow of his vehicle, the wheel of the side-car brushes it and sheds a gleaming chrome hub cap which spins away. Above us, beyond the crackling sparks on the tram wires, the hot sky is shredded with crimson cloud like the banners of evil armies . . .

The same evening? Certainly. We are in the apartment, I am stripped to the waist, and Juana has my head over the bathroom basin, is dousing me with water . . . to wash off the blood and tissue of the poor woman Miguel killed, I suppose. Mama is rushing about the apartment, piling clothes into a big leather bag with straps, its twin, already full, stands in the hall. Suddenly a huge pounding on the big internal front door, and shouts, enraged shouts, '*Ma-a-adre*, you cow, let us in, you bitch!'

Juana seizes my shoulders, spins me round, thrusts the grey chemise I was wearing before into my hands, yes, I am still wearing the black skirt, and pushes me towards the kitchen and the fire escape. There is a crash behind us, and I see the varnish or paint on the door crack, and then again it comes: they are using the fire-axe taken from its glass case on the landing. Here comes Miguel. Mama with an unclosed bag shedding underwear and stockings is behind us as we spill out on to the clanging stairs and stumble and hurtle down through three right-angles to the area below.

The three of us sprint across it, out through the service door and on to Ayala where once again the Norton awaits us. Mama in a gesture of magnificent despair hurls the bag from her, turns to Juana. 'I've got no money,' she screams.

'I've got some.'

'Enough?'

Juana shrugs broadly, swings her leg over the petrol tank, and again we pile into the side-car.

On the concourse of the station there are enormous queues at the ticket kiosks, arched holes framed in wood like dovecotes, crowds of people of all sorts fleeing Madrid, heading for relatives in the country, home towns, places where they, like us, might feel safer when the catastrophe comes. Clearly we are going to be part of this log-jam for some time and, with that innocent blend of boredom and curiosity typical I suppose of lads in their very early teens, I look around me, pick out the details. Much of the huge hall we are in is decorated with turn of the century art nouveau: swirling flowers and foliage, with allegorical ladies draped in flowing garments representing the virtues and attractions of Andalusia and the south. Here and there a naked breast peeps out. None is as beautiful, as full and rounded and perfectly shaped as Mama's.

Juana has left us to keep our place in the line while she has gone to the front to make enquiries. Now she returns.

'It's no good,' she cries. 'The Granada train is fully booked; if you get on at all it will be standing room only, but it leaves in half an hour and anyway I am eight pesetas short of the fare. There is a later train, not fully booked, for Badajoz and the Portuguese border. Won't that do?'

'No,' Mama cries, and stamps her foot. 'Granada is the nearest large town to Don Gabriel's villa, and he promised he would shelter us if ever we got into the sort of trouble we are in now. It has to be Granada.'

'I have more cash at home.' Juana chews her lip doubtfully. 'Or I could borrow some from a friend. Should I bike back to Desengaño? I could be there and back before you get to the ticket window.'

'But not before the train leaves. Oh, I don't know what to do. Juana think of something. You saw what happened. That brute Miguel tried to kill my David. And the next bullet would have been aimed at me . . .'

I shudder now, for two reasons. First, because in all the excitement and noise and the adventure of the meeting and then the bike ride, it has not dawned on me that our situation is indeed that serious. It is only now, I realize with hindsight, that I know for sure that that shot was aimed at me. Personally. But a worse consideration crosses my mind: if Jorge is around, things will be ten times worse than if we have to deal with Miguel alone. But just then Mama lets loose a high cry filled with surprise and hope.

'Federico! Federrreeeee-co!'

Twenty paces away two men are crossing the concourse towards the departure platforms. Both are suited in double-breasted dark grey, and wear wide-brimmed fedoras, and they are followed by a porter with three large suitcases on his hand-cart. The shorter of the two men stops, as if shot, turns, and gazes in our direction with large eyes beneath thick eyebrows wide, yes, with fear. Mama waves frantically, then breaks ranks and swoops across the space between.

'Who is it?' I ask Juana, who is frowning, possibly sneering.

'Federico García Lorca.'

I sense her disapproval.

'But he's all right, isn't he? Mama is always talking about him and we've read all his plays and poetry . . .'

'Oh, he's fine.' She attempts to sound bored. 'Spain's greatest playwright and poet. And about as politically useful to us as Shakespeare was to the English revolution. But . . .' she pauses, and her face lightens, 'he comes from Granada so that may be where he is going . . .'

XXXII

Leaving Granada the traffic for the first fifteen miles was heavy, slow, the narrow old road constantly interrupted with massive roadworks that would modernize it and link the new by-pass with the already modernized route to the coast. Meanwhile it was a hot, noisy, fume-laden hell threading together a chain of small old villages with greyish-brown stucco frontages and, between them, new urbanizations, clusters of tiny white villas crammed into congested terraces. As she drove Petra recalled the story of Querubín's and his mother's flight to Granada from Madrid in July 1936, as it appeared in Kepler's transcript.

The traffic came to what seemed a terminal halt with the military airfield on her right. She let out a long troubled sigh and spelled out the problem to herself for maybe the fiftieth time.

Gibson's *The Death of Lorca* has Lorca leaving Madrid for Granada on the night of the sixteenth of July, 1936. And that's what Hugh Thomas acknowledges as a source. But Querubín's hypnotically induced memory has it on the day after the shooting of the pro-left Assault Guard Castillo, the evening of the morning on which Calvo Sotelo was assassinated. That was the thirteenth of July. It's things like that make these memories not memories but fantasies.

She glanced down to her side at the Librería Urbana bag. She had bought the big biography on impulse, and the guide to Lorca's Granada, and both were still wrapped. She wondered at herself; there was no reason to suppose that either would change the record. The traffic edged forward, she shrugged, bit her lip, and let out the clutch.

∽

I am in a long railway carriage, the corridor. Everything is wood. Hard dark wood. Not only the door-frames and the window-frames, but the panelling between, above and below. The fittings are brass, and the windows are raised and lowered by thick, heavy leather straps which have holes that can be buttoned over brass nipples.

I see a girl, tall and thin, with large bony hands and large feet, with close-cropped black hair, wearing a dark grey chemise, damp and stained about the neck, above a full black skirt. The top part of her back is leaning against the wood-panelled space between two compartments, her feet which are shod in unblancoed tennis shoes, no socks, are thrust forward, her head and shoulders hunched over above them. Behind her cupped right hand she is surreptitiously smoking a cigarette, black Canary tobacco. A black, jet-beaded purse dangles from her left wrist. It is empty apart from the cigarettes and matches. Seven or eight other passengers are in the corridor, migrants from third class, waiting to be shooed back into the sardine cans they have left by a railway guard who today is armed. Knowing they have no right to be where they are, they ignore the girl and she ignores them.

Outside, the interminable cliché of the interminable Spanish *meseta* rolls by beneath a sky that is not quite dark. Indeed, as she watches, the last sliver of a water-melon sun sinks below a distant low escarpment and the clouds of black smoke belched from the smoke-stack ahead to spew across the *campo* merge with the white smoke rising in fog-banks above the streaks of red flame where labourers are still burning off the stubble.

Two hours later she is there again, for the grown-ups talk and talk and talk in their compartment and though it can be converted into a sleeping chamber with four couchettes, the offer of the conductor to do so has been refused, twice. Mother and the Poet gossip on. So, bored and weary, she, or he, is out here again for his or her third cigarette.

The throb and racket of steel wheels on steel rails slowly drops in beat and tone and at last comes to a juddering standstill. Outside, a small signal box, yellow stucco framed in grey corner stones, carries the name of the station they were approaching but have not quite reached: MANZANARES. *Manzana*: apple. Town of apples. Name of a river too, Madrid's river.

But it means more than that. This, she, or he, remembers, is the small town where the Poet's great friend the *torero* Ignacio Sánchez was fatally gored not quite two years ago, inspiring the Lament which, long though it is, he knows by heart and now recites to himself.

'"*At five in the afternoon, at exactly five in the afternoon, a boy brought the white sheet at five in the afternoon. A basket of lime was already bespoken, what followed was death, just death. At five in the afternoon."*'

He can hear the engine wheeze and clank in front, like an iron bull panting, hauling in air over its grey swollen tongue, still trying to shake free from its withers the papered darts that torment it. He hauls on the leather strap, unbuttoning it, and lets the window drop. The air outside is cooler than the air inside but heavy with the deep odour of coal and hot metal.

'"*When the sweat streaked the bull like snow, when the bull-ring was covered with iodine, at five in the afternoon, then death deposited eggs in the wound; at five, five in the afternoon, precisely at five."*'

Something sets them off; a sudden storm of frogs croaking in a nearby marsh, and then the crickets too.

The door by his elbow drags open, he drops his cigarette and tries to cover it with his tennis shoe, but it is the Poet, not his mother.

'Where are we? Why have we stopped?'

Proud that he can provide the answers to both questions, knows things this most charismatic (apart from his mother) of adults does not know, he speaks with elaborately nonchalant ease.

'In a siding, taking on water, and waiting for the express from Seville to come through. We are just outside Manzanares.'

'Manzanares.' The Poet pushes his hand across his forehead and the widow's peak of his hairline, and sighs. He steps to the half-open window and places his elbows on the ledge.

'"*But now his sleep has no end. Now the moss and the grass open with sure fingers the flower of his skull. And his blood comes singing, singing through marshes and meadows, sliding along unfeeling horns . . ."*'

'"*Now the mosses and the grass* . . ." Not "*the moss*".'

'Really?' The Poet turns, leans his back against the door, the window. 'The mosses? The moss?' He smiles. 'Yes, you are right.'

'I know I am. I learned it by heart.'

'Well, so did I. Moreover I wrote it. But why "*the mosses*", and not "*the grasses*"?'

'Too many "s" sounds? And perhaps you were thinking of the different types of moss, and that interested you, while the fact that there are different types of grass did not.'

'Of course.'

The Poet pulls a cigarette packet from his jacket pocket, pushes up the inner casing, offers it. The boy hesitates, throws a swift glance at the compartment door. The Poet smiles.

'She is getting ready for bed.'

The boy takes one and the Poet lights it for him with a tiny gold lighter and then lights his own. The boy gags on the smoke which is acrid and harsh, American, an instant sore throat.

When he has recovered, he finds the Poet's smile is now, through the blue smoke, a touch devilish.

'She knows, you know.'

'Knows what?'

'That you smoke.'

'She does?'

'There are two things no man can hide, and you are almost a man. Love and smoking. You are in love and you smoke.' He sighs. 'One of them will kill you, but which?'

The boy coughs, aware of tightness in his throat. They hear a distant train whistle, a banshee in the far away night. Disconcerted, the just-fourteen-year-old boy reasserts adult equality.

'That will be the express from Seville. Soon we will be moving again.'

'Yes.' The older man draws on his cigarette, then removes it from his mouth with his left hand. His right reaches out, strokes then cradles the boy/man's cheek.

'Soon . . . you will have to shave.'

A huge deep sigh, drowned in a shudder.

218

The metal roar rushes closer, and the Poet just manages to hoist the window in time. Nevertheless the pandemonium of the passing train rocks their carriage and its sulphurous heavy breath fills the narrow corridor they share.

On the third of January 1492 Boabdil, the last Sultan of Granada, paused on the crest of a low rounded spur, the most western of the foothills of the Sierra Nevada. It juts out into the *vega* that made the area rich and the city happen. He looked back.

He wept.

His mother remarked: 'You do well, my son, to weep like a woman for the loss of what you could not keep as a man.'

In 1992 there was a pub there called *El Ultimo Suspiro del Moro*, the Moor's Last Sigh. It was a big brash place with restaurants, playgrounds and a huge loop of a bar, and from its outside terraces you could look back in the direction Boabdil looked and see, not what he saw, but Granada today.

It promised respite from the heat and traffic which was now trickling noisily and noxiously through a bottleneck ahead caused by roadworks rather than village high streets. Petra parked her car, got out, locked it, then opened it all again to retrieve the Librería Urbana bag. She knew very well how a book can discourage unwanted attentions in such places – that at any rate was how she rationalized what she was doing.

She sat on a terrace table facing south and west and the mountains she was heading for, ordered a beer from the tap, and sat back for a while to enjoy the late afternoon sunshine and a view across the rolling but basically flat *vega* – a huge patchwork of brilliant greens interrupted by stands of cherry and apple in full bloom.

On this side of the pub the traffic noise was distanced enough to be ignored, the peaceful perfection of the Alhambra still ran through her veins, subduing the moment of panic she had felt on the edge of the wood. Presently she pulled the larger packet from the bag, shredded off the thin paper wrapper, laid the book with its big black and white photo of the poet on its dust-cover in front of her, and sipped the icy beer which had arrived at her elbow, together with three garlicky olives in a tiny oval saucer. A hawk, no, it was too big, a bird of prey, anyway, cruised the fields a mile away, then slowly soared in slow wild spirals that took it towards the sierra, her sierra, and, above them, into the deep, pure blue which subsumed it. A juke-box in the rooms behind her played 'Let's go-o-o – to San Francisco-o-o'.

She opened the book, leafed through the opening impedimenta to chapter one:

Of all the *vegas* of Spain – the word, pre-Roman in origin, denotes a fertile plain between hills – that of Granada, which forms the Andalusian backdrop to the life and work of Federico García Lorca, is arguably the most beautiful . . .

She sipped beer, looked up and over it all again, and conceded that in spite of strong evidence of industrialized agriculture he might well be right. She turned back to the book. There seemed to be an awful lot more about the *vega*, and then the land the poet's forebears had farmed, and indeed there were another nine pages before he was even born. Irritated, for she had after all bought the book on impulse, in pursuit of a probably impossible quest, she pushed it aside, her attention caught again by the juke box . . .

Two voices, she recognized both, admired both enormously, but together? On the same track? And what was this . . . ? The hair rose on her head, and the sparse down on the back of her arms, at their bravado, their certainty they could convert kitsch to art. She waited, relaxed and delighted by the enormity of it as the track stormed to its inevitable end heralded by triumphant arpeggios . . .

'*!Viva Barcelona!*'

She let the mundane sounds of children playing, traffic and conversation seep back, then shifted a big chunk of the book from right to left, almost at random, and found she was looking at the opening of the last chapter. The first words were: *The city to which Lorca returned on the morning of 14 July 1936* . . . Heart in her mouth she turned back one page and again the words leapt out at her from the verso: *Lorca left Madrid on the night of 13 July, not the 16th . . .*

XXXIII

On the train Mama told Federico we were on our way to Villa Goya, that we were on the run from my brothers who wanted to kill me, perhaps both of us, and that Gabriel Melchor had promised to hide us if ever our secret came out. And Federico told us that Don Gabriel would not be at Villa Goya: that he always went to Biarritz in July and August to escape the heat, and that was confirmed when we arrived and telephoned the villa. So now we are in this big hotel called the Alhambra Palace Hotel on the Alhambra hill. We have two rooms and a bathroom and for nearly a week I have been shut up in them.

The problem is we have no money. Federico gave us what he could, but already he had used most of his cash to get us on to the train and into the couchette compartment, though actually I don't think that cost him much, no more than a tip to the conductor. He'd booked the whole compartment for himself that morning at Cook's in Gran Vía. I know, I saw the ticket. Anyway he gave Mama what he could, which was enough to get us in here for a couple of nights, and since then we have been living, according to Mama, 'on tick'. She will use these English expressions. She knows, she says, about living 'on tick'. Apparently her father lived 'on tick' for most of his life, and only got out of debt by selling her to my father. So. Both of them were scoundrels!

Anyway I can't leave these rooms: all I have to wear is that grey chemise, black skirt, and the tennis shoes, and she says I have lost the ability to look like a girl: my hands and feet are now definitely too big, I have a haze of hair on my lip, arms and legs (but so does Doña Pili back at home) and if I'm not careful my voice cracks. Not though when I am singing, and she makes me sing a lot: she says, she has always said, it's a lovely sound and soon it will be lost. I want to cry when she says that but she says no, don't cry, probably you will end up singing like Caruso, or this new young man Gigli, and I say I'd prefer to be

222

like McCormack, and she says I am right. Anyway, she wants to get my singing phonographed, like the English boy's we heard on the wireless singing Mendlessohn's 'Oh, for the Wings of a Dove . . .' I'm not singing THAT, I said, and she said no, of course not, but something jolly and Spanish, Valverde perhaps. '"Clavelitos",' I suggested, with some scorn. 'Why not?' she laughed. 'David, promise me, you must never be pompous about popular music.' 'Certainly,' I replied. 'Right now, I should be happy to sing "Adió' Granada". And you could do your flamenco thing on your guitar.'

She goes down to the town every day and argues and beseeches and shouts at the director of the local branch of Uncle Miguel's bank, but he refuses to give her any money without proof of identity, and of course, in the rush and everything she left all our papers at home. And now the management of this great big ugly hotel are getting restless and want to throw us out.

I can hear the lift whirr on the landing outside, the metal concertina doors clang. Is it her? Yes, her key in the lock. Shit, I'm still smoking the cigarette I bummed off the chambermaid . . .

'David. David, damn you!'

She sweeps past me, throws back windows already open, fans the air with a grotesquely large newspaper, turns on me with anger spilling out of her eyes and her mouth.

'It's a filthy habit. Your father did it and stank of it. It will ruin your voice. Do you want to sound like Uncle Miguel? Do you want a voice like coal sliding down a chute? Do you?'

But what I want is to get out, and at last it looks as if it might be possible for she is wearing a new dress and a new hat, a sort of flattened trilby with a feather. It must mean she's got some money out of the bank.

She unpins the hat, tosses it on to the sofa, and slumps beside it. Then she picks it up and tosses it away.

'Oh I'm sorry, David, but I've had a horrid morning, come and sit beside me and give me a kiss, a real kiss.'

I do, and she holds me very tight, as if I am her only anchor on earth and she might float away like a ghost into the dark woods above the hotel if she does not have me to hold on to.

'But, Mama, you got some money,' I say at last.

'Yes, David. But I had to tell them where we are, where we are staying, before they would release it.'

'Oh God.'

'David. I'm sorry. But the people here would have had us out on the street . . .'

'Well, at least we can go down to the town and get me some clothes I can wear.'

'No, David. Not even that. Look.'

She shows me the newspaper. Huge headlines: *General Francisco Franco y Bahamonde declares a National Movement*.

'What does it mean?'

'It means the most important general in the army has sided with the rebels in Morocco and that the rising will spread to the mainland. Already there is fighting down in the streets and nearly all the shops are putting up their shutters.'

'But you got yourself a new hat.'

She giggles. 'I was the last customer, David. Don't be angry with me.'

'I'm only angry because you might have got hurt. You should have come back as soon as you had the money.'

'Señora Iglesias, a gentleman called on the telephone and left you a message. I have it here, transcribed for you.'

We are in the big foyer of the hotel, lots of panelling and brass and copper, ferns and Swiss cheese plants in huge holders. The same day? No, I think a couple of days later. The flunkey behind the desk, in morning coat and striped trousers, flicks a folded piece of paper from the pigeon-hole into which he is about to put our key, and hands it to Mama with a flourish as if he were a conjuror and had magicked it out of his sleeve.

She looks at the end.

'It's from Don Gabriel.' She scans the note. 'It says he has come back from Biarritz because of the troubles and is now at the Reyes Católicos Hotel here in Granada. He ran into Federico who told him where we are. He says things are very troubled in the countryside with churches burnt and civil guards murdered, which is why he has not gone straight to Villa Goya. He thinks we should stay here until things are quieter. However, he will call on us later today and discuss what will be the best thing to do. Well, that's good news.'

'Mama, perhaps we should not go for a walk after all. He might come while we are out.'

She looks at her watch. 'Don Gabriel will not move anywhere on a hot day between two and four.'

The flunkey intervenes.

'It would not be wise of the gentleman to leave the safety of his hotel today. Nor would I recommend you to take a walk.'

'Why not? You mean because the garrison rose yesterday against the Republic? And there is shooting and worse going on in the town?'

'Precisely, señora.' And he seems smug about it.

'And that is precisely why we shall go out. Why we shall go up to the Alhambra and see for ourselves what atrocities are being committed. For three days now the wireless has broadcast nothing but lies from that awful man in Seville, and the local newspapers are all owned by wealthy supporters of the rebels. Come Da . . . Serafina.'

And she sweeps out through the glass doors the crimson uniformed commissionaire is only just quick enough to open for her. I follow, trying to give my hips a provocative swing, and take her hand on the top step. The heat is like a wall, an invisible hot fog. She looks sideways at me and gives me the impish conspiratorial smile that makes me feel the pulse in my neck and tightens my scrotum.

But the entrance to the Alhambra, the great gateway with its hand on one side and key on the other (Mama has already told me the prediction – that the Moors will return when the hand reaches through the gateway and plucks the key), is closed and guarded with soldiers who eye us suspiciously and finger their rifles.

'Never mind. We shall try the other entrance, or go on up to the Generalife instead. The view from up there will be even better.'

To begin with I hum, and sometimes sing snatches when I can remember the words, Cherubino's song from *The Marriage of Figaro*. But it's a steep climb through an ancient wood of heavy, dark oaks, very still in the heat, and soon we are both perspiring. We hear occasional shots, and the rattle of machine-guns but very far away, and I recall that Cherubino has been condemned by the jealous count to be an ensign, a soldier. The gunfire seems no more dangerous than that which one hears out on the *campo* near Madrid, when the farmers go after partridges and larks. I cannot believe women and men, even children, are mutilated or killed by such sounds, but Mama looks pale and grim. Then as we near the top, a new noise, a deeper smack of a noise, then a short whine or whistle which ends with a distant thud.

We can see that the second entrance, again a stone tower-gate but this time protecting a short bridge over a ravine, is also closed and guarded, and without getting any closer Mama turns and follows paths into a pleasanter woodland of elms and beeches. A goldfinch sings from an oleander bough in bloom, then flutters off, flashing the yellow beneath its wings and the cherry red of its cap.

Presently the path opens out on to a parterre, a belvedere. Mossy flags flank a slowly moving channel of brown clear water between beds of roses, full-blown and bedraggled, unkempt, uncared for, but making the hot air heavy with perfume. Tall hedges of clipped cypress mark it off into a suite of roofless rooms whose back walls are ancient brick covered with bougainvillaea and plumbago, but whose windows look out to the hillside across the valley. The hillside is filled with narrow streets of red-tiled, whitewashed houses, the oldest, poorest dwelling places in Granada, the homes of the city's workers. And as we look down at it the clap of gunfire echoes across the spaces, then we see the flash on the corner of someone's roof, and as the smoke and debris balloon out from it the crack of the second explosion reaches us. Mama's fingers grip my upper arm, I feel her nails clamp into the bare flesh below the sleeve which I have pushed up.

'Sons of prostitutes and bitches.'

Fifteen seconds elapse between each round, and the space between is elegiacally silent with birdsong and the distant crackle of small arms like a bonfire. Dust and smoke spread across the roofs, and small fires, small to us a kilometre away, bloom like orange flowers. A whole house crumbles and falls in on one of them, and the sound, a second later, is like an old man clearing his throat. Then clap and crack again, another obscenity is born.

'Where is the gun?' I ask.

'In the Alhambra itself.' She thinks for a moment. 'Probably in the Plaza de los Aljibes. Where Federico and de Falla had their Festival of Deep Song. The year you were born.'

'We should go and stop them.'

'Oh, David.'

'Well, anyway, we should try.'

I wait for the next, then shudder when it comes and turn away.

'What shall we do, then? I don't want to go back to the hotel.'

'Nor me.'

'Nor do I want to stay here and watch this.'

'Me neither.'

I take her hand and we walk on, find a gap in the old wall and steps that climb to a terrace above it, shaded by the old trees. We stop, and look back once more over the gardens we have left, the valley, and the tiny houses jewelled with fires. Suddenly I want to put them away, leave them, leave the horror we can do nothing about, and seizing her hand more tightly I climb up the steep slopes into the woods, almost dragging her behind me, our feet slipping on the mast and old leaves. Then I trip on a root and, twisting, sprawl so she lands partly on top of me. She kisses me very firmly on the mouth and wriggles off me, but pulling me with her so I am now above her and her head is below me. She shuts her eyes and turns her head with a sudden gesture of impatience.

'Take off those stupid clothes.'

I kneel with my knees on either side of her waist and pull the grey chemise over my head.

'All of them.'

227

'You too.'

I stand, and first pull down the floppy knickers which used to amuse me but now embarrass me so I do not want her to see me in them alone, then the skirt. I have left the tennis shoes until last. I hook my thumb in the heel of one and then the other and marvel that she does not tell me to untie the laces. I turn to say so and see her spread before me, dappled with beech light, as glorious as Eve the mother of us all, and the smile dies.

I kneel between her knees and kiss her navel, her thighs, her sex, and feel her hands grip my elbows as she half sits and then pulls me firmly up so I cover her, and then her hand between our bodies and her fingers feed my sex into hers.

'Slowly, David, hold on and be slow.'

But I feel the pulse and the sudden rush almost straight away, yet her fingers are all over me especially my buttocks and, 'Go on,' she cries. 'Go on, go on,' and I do and feel no lessening of the power in my loins. I go on and on until she cries out that it is sweet, so sweet, and then I let heaven fall about me.

Slowly peace descends and blesses us and in the boughs above us a nightingale begins to sing, or perhaps it sang all through and only now do I hear it.

Then the gun. Then the gun again.

'David?' She murmurs.

'Vikí. Mama.'

'No, not Vikí. Dolí. Because . . . David? I feel a little sad.'

'Please don't feel sad. Not now.'

'But I do.'

'Why?'

'We had such fun together. When you were a boy.'

Then an excited baying sound, some way below us, but not far, and getting nearer, near . . .

'Oh shit,' I say, and I reach for those stupid clothes.

XXXIV

Petra pulled on the parking brake, put the BMW into neutral, knew something was wrong. The big shutters on the first floor of the locked studio were open. She turned off the engine and got out but instead of opening the garage door she walked round the car and looked up.

She screamed and ran, stormed up the narrow stone stairs no one ever used. At the top the door that was never opened was ajar. A shaft of almost horizontal sunlight streamed through the space she had seen from below, cast a long dark shadow right across the bare boards to the window on the other side, the one that looked over the pools. The shadow shifted as the body slowly turned, the toe of one shoe scrabbling the floor, marking a repeated spirograph pattern in the dust.

It had been a hay and fodder loft and the large iron hook from which the farmers had hung the pulley for hoisting in sacks or bales of feed had been left in place. Querubín had placed a small stool below it and hanged himself in a noose made from the silk scarves Melchor had rescued from his mother's Madrid apartment over fifty years earlier. The silk had stretched and the drop from the stool had not been big enough. He was still alive . . . but only just.

Petra struggled to get him down and screamed for help as she did so. At last Carmen came, waddling, stumbling up the stairs, breathless before she got there. Together they held the dying man, for by then he was dying, so there was no longer any weight dragging on his neck, and bellowed and screamed for further help. Then Petra said, 'You must take all his weight while I undo the knot.' As her fingernails wrenched at the twisted silk she realized that his body was smirching her dress with urine and liquid faeces.

Paco arrived. He had been down in the orchard clearing out the irrigation channels which he planned to fill the next day with the stagnant water from the pool, and was back in a moment with a knife from the dining room table below. The silk did not part easily for the blade of a table knife and it was some moments before they were able to lay Querubín on the floor.

Molí, the silver tabby queen who had cringed in a corner since their arrival, came closer now, seemed puzzled, wary, then pushed her cheek against Querubín's silvery hair.

They got the knot undone. Because the rope had been made from scarves knotted and twisted – the last a red one – the slip knot had snagged on one of the smaller knots and had failed to make a viable garotte. The skin on his neck was dreadfully chafed. Blood and ichor leaked from the grazes. Nevertheless, it now seemed possible that the man who had been dying was no longer dying. They wrapped him in blankets, Petra dredging her memory for the correct treatment for shock. They chafed his wrists and feet, there was no clothing to loosen, all he wore was his night-shirt. Carmen went to the phone.

An ambulance came, a converted Renault 21 estate: it had oxygen and a man who seemed to know how to use it. Some of the blueness around Querubín's lips receded. Dr Caridad Rocío Lorca was only a short time behind. Serious, unflustered, she administered two injections. Querubín responded, his eyelids fluttered, his breathing deepened, he seemed to choke on a cough.

'Right, the next thing we have to do is get him to a hospital.'

Petra tried to object: 'Should he not wake in his own room? He will feel so terribly disorientated . . .'

She felt too a residual distrust, passed on from her father, of foreign hospitals.

'Málaga has every modern facility. It is very important that he is X-rayed before he makes any serious attempt at movement. If there is even a minor dislocation in his neck it could kill him . . . Don't worry. I'll go with him.'

The men stretchered Querubín to the ambulance. When they and the doctor had gone Petra returned to the forbidden room.

Unlike the paintings in the rooms below, Melchor's last was horrible. As horrible in its way as the grotesque martyrdoms portrayed by Catholic painters of the counter-reformation. Real relevance in art always remembers, even if it does not actually portray, our ability to be good and happy and there was nothing of that here.

A naked woman hangs by her ankles from a tree. The cord has been wound out of her own clothes. Her throat, her breasts, her stomach, her pelvic area and the top of her thighs have been slashed. Many of the cuts are curved. Blood streams down from them. Below her swinging hands a young man, not much more than a boy, also naked, looks up at her. He is kneeling, but upright, and clutching his groin. Blood seeps heavily through his fingers. His silent scream is not for his physical pain, but for her.

A knife with a curved blade folded into a curved whalebone handle hung by a string from a nail in the wall beside the painting. Crudely scratched into the handle were the words – *Jorge: su navaja*, 'George: his sailor's knife', and a date: *Agosto 32*.

Later, when the first shock had faded, Petra recalled how the Granadino doctor who had taken David to the monks at Silos had told them that a friend had brought the boy to him. That friend had to be Melchor. The painting had to be his memory of how he had found him.

'His dreams are true,' Petra said to herself. 'But he has to be made to believe them.'

XXXV

She phoned the hospital four times over the next twenty-four hours but had to wait until the following evening before they were able to tell her that his condition was stable, that through the afternoon he had been intermittently conscious between long spells of real sleep. A visit might be possible the next day, but probably it would be better to wait for a day or two more.

She awoke after a second night disturbed by dreams and waking fantasies, with a deep ache of loneliness which sat on her chest like a giant white slug. As she lay on her back and listened to the roar of the dawn chorus she realized that a day in the villa, practising, singing, studying, with only the discreet movements and sounds of Carmen and Paco in the background, was an impossibility. Yet she was angry with this weakness, annoyed with herself, knew it was uncharacteristic and a luxury she could not afford.

It was a Saturday and the municipal market closed at one. She rang Mari-Elena and suggested they should rehearse in the villa's music room. It would, she argued, be useful to have the portative organ and there were also CDs and tapes of earlier performances they could listen to. She suggested driving over to Campanillas to fetch her but Mari-Elena said she had her own car. Meanwhile, Petra phoned the hospital again. Querubín's slow recovery continued, a visit on Monday should be possible. The relief she felt surprised her, filled her with elation, left her feeling that things were all right, would turn out well.

Mari-Elena arrived in her psychedelically painted Citroën 2CV.

It was a humidly hot afternoon and the music room on the sunny side of the villa was, though shaded by the arcade, in danger of becoming an oven. Mari-Elena pulled down the slatted blinds in front of windows open to the ground and showed Petra how the frames could be adjusted to pull the blinds out into the colonnade like the sides of a sloping tent to catch whatever draught might come along. With the brilliance of the light reflected from the pool cut off, the room was dark as well as warm, conferring a sort of conspiratorial privacy on what they were doing.

The concept of exercising a voice before singing seriously was one Mari-Elena would not be bothered with, and Petra had been practising for an hour before she came. They began right away with the sequence of passages alternating between Nero and Poppea at the beginning of the final scene.

'*Dá licenza al mil spirto*
Ch'esca dall'amoroso laberinto . . .'

'License my spirit to leave this amorous labyrinth
Of fulsome praise
and bow myself to you, as I should:
My king, my spouse, my lord, my blessing . . .'

'Not bad, not bad. But it's too pure, too innocent. Poppea wasn't like that. She was a mature woman, no virgin. She was also a schemer, a conniving bitch. Get some edge into it.'

Mari-Elena tried again, but it sounded forced, strained.

'It's not in the music,' she complained.

'It's in the character. Sing the score and we're done for. Sing the character.'

Mari-Elena took a deep breath, hand pressing on her upper diaphragm, looked down at Petra, who led her through the undulating line with her right hand using a reed-stop this time, trying to get her to linger in places, draw out a vowel here, hold a high note there before tumbling down in swooning cadence.

'Better? Yes, I think so.'

'I don't.'

'No?' Petra looked up at her in surprise. 'Why not?'

Frustrated, Mari-Elena shook her dark head.

'It's like when we practised before. We're just two women with beautiful voices making beautiful music . . .'

'Whereas I'm asking you to be a woman throbbing with delight in the physical presence of your lover, about to ascend the erotic peak of a life already filled with erotic experience.'

Again it was a declaration, and in spite of the ironic inflection she gave it, a proposal. Mari-Elena laughed a little, but nervously, shy.

'Something like that.'

Petra, heart beating now, sweat glistening in the shadows on her temples and her breast-bone, made an effort to be brusque.

'Right,' she said. 'From the top, we'll take it apart, line by line, phrase by phrase. "*Il mio genio confuso* . . . My spirit confused."' She peered at the score, wiped her palms on her thighs, spread a chord, struck an entry note which rang round the cuboid room and drew a response from the gilded guitar.

But Mari-Elena was not used to such intensive rehearsal and within an hour they were hot, frustrated, almost on the edge of being annoyed with each other.

'Let's stop. I think we ought to.' Petra got up from the organ, walked across to a table between the darkened windows, took a peach from a bowl which Carmen had filled from an espalier on a south facing wall.

'Want one?'

'Please.'

Facing each other they bit into the large, downy fruits, let the juice spill into the palms and fingers of their left hands. Petra caught Mari-Elena's, forced her narrow open palm down her own cheek, then licked from it what was left of the juice, savouring the salty tang behind the tart sweetness. Mari-Elena pulled her hand free, slipped it behind Petra's neck, her tongue caressed the juice on Petra's cheek, then, reaching up on tiptoe, found her ear. Petra's fingers and thumbs were long enough to meet round the Spanish woman's waist. She bent her head slightly and kissed her slowly and longingly on the lips, let her feel her tongue. Mari-Elena opened her mouth and her hands dropped to the small of Petra's back, pulled her in, even closer than before. They kissed and caressed for some time, then Mari-Elena asked if they could not go to bed.

An hour or so later Petra woke from the sweetest doze she had ever had to find the Parma Violet Lady was stroking her cheek with the back of her hand.

'I have to be home by five. Half-past at the latest. Can we have a swim before I leave? I have my costume with me.'

But the pool was empty. During the morning Paco had siphoned out the old water into the irrigation channels below and the spring had not had time to replace it with more than a few inches at the deep end.

'*Kein problem!* We'll go to Playa de Campanillas.'

'A beach at Campanillas? How can that be?'

'The dam, the lake above the dam. There is a regular beach, but lots of other places too where one can swim.'

Petra collected towels and her costume. They went in the 2cv and Mari-Elena welcomed Petra's hand on her thigh as she drove. Almost immediately they were held up by a herd of goats with the goatboy in the rear wielding a big stick and throwing stones to head his charges off if they trespassed away from the verges and tried to scale the dry-stone walls into a neighbour's fields. For a moment or two they cruised through the herd at walking pace, which gave Petra time to marvel at the flowers: bronze-coloured foxgloves, long creeping vines of everlasting sweet-pea, a plant with tall spikes of pink waxy flowers. The goat smell scented the air, a cocktail of hay, sex and milk. Kids scampered close to their mums, whose heavy paired udders swung between their thighs. From behind they presented blatant labia and anuses beneath short, pertly flicking tails.

They drove on past fields red with poppies grown for their seeds, or fallow and sheeted with daisies. The orange groves were heavy with blossom, clouds of white stars in the dark green leaves.

'Will there be lots of people at the beach?'

'We don't have to go there,' Mari-Elena said. 'There are other places.'

They climbed, crossed a crest and trundled on and down through rolling hills of olives and almonds with an occasional gleam of the blue water of the artificial lake showing through and rising to meet them.

They rounded a bend and suddenly, beneath leaf buds like green flames on the tips of the upswung boughs of a fig tree, the road ended in three whitewashed boulders. As Petra opened her door two bee-eaters, enamelled blue, green, orange and yellow flew out of the fig tree, out over the still water, banked steeply, manoeuvred with their strange, spiked tails over an unlikely thermal, and soared away.

The still waters of the lake, full with the melted snows from the sierra, came right up to the boulders. To Petra it seemed a dead, artificial, unnatural sort of a lake, the water too still, the line which cut off the hills on the far side too straight, as if done by a cheese-wire. None of this bothered her lover. Mari-Elena piled out of the car, climbed into her costume, and scampered in. She turned and with arms folded across her breasts, shoulders hunched, screamed, '¡Qué frrriiiiioo!'

It was cold. For a moment Petra, in her costume now, felt awkward, uncomfortable, almost cheated, up to her knees in water that had been snow not long before, her feet cringing at what lay under them, while the warm air around her was still and heavy apart from the flies that were beginning to seek her out. But Mari-Elena surged on into the lake in a neat fast splashless crawl which took her twenty metres out and then back to a point where she could stand in front of Petra with the water lapping her thighs. Hands on hips, head on one side, wet hair, blacker than ever, twisted across her white throat, brown nipples pert from the cold showing through the scant material of her costume, she looked a perfect Venus, born from the foam.

'You can swim?'

'Of course.'

'Can you swim for half an hour without stopping?'

'Yes.'

'Come on, then.'

And she turned again, launched herself back into the lake but this time did not turn. Made breathless again by her beauty, but wondering too, Petra followed.

Mari-Elena swam with slower, more graceful ease for a hundred, then another hundred metres, only looking over her shoulder once to see if Petra was following. Suddenly she stopped, trod water for a moment, then rolled on her back and waited. Petra came up to her and to her amazement found the water suddenly warm, with a bluish tinge like tonic water, and indeed it was slightly fizzy too. An odour of sulphur, not strong enough to be unpleasant, hung above it. There was even a buoyancy in it, a lift the water around did not have. It warmed her toes, flowed up her thighs like a caress.

'I don't believe this, it's . . . wonderful.'

For a moment they trod water facing each other, then Mari-Elena put her hands on either side of Petra's waist and kissed her firmly on the mouth. Her legs, still pummelling the water, briskly caressed Petra's hips with her inner thighs. Then she launched away again with a laugh.

'Good, isn't it?'

Turning to follow her, Petra found she was looking up the hillsides on the other, farther side of the lake. Through eucalyptus and above the olives and citrus but beneath stacked orangy palaces of cloud she could see a church and roofs and the name of the village came to her: Alhamilla.

XXXVI

That evening the weather collapsed as cold fronts rolled in off the Atlantic and fumbled the rotundities of Mediterranean heat with icy fingers. Thunder rumbled in the mountains around and sabre-slashes of sheet lightning sliced the sulphurous air beneath the black, stacked clouds, making the kitchen seem a safe place to be. Without Querubín Petra had decided she did not want to be waited on by Carmen and she had asked if she could eat with them in the kitchen. She sat with Paco and cut circles of bread off a long crusty loaf while Carmen chivvied tiny black puddings cased in a bluey-grey skin around the base of her giant frying pan. The bright lights dimmed every now and then because of the distant storms.

'This afternoon,' Petra remarked, speaking slowly to give Carmen a reasonable chance of understanding her Spitalian, 'we swam in the lake below Alhamilla. We found a spot where the water was warm mineral water, bubbling up from a spring below. Does that mean Baños de Alhamilla is under the lake?'

A long silence filled the room like a chill mist, even the sausages ceased to sizzle as Carmen removed the pan from the heat. She pushed a strand of grey hair off her cheek and when it fell back used both big red hands to tuck it under a grip. She looked at her husband, he looked into his glass.

'Best place for it,' she said at last, and turned back to her cooking.

'Why?'

This was ignored and the meal went ahead as if nothing had been said. But at the end, while Carmen fussed over the coffee-pot and the other two nibbled plump blushing apricots, the thunder suddenly pounced, shook the shutters, put the lights out. Paco found a candle and then a lamp. By the time they were settled round the table again the rain was drumming on the roof, bouncing off the flags in the patio, hissing into the pool.

Petra took a deep breath and tried again.

'I want to know about Baños. I want to know why no one round here wants to talk about the place, or even admit it existed.'

Mari-Elena had been as mute on the subject as the lady who owned the Alhamilla bodega, disclaiming with a fervour that was suspicious any knowledge of a spa lost beneath the lake. Petra, afraid to spoil the day, their newly won closeness, had not pressed her.

The chiaroscuro of lamplight was the mask the old people needed. Bit by bit, not chronologically, correcting each other at times, and once agreeing to differ on a detail, they let the story unfold.

Originally there had been nothing but a hot spring whose water the locals found therapeutic for all sorts of ailments. As is usual in such places there was a chapel dedicated to the Virgin which Petra supposed had replaced the pagan shrine to a local water nymph. Some way from its source the stream had tumbled down a black cliff clad in emerald ferns, streaking the rock with a rusty deposit and carving out a ravine and then a little valley filled with sweet chestnuts. This became a tributary of the main river, joining it at a spot just above the place where the dam was later built. The spring itself was in a fertile bowl which supported three families of tenant farmers. They cultivated oranges and olives, tomatoes and potatoes, reared goats and chickens. Paco's father had courted one of the daughters, though the engagement ended when the landowner evicted his *novia*'s family in 1905, and thus pauperized them. Peasant sons marry paupers only in fairy tales and only when the pauper turns out to be a princess. The landowner who was an *Indiano* and therefore rich, no doubt he borrowed money as well, built a street of hotels, closed in the spring and created a spa. *Indiano*? asked Petra. Carmen explained: someone who has made their pile in the Americas and returned to the mother country to enjoy it.

The first hotel was burnt down, and out-of-work Galicians were brought in to break a construction workers' strike. The landlord, or the company that he had become, persuaded the authorities, no doubt by bribery, to build a fortified Civil Guard *cuartel* to protect their clients. It was manned by a section of ten men under a sergeant. They were equipped with a heavy Maxim machine-gun and hand-grenades as well as the usual carbines and pistols. And once the spa was opened, in 1920 they thought, there was no more trouble. Apart from anything else it provided employment for some of the children and grand-children of the dispossessed peasants; and it flourished.

On 20 July 1936 the garrison in Granada declared for Franco and the rebels. Forty or fifty men, known anarchists from the villages around Alhamilla, including Campanillas, felt they needed to protect themselves. They gathered in Baños and asked the sergeant to surrender his weapons. If he did, he and his section of Civil Guards would be allowed to take a lorry and go to Granada – a refuge which the doctors, priests and landowners had already been allowed to reach, unharmed.

The sergeant refused and ordered his men to fire on the anarchists. Two were killed, three wounded.

There are many mines in the Sierra Nevada and neighbouring ranges, silver and lead mainly, and most were already occupied by the miners. Which meant they had access to dynamite.

They blew up the *cuartel* and all ten *guardias* were killed.

Within weeks the front line between the Republicans and the rebels was established and remained fixed for most of the war. It followed the course of the Río Guadalfeo, forty kilometres away to the east, which meant the countryside round Alhamilla was subjugated by Catholic Youth Movement death squads, made up of local señoritos and their lackeys, all known to the villagers. It was a death squad of this sort that murdered Lorca himself on 18 August 1936. No one was safe and soon all the anarchists and committed Republicans were betrayed or sought out. Baños became the place of execution, the ravine and chestnut wood below where the bodies were dumped.

When, early in the fifties, the authorities declared that a dam was to be built and that Baños, now a place of ghosts who haunted them all, would be submerged, a great weight was lifted from the communal conscience. Once the bloodshed was over (and it continued sporadically into the forties) there was hardly anyone amongst the survivors who did not bear a burden of guilt. Apart from the murderers themselves, those who had not been directly implicated had escaped only by denying their relatives, their loved ones and their faith in the anarchist creed of Mutual Aid. When the water rose and finally covered the smashed hotels and the half-buried skeletons of the hundreds who had been murdered, the survivors accepted an unspoken covenant. Baños de Alhamilla might never be forgotten, but it would never be mentioned again. To outsiders it would be as if it had never existed, and, hopefully, with the passing of a century or two, it would become mere folklore, an evil spell that had lost its power.

Towards the end of the story the thunder receded, the rain became a softer fall rather than a deluge and presently the light bulbs glowed and then came full on. Paco turned out the lamp, and Carmen snuffed the candle between her moistened thumb- and finger-tip.

'I have two brothers under that lake,' she said, and dabbed her eyes with her apron. 'They were older than me, of course. In my dreams they still play with me: giants in their gentleness and beauty.'

Petra reached across the scrubbed table and squeezed the old woman's knobbly knuckles.

'Thank you for telling me,' she murmured. 'I did not mean to upset you.'

She needed solitude, a space to be quiet in and reflect. She sat at the long black table in the library with the score of *L'incoronazione di Poppea* open in front of her but not reading, just listening to the weeping eaves and the rumbling thunder which was circling back. She wanted to mourn the dead of Alhamilla, María Dolores Iglesias y Corazón, whose portrait was behind her, and her lover-son David, who might or might not be dying in Málaga. Presently she heard a voice in her head, her own voice, yes, but not entirely in her control. She mouthed the words, almost aloud.

'I think I should go to Málaga.' She looked at her watch. Half-past two. 'I think I should tell him about Lorca and Baños as soon as I possibly can. When he knows about them he may choose to get better.'

On the way out her fingers caressed the unglazed portrait of Dolí.

She murmured to it, 'Come with me. Please.'

XXXVII

As she opened the garage the thunder cracked again in the mountains behind her and the rain returned in big, warm, heavy drops. The air smelled of sulphur and dust recently laid. She slotted in the third act of Poppea . . .

'Ascendi, ascendi, o mia diletta, mia diletta
della sovrana altezza all'apice sublime . . .'

The mezzo voice, strong but recognizably female, soared and swooped on above a continuo of bass-viol and harpsichord to the final phrase of Nero's command that Poppea should ascend to the highest peak of glory.

'Climb, climb, my chosen one from sovereign height . . .'

The voice unwound its chain of melody above the rich hum of the engine, the headlights swung through silver rain over ancient olives and dry-stone walls, and Petra suffered in the warm space that enclosed her a sudden surge of almost unbearable happiness.

But by the time she had reached the wide deep gorges the main road and river thread on their way to the sea, reaction had set in and exhaustion began to surge over her in waves. And it was then the storm broke right over her. The rain roared on the car roof but could not muffle the terrible cracks of thunder that bounced between the towering rock faces, themselves illuminated by lightning flashes that came so frequently it was as if she were lit by some manic stroboscopic device. And its intensity seemed to get into the souls of the few who were up at that time of night, stirring up hidden madness.

As she climbed into the corniche above Salobreña a youth broke out from the side of the road and ran across, almost under her wheels, lit by lightning and headlights, a ghostly figure curtained in the rain. But worse was to come. For thirty kilometres between Salobreña and Nerja the mountains came close to the sea. For the most part the road circled the capes and promontories high above it or cut through them in tunnels, but twice it dropped to sea level before climbing and twisting up steep slopes. At the bottom of the first long climb, two cars roared past her, a VW Golf convertible with the roof down, the other a Ford Fiesta. There were three youths in the Golf, the one in the back standing and howling into the rain and wind which plastered his shirt to his body and whipped his long hair out behind him.

For a minute or so she could see their headlights swinging up the hairpins above her and felt relieved that their speed was taking them away from her so quickly, but as the road levelled and the black semi-circle of the first tunnel loomed like a giant mouth two hundred metres away there they were again, lit by her lights and by their own reflected off the cliff face. The Golf was slewed across the road with its front almost touching the stone facing of the tunnel entrance, the Fiesta was behind it, angled the other way so both cars together blocked her carriageway and about a third of the other side too.

There were five of them now, all men, strung across the road between her and their cars, still curtained by rain silvered by the lights, waving, waving her down.

'They've had an accident. They need help,' she said to herself.

'Don't stop,' a voice in her head said.

Nevertheless she slowed and at that moment the four headlights of a huge tanker filled the far end of the tunnel, hurtling towards her.

'Don't stop.'

At fifty metres she saw that the youth who had been standing in the back of the Golf was swinging what looked like a baseball bat. She put her foot down, the powerful little car surged forward, the youth swung the bat but, possibly surprised by her sudden speed, smashed it at the panelling of her door rather than her windscreen. She got round them, but only just. The bat was torn out of the youth's hand, twisted into the air above him, she braked, pulled to the right, and corrected the skid which still could have taken her into the path of the tanker.

244

'Oh Jesus,' she cried, as she came back out into the rain. Then her wing-mirrors bounced the glare of headlights behind her into her eyes, she glanced in the rearview mirror and saw circles of light framed in the receding blackness.

'Is it them? Are they coming after me?'

And as the road dropped and hairpinned again she could see there were indeed two sets of lights behind her.

She knew her BMW was potentially faster than either of them, but in this storm? On this twisting road? Going downhill the gap steadily narrowed, as if they were reeling her in, but when it climbed again she felt more confident, more in control should any emergency appear in front of her, and she drew away again and occasionally the bends took their lights out of the rearview mirrors. In the second tunnel, longer than the first and dead straight, she pushed the needle up to a hundred and seventy, the revs climbed to forty-five and vibrations she had never felt before shook the car, but she got away, hurtling back down towards the sea well before they were clear of the tunnel.

The surf beneath the rain pounded the low sea-wall, some-times fountaining up on to the road, carrying shingle, drift-wood . . . and all that at the nightmare time of night, between three and four in the morning.

'There aren't any more hills between here and Málaga, and most of the road is built-up from now on. Even if they do catch up they won't do anything, will they?'

And the voice that had been with her through it all answered, 'No, they won't. Of course they won't.'

Petra looked across to the empty passenger seat, and then the back seats, checking there was no one else there. Of course there was not. Not at all.

She reached the hospital shortly before five in the morning and was told there was no possibility of seeing Querubín for at least two hours. She was shown into a wide, bare waiting area with terrazo flooring, plastic and metal seating, vending machines and copies of ¡Hola!, two months old and more. She was drained now, worn out, cold, and wondered what the hell she was doing.

'I could have phoned him, he's in a private room, he'll have his own phone. Bloody machine's given me chocolate and I'm sure I pressed the button for coffee.'

The woman on the desk was relieved by another. Cleaners passed through chattering like sparrows about the storm; one came back carrying a big mop with a long rectangular head which she pushed briskly over the floor, making Petra lift her feet, leaving swirls of grey sudsy water in her wake.

At half-past eight Petra went to the desk again, and discovered that the new receptionist had no idea who she was nor what she wanted. She used her phone and presently a white-coated intern came out of the lift and walked across to them.

'Señor Querubín is still very ill, you know. Not really fit enough yet to have visitors. In fact his temperature and respiration have risen more than they should.'

Touched with dread, Petra tried to explain: 'I think I know why he made this attempt on his life, and I am certain I now have information that will make him feel much happier.'

But the doctor wanted to know who she was, what her connection with Querubín was.

'Look. I saved his life in the first place. His personal doctor knows me. Can't you phone her?'

After another hour the intern returned to agree to a five minute visit, with warnings that she must not excite the patient, and above all be very careful not to cause him to move his head suddenly. 'There are severe lesions to the neck cartilage which could still be a problem . . .'

Querubín was propped up on piles of pillows like a broken doll; massive bruising had begun to spread up the side of his face and his right hand, clenched on the sheet in front of him, shook spasmodically. His neck was cased in a support. A drip-feed was attached to his left arm. His skin was pallid, waxy, not just on his face but on his chest too, which was exposed. His eyes opened, searched the light for some sign that would tell him who his visitor was.

'Petra.'

There was a chair by the window. Petra picked it up, brought it to the side of the bed. She sat down, reached across, took his shaking hand in both of hers and applied what she hoped was soothing pressure.

'David, there really was a Baños de Alhamilla. It really existed. I am sure now you were there. With your mother. And there's another thing I've worked out . . .'

'There's no one with you?'

'No.'

His eyebrows furrowed, his blind eyes searched the spaces around her, seemed to focus.

'Maybe.' She shivered then hurried on. 'In nineteen seventy-two you knew the date Lorca left Madrid, knew the right day, when historians at the time had got it wrong. Do you understand? It was something you could not have got from Hugh Thomas or Gibson's earlier book or whoever. The only way you could have got it right was by being there yourself, doing the things your dream-memories say you did.'

His reaction was slow, but a gentle smile spread across his mouth and she felt his eyes were smiling too, though the swollen lids had closed again. Then his head turned the other way and his other hand moved out too, and half closed on . . . nothing at all.

∽

I am lying with my head in my mother's lap, looking up into her face. Behind her head I can see bright, bright red flower buds, small like drops of blood amongst dark glossy foliage, a greenish brown. There are thorns too. It is very warm and we are in a wild sort of orchard place. I am very, very happy. She is twining starry white flowers on long tendrils into my hair. The scent is heavy, orange blossom or jasmine, or maybe both. She is singing a song, a love poem, a poem about love.

∽

He opened his eyes, cleared his throat.

'You'll take me home?'

'Of course. As soon as they say I can.'

A rippling chord from Dolí's guitar rang across the water.

'*Ascendi ascendi . . .*

O mia dile-e-e-etta'

'Climb, climb my chosen one from sovereign height to zenith sublime . . . From earth and from the stars your triumph is acclaimed . . . Adored Poppea, my loved one . . .'

Sitting in a big wicker chair at the other end of the pool, in the central arch of the cloister, Querubín lifted his head: on the second *dile-e-e-etta* an unscored improvised ornamentation, straight from the heart, spontaneous, convincing.

Then Poppea answered:

'*Il mio genio confuso*

al non usato lume . . .'

'My soul, confused by unaccustomed light, almost forgets good manners, sir, and fails to thank you . . . ' An amateur, Petra warned me, not bad, but she, whoever she is, has missed the false modesty, the irony. This after all, is Poppea's triumph, her coronation. Sing the character not the score.

Then Petra's voice again, yes, like an emperor, but an emperor in love: '*Per capirti negl'occhi, il sol . . .*' 'To arrive in your eyes the sun has diminished itself, to be harboured in your breast the dawn leaves the sky . . .'

His lumpy hands gripped the arm-rests; his head came up and forward, thrusting to catch the sound; his eyes fixed on the distant figures which had been blurred and little more than blobs of white light in darkness but now took on shape and form and substance, and Petra sang on, sang love not hate, sang the love a man might feel for a woman.

Then for a moment or two silence spread a mantle over the rose-petalled water. The moon rose into the glow it had already cast above the sierra, a three-quarter waning moon, on cue. Petra had timed it. The women took a step forward: not even the doves dared intervene, though Querubín now pushed down with his hands and stood, and with head still thrust forward, moved to the very edge of the pool.

'*Pur ti miro, pur ti godo . . .*'

'Now I behold thee, now I enjoy thee . . .'

Petra put the guitar to one side and heard the blend as for the first time they sang two notes together. She glanced at Mari-Elena, noted the sweat on her brow, her pallor, the way the tendons in her neck stood out as she reached for notes at the very extremity of her range.

'*Si, mio cor, mia ben, mia vita, si.*'

'Yes, my heart, my love, my life, yes . . .' then the reprise of the first verse sung this time with a succession of resolved dissonances to end on *mío tesoro*, a dying fall.

Querubín shrugged off his cotton dressing gown, the long shirt beneath and his slippers, and walked into the pool.

The warm water, warmer than the warm night air, climbed his shins, his knees, his mutilated genitals, his waist, and the rose petals swirled around him like floating archipelagos. He stooped, scooped up water and petals in both hands, let them slide over his shoulders before folding his arms across his chest.

'*Madre,*' he called, high like song, '*Veo. ¡Qué veo!*'

'What did he say?'

'He said he can see.'

Petra pulled off her shirt and jeans, took three steps and dived noiselessly in. Her head broke the surface in front of Querubín. He took both her hands.

'You were good,' he said. 'As good as I ever was,' and he kissed her, first one cheek, then the other.

They took him back to the chair, dried him, got him back into the few clothes he had been wearing. He would not go to bed. They ate grapes, the very first, and nuts, and drank the wine. The two women remained beside him while he slept – Petra held his hand, Mari-Elena sat at his feet with her knees tucked under her and stroked her cat. She left before dawn, saying she had Emilio and Wilf to think of.

Querubín stirred in his creaky chair, opened his eyes.

'Sometimes,' he said, 'at sunrise, you can see Africa from the mountains.'

Half an hour later they walked slowly off the road and into the short grass of the mountainside dotted with boulders and cropped hemispheres of thyme. The light grew, tinged with shades of lavender. The sky above turned from purple to violet to blue and the stars went out, all but one. In front of them the mountain, riven with mist-filled valleys, tumbled down to distant beaches. The colour of ripe sloes, the sea climbed to a high horizon veiled in mist. Above it the three-quarter moon hung like a slice of mother-of-pearl.

'It's too misty,' Petra murmured.

'Wait.'

The light grew, and then behind them and on their left the first gold shard edged above a distant crest. The warmth was an instant caress, the transformation from night to day as quick. Fifty yards away a lark took off on busy wings, spilled song, and then a hundred yards on the other side another. A white-breasted brown alpine swift skimmed the slopes only inches above the grass and rocks, too quick for the eye to hold it for more than a second or two.

The sea took on new colours, green near the beaches, then deep blue fading to mauve. The mist lifted and suddenly it had an edge, a seam which sewed it to the sky, an unbroken string of tiny seed pearls above a thread of black. Africa. Just as it had been when Petra had first found this spot back in January, but at sunrise even clearer.

'Can you see it?'

'No, of course not.' He laughed, almost silently. 'I can see the light. I can tell the difference between the moon and the sun. I can see you. And that is enough. For now.'

Then:

'Thank you,' he said. 'You are very, very good, but we still have a lot to do.'

❧

A year's work was followed by a concert tour arranged for Petra by Querubín's agent. She returned in the autumn to find him ill again, suffering from severe pain in his vocal cords. Together with Carmen she nursed him and, when he could, he continued to coach her almost until he chose to die.

The week following the funeral was filled with the pain of bereavement: she almost felt her voice might go, her throat and chest suffered so. But she had people to see, long telephone calls to make putting in train the provisions of Querubín's will, including giving Paco and Carmen the means to live near their children in Campanillas. They moved out the day before Petra, leaving Villa Melchor for one night to her alone. They even took Molí with them.

It was a vigil. She wandered from room to room – reading a book here, touching an instrument there, playing discs for a few minutes before turning them off. When daylight returned she climbed the turning stairs to the forbidden studio, hoping that somehow a transformation had taken place, that the horror would be gone.

In the dawn light the painting was even harsher, more unrelentingly descriptive of the event it recorded than when she had seen it the first time. She wanted to tear it down, rip the canvas from the stretcher, burn it. But then she recalled Nero the tyrant, the man who kicked Poppea to death when she was pregnant with his child, as well as the Nero who loved, and she knew she must hold them both in her soul if she was to be the artist she wanted to be.

She came last to the portrait of Dolí. And here there was a sort of disappointment. It no longer seemed such a magical painting, the technique was too perfect, and when she sought again some spark in the reflected eyes, some signal of gratitude perhaps, or just complicity, she found the light had gone.

She left at half-past one, hoping to find the roads free of heavy traffic, but on an impulse parked in the municipal car-park at Campanillas and walked back to El Molino. Mari-Elena was singing and accompanying herself on her guitar: Paco Ibañez arrangements of Spanish poetry to a small circle of friends. Petra listened to a couple of songs then went over to her.

'I've come to say good-bye, and to thank you.'

The Parma Violet Lady reached up her lean brown hand, pulled down her head and kissed her.

'It was like a fairy story.'

'Yes.'

Her fingers trickled over the strings and she sang.

> 'Erase una vez
> un lobito bueno
> al que maltrataban
> todos lo' corderos
> y había también
> un principe malo . . .
> Una bruja hermosa
> y un pirata honrado'

Petra felt the hair on the nape of her neck prickle, and a slight sweat broke out in her palms.

'What do the words mean?' Though she knew already.

'Once upon a time there was a good wolf who was mistreated by all the sheep. There was also an evil prince, a beautiful witch and an honourable pirate.'

'Who wrote them?'

'José Agustín Goytisolo. The eldest of the three Goytisolo brothers.'

'He's still alive, then?'

'Oh yes.'

'So he could not have written them in 1936.'

The Parma Violet Lady smiled and shrugged. 'No. He would have been about seven years old, I think.'

She sang on:

> 'Todas estas cosas
> había una vez
> cuando yo soñaba
> un mundo al revés'

'What does that last bit mean?'

'All these things belong to a time when I was dreaming, dreaming a world turned inside out.'

'Ah.'

It did not matter, she said to herself, as she drove on towards Granada, Europe, London, that the words Mari-Elena had sung were the same as or echoed the ones María Dolores had used, when, hiding with David from a roaring lion, she had been asked to tell a story, a fairy story, inside a wardrobe. It did not matter at all. Nothing really matters.

She grinned to herself, found the tape she wanted, slotted it in – and it wasn't Monteverdi.

¡LIBERTAD!